HANDING ON THE FAITH

HANDING ON THE FAITH

Matthew Lewis Sutton
and William L. Portier
editors

THE ANNUAL PUBLICATION
OF THE COLLEGE THEOLOGY SOCIETY
2013
VOLUME 59

ORBIS BOOKS
Maryknoll, New York 10545

Founded in 1970, Orbis Books endeavors to publish works that enlighten the mind, nourish the spirit, and challenge the conscience. The publishing arm of the Maryknoll Fathers and Brothers, Orbis seeks to explore the global dimensions of the Christian faith and mission, to invite dialogue with diverse cultures and religious traditions, and to serve the cause of reconciliation and peace. The books published reflect the views of their authors and do not represent the official position of the Maryknoll Society. To learn more about Maryknoll and Orbis Books, please visit our website at www.maryknollsociety.org.

Library of Congress Cataloging-in-Publication Data

Handing on the faith / Matthew Lewis Sutton and William L. Portier, editors.
    pages cm. —(The annual publication of the College Theology Society ; VOLUME 59)
    Includes bibliographical references.
    ISBN 978-1-62698-079-2 (paperwork)
    1. Christian education.   2. Theology—Study and teaching.
3. Catechetics.   I. Sutton, Matthew Lewis, editor of compilation.
BV1471.3.H363 2014
268'.82—dc23
                        2013046651

Contents

Part II
Teaching Theology

Part III
Implications

With deep gratitude and respect,

Matthew Lewis Sutton dedicates this volume to
Dr. Christopher Thompson
who handed on the faith to him in charity and prayer;

William L. Portier dedicates this volume to Bonnie,
his wife of forty-two years.

Introduction

Handing On the Faith

Matthew Lewis Sutton and William L. Portier

Just about midway through the four-year commemoration of the fiftieth anniversary of the Second Vatican Council, members of the College Theology Society (CTS) gathered in May 2013 at Creighton University in Omaha for the fifty-ninth annual meeting. In a signature passage from the Introduction to *Gaudium et Spes*, the Council recalled the church's "duty in every age of examining the signs of the times and interpreting them in light of the gospel. . . ."[1] One of the signs of the times needing interpretation is what Sandra Yocum, in her 2007 history of the CTS, described as a "revolution in theological studies in every aspect from who produces theology to what is produced, from who teaches to who learns, and from where theological studies take place to what is actually taught in the undergraduate college classrooms."[2] Professors and students are still changing. The "revolution" continues.

Preceding generations secured the academic legitimacy and legitimate autonomy of theology as an undergraduate discipline. Our predecessors' students, however, were most often descendants of European Americans, catechized in the networks of elementary and high schools that helped make up an immigrant Catholic subculture. It peaked around the time Vatican II ended. Now more diverse, and often culturally segmented, our students come from a pluralist mix in which religious disaffiliation is on the rise, and in which religious affiliation of any kind tends to be intentional and fluid rather than culturally inherited.

Under the broad heading of "Teaching Theology and Handing on the Faith," participants in the 2013 meeting did their best to interpret these new signs of the times and to reflect on new paths opening up for our discipline. Three plenary speakers, Robert Imbelli of Boston College, Aurelie Hagstrom of Providence College, and Curtis Freeman of Duke University, oriented our reflections in directions that were respectively Christological, inspired by Scripture and the Second Vatican Council, and authentically evangelical.

Speakers and panelists addressed new situations in demography and higher education, particularly in the Catholic institutions where most of our members teach. Recent studies show that religious illiteracy in the United States is widespread.[3] According to a recent Pew Forum study, Catholic students, while generally committed to ideas about social justice and volunteering, do not evince a deep or even foundational understanding of the Christian tradition.[4] As is well known, another Pew Forum study detected a decline in Catholic affiliation, particularly in young people.[5] Similarly, a recent study by the Center for Applied Research in the Apostolate shows that college students drift away from the practice of religion, even though Catholic colleges and universities tend to slow the drift.[6] At most Catholic colleges and universities, the demographics of students' relationship to the Christian faith are changing rapidly, if not radically.

In the face of these challenges, many discussions at the annual meeting explored the Catholic theologian's complex relation to the publics of academy and church and revisited past assumptions about possible convergences between teaching (*docere*) theology and handing on (*tradere*) the faith. For many students attending a Catholic college, courses in theology often represent their first substantive adult engagement with the Christian tradition. Their theology professors might represent their first encounter with an intellectually committed Catholic Christian. These observations raise questions about core curricula and the responsibilities Catholic colleges have to give explicit attention to Catholic intellectual and cultural traditions.

They also bring into view questions about the relationship between the academic position of teaching theology and the ecclesial mission of handing on the faith. Some would question the possibility of a convergence between these two separate spheres and wonder if suggesting a convergence makes improper impositions and oversteps legitimate, distinct lines of competence and responsibility.

Nevertheless, whether professors intend it or not, their implicit understandings of this relationship between teaching theology and evangelization affect their students as they read the Bible and learn the history and doctrines of Christianity. Evangelization need not be understood in a narrow sense. Rather, for the sake of this discussion, it is best understood in the complex, multidimensional way set forth by Paul VI in *Evangelii Nuntiandi* (1975). For the future of Catholicism in the United States, particularly in our Catholic colleges and universities, explicit attention to the relationship between theology and evangelization is absolutely critical both for self-aware teaching and for the ecclesial mission of evangelization.

Pope Francis likes to recall that it was his Italian-Argentine grandmother who handed on the faith to him.[7] Reflecting on this experience, Francis wrote in *Lumen Fidei*:

> Since faith is hearing and seeing, it is also handed on as word and light. . . . Faith is passed on, we might say, by contact, from one person to another, just as one candle is lighted from another. . . . The transmission of the faith not only brings light to men and women in every place; it travels through time, passing from one generation to another. Because faith is born of an encounter which takes place in history and lights up our journey through time, it must be passed on in every age.[8]

We have come to understand God's revelation in the Scriptures not primarily as doctrine, but as encounter with the Triune God. A faithful response to revelation demands more than intellectual knowledge and includes obedient, loving life in the Holy Spirit.[9] Such obedient, loving life is performed, and since it is performed it is already creative imitation.[10] And is this not a way to interpret handing on the faith through witnessing, performing, and imitating the reception of the revelation of God into the next age?

The Synod of Bishops met in October 2012 to consider the "new evangelization." Their reflections inspired the topic for a dialogue between bishops and theologians, hosted by the USCCB's

Committee on Doctrine in March 2013, on the role of Catholic colleges and universities in the new evangelization. As CTS president, Sandra Yocum addressed this meeting on the topic of the gospel and undergraduate education. Her presentation raises the question with which the editors want to begin this book: "What do our students need?" Undergraduates, she concluded, need witnesses, companions to accompany them on the way, and, above all, time and space to grow. The following chapters explore how theologians might respond and witness to these needs.

Convergences

Theologians offer students possibilities for new "convergences," Balthasar's word for the return of multiplicity into originating unity. In a 2001 homily to university professors, Pope John Paul II called for a new synthesis.[11] Robert Imbelli addressed the first night's opening plenary on "The Heart Has Its Reasons: Giving an Account of the Hope That Is in Us." In tones reminiscent of Cardinal Avery Dulles, he urged that our witness as teachers converge on Jesus Christ. If it is Christ who is being handed on, then teaching theology is rightly centered on Christ. In his own undergraduate teaching, Imbelli concludes that a Christocentric approach means that his students must, in Newman's terms, achieve a notional apprehension of Jesus Christ. Such notional apprehension remains open to a real assent, but the latter depends on a student's free intentions and the movement of the Holy Spirit.

Dulles's secretary, Anne-Marie Kirmse, O.P., offered her thoughts on the convergent work of the late cardinal as an example of a theologian seeking to teach from within the church's call for a new evangelization. Her analysis of the cardinal's enthusiasm for *Evangelii Nuntiandi*, along with his last book, *Evangelization for the Third Millennium*, stimulated reflection on what is new about the new evangelization. Dulles worked on the final edits for his last book from his hospital bed, a witness to a distinguished theologian's unreserved dedication to handing on the faith.

Continuing to imitate the Ignatian spirit of Dulles, this book includes chapters by two younger Jesuits, Christopher Collins and Christopher Hadley. They provide accounts of handing on the faith in the classroom, focused respectively on the importance of

Scripture and on the importance of an integrating spiritual theology. Both chapters emphasize teaching theology as a spiritual encounter with the Word. Collins achieves this encounter with Flannery O'Connor and Hadley with Hans Urs von Balthasar.

Maureen O'Connell argues that thinking about Catholic moral theology with our mostly millennial students necessitates new strategies. Respectful of the great accomplishments of post-Vatican II-era theologians, O'Connell warns against an all too easy nostalgia for the theological arguments of that period. She challenges teaching theologians to make the experiences of the millennial generational cohort the focal point for theological investigation in our courses, inviting students to resource both the tradition and their own campus cultures to remix new alternatives for Christian living.

Teaching Theology

The lasting goodness of the Society is the scholarly analysis of the practicalities of teaching. Members responded to the theme "Teaching Theology and Handing On the Faith" with a wealth of personal reflection on what happens in our classrooms. From these riches, the editors, with the help of peer reviewers, chose the chapters that make up the section of the book on "Teaching Theology." These chapters describe in personal and confessional fashion the lived experience of teaching theology as handing on the faith.

The section begins with Aurelie Hagstrom's plenary address. She takes the title of her reflection on theologians and handing on the faith from St. Paul in 1 Corinthians, "For I handed on to you as of first importance what I myself had received." Facing squarely the challenge that many Catholic theologians in U.S. colleges and universities tend to "bristle" when they hear themselves described as "agents" of the new evangelization, she deftly negotiates her way between a classic academic approach to teaching theology on the one side and a catechetical approach on the other. Her "third way" between theology and catechetics relies on a perceptive interpretation of *Dei Verbum* motivated by simultaneous Pauline and Marian hermeneutics. Hagstrom's back and forth between theology and catechetics as we have understood them over the past forty years offers wise direction for reading the signs of the times anew.

The chapters that follow display something like Hagstrom's "third way" as practiced by teaching theologians across the United States. Beginning in California, David Gentry-Akin presents the third way as serving a living Catholic intellectual tradition. Presuming faculty members enthusiastically evangelical and deeply intellectual about their discipline, he navigates the terrain of the discourse of diversity in Catholic universities. He offers his teaching methodology as a way forward that honors diverse students while also presenting to them a real apprehension of the faith designed for a new generation of Catholic intellectuals.

Now traveling through the Midwest and in a different context, Andrew Black discusses the evangelical character of teaching theology as a Baptist faculty member at a Catholic institution. These thoughtful reflections of "a Catholic-Baptist theologian" describe Black's rich ecumenical experiences of teaching and learning in the theology classroom. Though somewhat haunted by the idea that what students take from his required general education courses might be "the only Jesus they'll ever see," he concludes that nothing could be more "practical" than finding God in the company of others.

Continuing in the Midwest, Katherine Schmidt addresses the meaning of conversion and its role in teaching theology. She offers a Lonerganian analysis of conversion that draws on the doctrine of the communion of saints. In her teaching, she guides students through an evaluation of their horizons while also helping them consider the Christian horizon engaged rigorously, critically, generously, and compassionately.

Arriving on the East Coast, for Mary-Paula Cancienne the "third way" means attention to the aesthetic dimensions of her students' humanity. She argues that the diverse cultural fragmentations that separate the teacher from her student can be traversed by nurturing their aesthetic sensibilities and religious imaginations.

Returning to the Midwest, three faculty members from Viterbo University, Emily Dykman, Michael Lopez-Kaley, and Laura Nettles, describe the "third way" in the context of their institution. Acknowledging a certain tension between their Franciscan university's ecclesial and academic missions and the practicalities of teaching required introductory courses in Christianity, they revisit *Ex Corde Ecclesiae* (1995). For them, affirming faith and challenging knowledge will neither water down Christianity nor belittle rigorous critical reasoning. They advocate openness to campus ministry and the Franciscan charism of handing on the faith through witness, as in the maxim often attributed to Francis but certainly Franciscan in spirit, "Preach the gospel at all times. If necessary, use words."

Ending back on the West Coast, we complete our round trip in California to see, with Felicidad Oberholzer, the "third way" applied to the concrete teaching of a Christian marriage and family course. The disconnections between Christian teachings on sexuality and her students' easy acceptance of popular notions of sexuality might tempt one to despair. Instead, with real appreciation for her students and their experiences, Oberholzer takes these disconnections as an opportunity to invite students to see human sexuality in alternative and ennobling ways.

Implications

The book's final section takes up three stories of handing on the faith in settings that, though not directly academic, have much to teach. They include an eighteenth-century piece of fiction and its evangelizing role, the renewal of the identity and mission of Catholic Relief Services through a re-appropriation of Catholic social teaching, and the story of more than thirty years of ecumenical hospitality in Rome's Lay Centre at Foyer Unitas.

Curtis Freeman, the annual meeting's third plenary speaker, blended personal narrative and historical theology as he described the role of Daniel Defoe's *The Life and Adventures of Robinson Crusoe* in forming his own faith. Highlighting the narrative dimension of the transmission of Christian doctrine, Freeman enlists Defoe's help in understanding an age of castaways "whose ecclesial ships have crashed on the grounds of modernity." From Defoe's story, he takes implications for the ongoing development of doctrine among Baptists and other Christians.

Christine Tucker narrates "a crisis in Catholic identity" in the 1990s at Catholic Relief Services (CRS). Prior to the fall of the Soviet Union in 1989, the Cold War shaped and even funded much of CRS's international development work. Without sacrificing professional standards, CRS adapted itself to a post-Cold War world by rediscovering and integrating into its work an important aspect of the tradition, Catholic social teaching. Tucker's story serves as a parable for theologians seeking to renew their teaching mission for a post-Catholic-subculture time.

This book ends in Rome with Donna Orsuto's talk on the occasion of her receiving the 2013 CTS Presidential Award. 2013 marked the seventeenth consecutive year that members of the National Association of Baptist Professors of Religion (NABPR) have met jointly with CTS. Orsuto began with expressions of gratitude to three Baptist professors at Wake Forest University who had occasioned her first trip to Rome in 1979. One of those professors, Ralph Wood, was present at the banquet when Orsuto received the award. Her 1979 trip began thirty-three years of ecumenical and interreligious hospitality at the Lay Centre. To convey a sense of Rome's impact on her, Orsuto invoked testimony from Dietrich Bonhoeffer and Thomas Merton, as well as Francis de Sales's wise advice, "Let us be what we are and be that well." Her conclusion, citing William Wordsworth, captures the spirit of the Omaha meeting as well as everything in this book: "What we have loved, Others will love, and we will teach them how."[12]

The book you hold in your hands is the work of eighteen CTS members, eleven women and seven men. They come from a wide spectrum of colleges and universities and, in some real sense, represent all who gathered at Omaha last spring. We hope their work will promote continuing reflection for a new time on the relationship between teaching theology and handing on the faith.

Acknowledgments

Matthew Lewis Sutton thanks the many people who made this project available to you, particularly Dr. David Gentry-Akin, who believed; Dr. Sandra Yocum, who encouraged; and Dr. William Collinge, who delivered. He also thanks his graduate assistant, Mr. Andrew Outar, and especially his co-editor, who was the *petros* of the project. What is good here comes from them. Lastly, he would like to thank Jesus, who is forever our good, and His mother, the Seat of Wisdom, who is the patron of our society. Lord, grant that we may hand on your everlasting love in wisdom and fire.

William L. Portier is grateful to the NABPR members with whom, since 1996, we have shared Christian fellowship and scholarship.

Notes

[1]*Documents of the Ecumenical Councils*, vol. II (Trent to Vatican II), ed. Norman P. Tanner, S.J. (London and Washington, DC: Sheed & Ward and Georgetown University Press, 1990), 1070.

[2]Sandra Yocum Mize, *Joining the Revolution in Theology: The College Theology Society, 1954-2004* (Lanham, MD: Rowman & Littlefield, 2007), 4.

[3]See, for example, Stephen Prothero, *Religious Literacy: What Every American Needs to Know and Doesn't* (New York: HarperCollins, 2008). See also the work of a number of sociologists such as Dean Hoge, James Davidson, William D'Antonio, and others affiliated with the Center for Applied Research in the Apostolate at Georgetown University.

[4]See the Pew Forum, "U.S. Religious Knowledge Survey (2010)," September 28, 2010, http://www.pewforum.org.

[5]See the Pew Forum, "Faith in Flux: Changes in Religious Affiliation in the U.S. (2009)," April 27, 2009, http://www.pewforum.org.

[6]The Center for Applied Research in the Apostolate (CARA) gives a lukewarm assessment of Catholic higher education, because "[m]ore often than not, Catholic students at Catholic colleges are slightly *less* likely to shift away from Church teachings than Catholic students attending other types of colleges and universities." See the full report at http://cara.georgetown.edu/Publications/workingpapers/CARAWorkingPaper9.pdf. The study was responding to a Cardinal Newman Society report of several years earlier that suggested that Catholic colleges and universities were actually harming the faith of their students. The CARA report shows that assessment to be false. Yet it does not show that Catholic colleges and universities are leading students to a robust engagement with Catholic faith.

[7]Pope Francis, "Homily from the Celebration of Palm Sunday of the Passion of Our Lord," Saint Peter's Square, March 24, 2013, http://www.vatican.va.

[8]Pope Francis, *Lumen Fidei*, June 29, 2013, paragraphs 37-38, http://www.vatican.va.

[9]Hans Urs von Balthasar, *Convergences: To the Source of Christian Mystery*, trans. E. A. Nelson (San Francisco: Ignatius Press, 1983), 39.

[10]For more on this stream of thought, see Andy Crouch, *Culture Making: Recovering Our Creative Calling* (Downers Grove, IL: IVP Books, 2008) and Gregory Wolfe, *Beauty Will Save the World: Recovering the Human in An Ideological Age* (Wilmington, DE: ISI Books Intercollegiate Studies, 2011).

[11]In his homily to Catholic university professors, Pope John Paul II said, "The young generations expect of you new syntheses, not of an encyclopedic type but of a humanistic form of knowledge." Thus, we should "acquire a fresh approach to fostering the meeting of human minds, giving greater incentives to the quest for truth, scientific advances and the transmission of

culture. Today too, we should rediscover a renewed trend toward the unity of knowledge—that of the *uni-versitas*—with innovative courage in planning a curriculum of studies for a high-profile cultural and formative plan that serves the whole man" (*L'Osservatore Romano*, Oct. 17, 2001).

[12]William Wordsworth, *The Prelude*, ed. Jonathan Wordsworth (London: Penguin 1995), 2:446-47.

The Gospel and the Education
of Our Undergraduates

Sandra Yocum

The style, format, and specific content of the following reflection on the theological education of undergraduates require
contextualization. It originated as one of several presentations
in a dialogue hosted by the United States Conference of Catholic
Bishops (USCCB) between representatives of the various theological academic societies and episcopal and staff members of
the USCCB Committee on Doctrine on March 16, 2013, at The
Catholic University of America in Washington, DC. The focus of
the dialogue was the role of Catholic colleges and universities
in the New Evangelization. New Evangelization was, of course,
the theme of the General Assembly of the Synod of Bishops in
October 2012.

The invitation to each society requested that they select no more
than seven representatives from their membership. The academic
societies represented were the Academy of Catholic Hispanic
Theologians of the United States, the Academy of Catholic The-
ology, the Black Catholic Theological Symposium, the Catholic
Theological Society of America, the College Theology Society,
and the Fellowship of Catholic Scholars. The College Theology
Society representatives were Christopher Denny, Ph.D., St. John's
University, NY; David Gentry-Akin, Ph.D., St. Mary's College of
California, Moraga, CA; Julie Hanlon Rubio, Ph.D., St. Louis Uni-
versity, St. Louis, MO; Bradford Hinze, Ph.D., Fordham University,
Bronx, NY; Timothy Matovina, Ph.D., Notre Dame University,
Notre Dame, IN; William Portier, Ph.D., University of Dayton,
Dayton, OH; and I, Sandra Yocum, Ph.D., University of Dayton
and president of the College Theology Society.

Discussion centered on three topics which appeared on the program using the following descriptive phrases: "the relationship between catechesis and theology in a university setting in light of the New Evangelization," "the role of the Catholic university or college in the promotion of the New Evangelization," and "the intellectual, theological and moral needs of contemporary undergraduates in the age of the New Evangelization." Ten-minute presentations from a bishop and an academic on each topic set the stage for free-flowing discussion among all the participants that lasted from forty-five minutes to an hour. Archbishop William Lori, S.T.D., Archdiocese of Baltimore, and Aurelie Hagstrom, Ph.D., Providence College, Providence, RI, representing Catholic Theological Society of America, addressed the first topic on the relationship between catechesis and theology. Bishop John O. Barres, S.T.L., S.T.D., J.C.L., Diocese of Allentown, and Brian Benestad, Ph.D., University of Scranton, Scranton, PA, representing the Fellowship of Catholic Scholars, addressed the second topic on the general role of Catholic colleges and universities in the New Evangelization. Archbishop Allen H. Vigneron, Ph.D., S.T.L., Archdiocese of Detroit, James Keating, Ph.D., Providence College, Providence, RI, representing the Academy of Catholic Theology, and I, representing the College Theology Society, addressed the third topic concerning the needs of undergraduates.

Discussion was lively and heartfelt. All of those who attended came away with a better understanding of the varied challenges that college professors and bishops face in "teaching theology and handing on the faith," the theme of the 59th annual convention of the College Theology Society (Creighton University, Omaha, NE, May 2013) and the theme for this volume. What follows is the text of my ten-minute presentation on the "intellectual, theological, and moral needs of contemporary undergraduates in the age of the New Evangelization." Preserving the oral quality of the text seems quite appropriate in a volume on "teaching theology and handing on the faith," activities rooted in stories told and visions proclaimed. I hope that you find something of your own work with our sometimes exasperating and often remarkable undergraduates reflected here.

Presentation on "The Intellectual, Theological,
and Moral Needs of Contemporary Undergraduates
in the Age of the New Evangelization"

Thank you for this opportunity to reflect with you this afternoon. I begin with a couple of points for clarification. The undergraduates whom I have in mind are eighteen to twenty-five years old with some affinity for Catholicism, and yes, I recognize not all our students have any such affinity. Second, the sources of my remarks are not limited to my experience but reflect conversations with my College Theology Society and University of Dayton colleagues. I am, however, the interpreter, and take full responsibility for any misstatements in what follows.

Intellectual Needs

Those of us who teach undergraduates have the privilege of witnessing remarkable intellectual development in many of our students. Most eighteen-year-olds arrive on our campus with limited skills in critical thinking, including recognizing different kinds of questions (informational, interpretive, moral) and formulating such questions, understanding complex material using summary, comparison/contrast, analysis, evaluation, and synthesis, and articulating their understanding orally and in writing. Students develop these skills as they engage in learning something substantive, in this case, about Scripture and Catholic tradition (intellectual, spiritual, moral, material). They also need to develop an understanding of what informs their worldview and other worldviews, religious and secular, which a colleague aptly described as being "formed dialogically," and noted was so necessary for the Christian work of reconciliation. Perhaps it even enables them to claim with a measure of confidence: "The joys and the hopes, the griefs and the anxieties of the men [and women] of this age, especially those who are poor or in any way afflicted, these are the joys and hopes, the griefs and anxieties of the followers of Christ. Indeed, nothing genuinely human fails to raise an echo in their hearts" (*Gaudium et Spes*, 1).[1]

I recognize the difficulties in accomplishing what I have just described from two vantage points. First, our students can too easily experience their four years of coursework as exposure to disparate bits of knowledge with little underlying coherence, or as irrelevant (especially theology) to the desired end, a degree. How do we help students, as a colleague wrote, "to appreciate and appropriate university education as a quest for the truth, rather than as an instrumentalist tool by which to gain financial success"? Second, engaging in "a quest for the truth," learning how to think critically, proves a difficult task. Another colleague describes the challenge of navigating "between two extremes [in undergraduate understanding]: (a) the sense that Catholic tradition can be assessed and accepted subjectively; (b) the sense that the proper response to the tradition is blind obedience." The first extreme moves between a subjective fideism (what I believe is true for me) or a reductive rationalism in which critical examination reduces tradition to mere opinion. The second easily devolves into a fundamentalism that truncates the richness of the tradition or into a fideism divorced from reason. So, intellectually, our students need to be schooled in what John Paul II so beautifully described in the opening lines of *Fides et Ratio*: "Faith and reason are like two wings on which the human spirit rises to the contemplation of truth; and God has placed in the human heart a desire to know the truth—in a word, to know himself—so that, by knowing and loving God, men and women may also come to the fullness of truth about themselves (cf. Ex 33:18; Ps 27:8-9; 63:2-3; Jn 14:8; 1 Jn 3:2)."

Theological Needs

Students need to study the Bible, to be thoroughly grounded in that text. What do I mean by study? Certainly, the historical and cultural contexts of individual texts, as well as their literary genres, are important components. Just as important, borrowing from *Dei Verbum*, "Attention must be given to the content and unity of the whole of Scripture if the meaning of the sacred texts is to be correctly worked out. The living tradition of the whole Church must be taken into account along with the harmony which exists between elements of the faith"(12). Scripture lives within the Church, as the community's book. Reading this book is a communal activity even when a lone individual reads it. To understand Scripture's life within the Church requires some knowledge of the living tradition. The written word reveals God as One who enters into relationship with us, ultimately manifest in Jesus Christ, the incarnate Word, present in the beginning, at creation, one who comes in flesh and in spirit to redeem and sanctify. As *Dei Verbum* explains, "There exists a close connection and communication between sacred tradition and Sacred Scripture . . . [which] flow from the same divine wellspring, in a certain way merge into a unity and tend toward the same end"(9). Students can study the creed as the premier example of that "close reciprocal relationship." In his Apostles' Creed commentary, Nicholas Lash pithily expresses this point: "What Scripture says at length, the creed says briefly."[2] Students also need exposure to the expansive watershed that flows from this divine wellspring. Sacraments, liturgy, and other forms of prayer mediate God's ongoing invitation for personal and communal participation in the life flowing from the wellspring.

Two thousand years of practicing the faith provide many inspiring examples of "the whole church's living tradition," as well as examples of failures to live the sacred tradition and scripture. Think of an Ignatian-inspired examen of the Church's life. Let us be willing to ask about what has brought the church community closer to God, and what has not, all in the spirit of gratitude to God. A colleague reflects beautifully on exploring with his students this watershed flowing from the wellspring: "In my intro courses I work more and more with sacred texts from the perspective of examining how particular texts . . . have inspired Christian living and understanding of the faith in different moments of our history." Today, we enjoy a particular blessing, access to many expressions of Catholic faith across the globe; we can bear witness to the gospel's catholicity manifest in its fruition in many different times and places. Such examples may spark our students' sacramental imagination to recognize how the world they inhabit is enlivened with God's redemptive and sanctifying presence revealed in Jesus Christ.

Moral Needs

This final topic proves the most challenging to me. A colleague observed, "Morally, students should learn religious and secular

alternatives to the dominant individualist and libertarian para-
digms that saturate even Catholic universities ... [and] appreciate
the concern for the common good and attempts to expand the
circle of justice to include those who lack access to those material
and spiritual resources necessary for human flourishing." This
description expresses the University of Dayton's and many other
institutions' commitment to teaching ethics across the curriculum.
Determining its effects in our students' lives remains elusive. I
think most undergraduates are aware of the "noes" in Catholic
moral teaching; their familiarity with the tradition's "yeses" that
animate the moral life is less clear to me.

At the heart of the new evangelization is an invitation to come
to know Jesus Christ. Jesus powerfully reveals what creation in
God's image and likeness looks like, for as Paul proclaims to the
Colossians, Jesus is "the image of the invisible God, the firstborn of
all creation" (Col 1:15). Teresa of Avila, in the opening paragraph
of *Interior Castle,* describes the soul as "a castle made of a single
diamond or of very clear crystal, in which there are many rooms"
and reminds her sister companions that God delights in us, "for,
as He Himself says, He created us in His image and likeness. Now
if this is so—and it is—. . . we can hardly form any conception of
the soul's great dignity and beauty."[3] How can we convey the self's
great dignity and beauty and the ways in which that is fostered or
undermined, made radiant or covered over, attended to or ignored
—on the personal, communal, and social level? Perhaps, in their
study of the Bible, students ought to be schooled in *lectio divina*
as much as exegesis, and invited to engage intentionally in moral
living. At the University of Dayton, for example, "Commitment to
Community," a rule of common life based on two Catholic moral
principles, the dignity of the human person and the common good,
articulates a guide and a standard for student living. Students
still make poor choices, but, as a Marianist brother explained to
me, the rule helps him reflect with students on the personal and
communal consequences of their bad behavior and spells out an
alternative way of living in community.

Of course, even more effective than a rule of common life is
a community living the common Christian life. "Above all the
Gospel must be proclaimed by witness." Imagine:

a Christian or a handful of Christians who, in the midst of their own community, show their capacity for understanding and acceptance, their sharing of life and destiny with other people, their solidarity with the efforts of all for whatever is noble and good. . . . In addition, they radiate in an altogether simple and unaffected way their faith in values that go beyond current values, and their hope in something that is not seen and that one would not dare to imagine. Through this wordless witness these Christians stir up irresistible questions in the hearts of those who see how they live: Why are they like this? Why do they live in this way? What or who is it that inspires them? Why are they in our midst? Such a witness is already a silent proclamation of the Good News and a very powerful and effective one. . . . Other questions will arise, deeper and more demanding ones, questions evoked by this witness which involves presence, sharing, solidarity, and which is an essential element, and generally the first one, in evangelization. (21)

Sound familiar? The inspiring scenario comes from Paul VI's 1975 Apostolic Exhortation, *Evangelii Nuntiandi*.

What do undergraduates need? They need witnesses who can serve as guides, pointing in the right direction, showing them the path, inviting them on the journey. They also need companions with whom they can break bread on the journey. Above all, they need time and a place—time to grow in wisdom and love of God like Augustine, whose *Confessions* appears sometime after his fortieth birthday, and a place to remain with the Lord. The first chapter of John's Gospel depicts a simple exchange between Jesus and two of John's disciples. Jesus asks, "What are you looking for?" No answer from the disciples; rather, a question: "Rabbi, Where are you staying?" And Jesus' simple response is, "Come and see" (Jn 1:38-39). Jesus never rescinds the invitation to the disciples, even with their misperceptions, missteps, even betrayals. At the gospel's conclusion, Jesus sought out those who had abandoned him, and he gave them his peace. Where is the place where young women and young men can "come and see" for themselves and, like the disciples, learn how to live in Christ's peace?

Notes

[1]All quotations from church documents are taken from the Vatican website: http://www.vatican.va.

[2]Nicholas Lash, *Believing Three Ways in One God: A Reading of the Apostles' Creed* (Notre Dame, IN: University of Notre Dame Press, 1992), 9.

[3]Teresa of Avila, *Interior Castle*, trans. E. Allison Peers (New York: Dover Publications, 2007 [1946]), 15.

PART I

CONVERGENCES

The Heart Has Its Reasons

Giving an Account of the Hope That Is in Us

Robert P. Imbelli

October 2012 was a true "kairos" moment, for it saw the conjunction of three significant ecclesial events: the fiftieth anniversary of the opening of the Second Vatican Council, the beginning of the Year of Faith, and the meeting of the Synod of Bishops on the New Evangelization. Thus, the convention of the College Theology Society took place in the light of an auspicious constellation of events. It thereby provides an opportunity to respond afresh to the challenge they represent.

Allow me a personal reminiscence. October 2012 was, for me, a particularly "graced moment." I was present in Rome for the Mass celebrating the fiftieth anniversary of the Council and the inauguration of the Year of Faith. It was a sun-drenched October morning, and present at the Mass, along with the participants at the Synod, were the Patriarch of Constantinople and the Archbishop of Canterbury. In his homily, Pope Benedict extolled the documents of Vatican II as the indispensable basis upon which to build as we confront the challenges of the present and the future.

I had also been present in Saint Peter's Square fifty years before for the Council's opening. I had just arrived in Rome as a first-year seminarian to begin theological studies at the Gregorian University. The four years I spent in Rome were remarkable by any measure. Though I had fine professors at the Gregorian University (men like Bernard Lonergan, Francis Sullivan, and René Latourelle—to name but three), there is no doubt that the events outside the classroom had even more of an impact. I was ordained to the priesthood in Rome in 1965, so my almost fifty years of priestly ministry and teaching have been indelibly marked by the Council.

Hence, being in Rome last October filled me with a deep sense of gratitude, a sense of personally having come full circle.

Fifty years is certainly a long period in the life of an individual— as I can fully attest! But it is a relatively short time in the life of the Church, and in the reception of a Council, especially one as "revolutionary" as Vatican II.

Signs of the Times

One of the phrases used by the Council has come into theological and even popular currency: "reading the signs of the times." The theme of the 2013 convention of the College Theology Society, "Teaching Theology and Handing on the Faith: Challenges and Convergences," indicates that a number of those signs have evolved in the past fifty years. I make no claim to originality in enumerating issues such as the following:

1. the decline if not the disappearance of the Catholic sub-cultures that formed and nourished folks like me (and perhaps a few of you);
2. the precipitous decline in the number of Catholic schools on the elementary and secondary level, with the consequent effect on both religious formation and practice;
3. the widespread biblical and theological illiteracy we encounter among our college students—acknowledged from all points on the Catholic compass;
4. polarization among members of the Catholic community (of which some blog sites serve as a house of horrors mirror);
5. as a sub-species of that polarization: tension among theologians and bishops, with particular instances too well-known to require further specification; and
6. drawing closer to the convention theme: the issue of the identity and mission of Catholic colleges and universities.

Current Concerns

Of course, we all inevitably read these signs of the times from a particular vantage point. Let me briefly sketch something of the perspective I bring.

I have spent twenty-seven years at Boston College—six as director of the Institute of Religious Education and Pastoral Ministry, and over twenty as a teacher of theology, teaching both undergraduate and graduate courses. For the past ten years, I have also been active in Boston College's "Church in the Twenty-First Century Initiative." In connection with the Initiative, I edited the volume *Handing On the Faith: The Church's Mission and Challenge* and, most recently, the Spring issue of *C-21 Resources* on "The Catholic Intellectual Tradition."

In these years, I have often voiced two concerns that bear on the topic of the convention. First is the tendency in college and university mission statements to camouflage "Catholic" and to substitute phrases like "in the Jesuit tradition" or its equivalent. Moreover, in parsing the tradition invoked, often the content has been reduced to some vague generality like "educating men and women for others."

The second tendency I've decried is the ritualistic distancing of theology from catechesis, as in the oft-repeated refrain: "We're doing theology, not catechesis." Often this eventuated not simply in a distinction, but in a divorce between the two.

These two tendencies may have been understandable in light of the signs of the times of the immediate post-Vatican II era. The Council rightly stressed the indispensable role of lay men and women in the total life of the church. It showed the deep bonds uniting Catholics with their fellow Christians and, indeed, with all people of good will. It spoke of the need for a revival and reform of theological studies.

The aftermath of the Council saw the loosening of the tight juridical and clerical bonds of our institutions of higher education. It also witnessed the growing conviction of the need for theology in the United States to establish its academic integrity and credentials. Paradoxically, this has led in some instances to a move from theology to a more neutral espousal of "religious studies."

But in light of new signs of the times, some of which I alluded to above, a new discernment seems called for. Indeed, I sense a course-change over the past fifteen years. I perceive a greater willingness to affirm the Catholic identity of colleges and universities, animated in part by Pope John Paul II's Apostolic Constitution *Ex Corde Ecclesiae*. This is sometimes done via an exploration of "the Catholic Intellectual Tradition" and its bearing upon curriculum decisions and design.

I also think there is a growing sense that kerygma, catechesis, and theology form a differentiated continuum, rather than completely discrete ecclesial tasks. Since this latter point bears upon the theme of the College Theology Society convention, let me elaborate further to stimulate and contribute to the discussion.

Catechesis and/or Theology

In a recent article in *Commonweal*, Michael Peppard of Fordham University wrote:

> Just about every day, theological educators must channel Paul at the Areopagus, tailoring our methods to an audience that has no idea what we are talking about (Acts 17). Following Paul's lead, we meet our students where they are, in order, God willing, to bring some of them forward on a path (*educere*). In that process of theological education—not catechetical instruction (*instruere*)—we learn and change together.[1]

I agree with much in Peppard's thoughtful piece, but the passage I just quoted struck me, because it seemed to suggest a dichotomy between "theological education" and "catechetical instruction" that I find problematic. I posted the quote on the *Commonweal* blog under the heading: "Theology and/or Catechetics." A lively conversation ensued.[2]

Enriched by that conversation, let me offer a few clarifications. First, Peppard's disjunction between the tasks of "*educere*" and "*instruere*" does not do justice to either the college classroom or the catechetical setting. *Educere* and *instruere*, I contend, are operative in both.

Second, however, there is a clear difference in audience and goal.

In catechesis the goal of the education is to form members of the community by "handing on the faith." In theological education, as it currently takes place in many of our institutions, the goal is to convey notional knowledge of a particular religious tradition to students who may or may not be participants in that tradition. Put in other terms: catechesis aims at personal transformation in light of the faith tradition handed on; theological education aims at intellectual appropriation of the matter conveyed: in the case I am considering, the Catholic theological tradition. Thus, by insisting on the nexus between catechesis and theology, I am not advocating the collapse of the two ecclesial undertakings in an undifferentiated fusion.

However, and this is central to my presentation, I maintain that the theological educator must respect not only the tradition which the individual student may espouse, he or she must also respect the uniqueness of the tradition which is being presented—in this case, the genius of Catholicism, its distinctive form or *Gestalt*.[3]

Hence, I do not deny differentiations. But I hold that both theological education and catechesis "hand on," communicate the faith's content. Thus my insistence on "differentiated continuity." In terms of the CTS convention's theme: I do not deny the "challenges," but stress the "convergences."[4]

I will try, in the main part of this essay, to illustrate the convergences by reflecting with you upon the theological task as I understand it. What are we teaching when we teach theology in the Catholic Christian tradition? Here is where the continuum of catechesis/theology needs to be extended to embrace the kerygma, the proclamation of God's salvation in Jesus Christ. Or, perhaps more to the point, the kerygma needs to be acknowledged as the matrix and ongoing reference of both catechesis and theology. I believe myself to be in the good company of Karl Rahner in making this claim. Rahner writes: "Since theology reflects and serves the giving of a critical answer for the faith, it is essentially oriented to testimony and preaching. Hence all theology is 'kerygmatic.'"[5]

An Understanding of Catholic Theology

A recent article in *America* by the Jesuit theologian James Hanvey, "*Quo Vadis*?: Reflections on the Shape of the Church to Come," contains this challenging observation:

Too often, in its migration to the university, theology has lost its sense of service, not just to the academy but to the church and its mission. It needs to claim its own freedom and legitimacy within the campus, without sacrificing its subject to the gods of secular reason. Theology must not allow itself to forget that only in service of the mystery of Christ and his church is it preserved from vacuity.[6]

I take my point of departure from the theme sounded in Hanvey's last phrase—"Only in service of the mystery of Christ and his church is [theology] preserved from vacuity." I propose, then, three variations on the theme of the mystery of Christ and his church as giving specific form to Christian theology. The variations take the theological virtues, faith, hope, and love, as ways of structuring an approach to Christian theology.

1. Many here will recognize and accept an approach to theology that takes its point of departure from Anselm's assertion that theology is "faith seeking understanding" (*fides quaerens intellectum*).

I want to draw out two implications of this understanding that are not always to the fore as they should be. One implication is that there is a *prior given* not always sufficiently acknowledged. The faith upon which theology reflects is responsive to a revelation that it has not itself generated. There is an *objectivity* of the Christian fact that precedes any subjective appropriation, including that of the theologian.

Let me illustrate this point with reference to the Second Vatican Council. Though the Council's four constitutions represent the key documents which must have pride of place in the ongoing interpretation and reception of Vatican II (fifty years later!), *Dei Verbum*, the Dogmatic Constitution on Divine Revelation, should be considered "*prima inter pares*," first among equals. For without the revelatory given, neither liturgy nor church nor mission and service to the world has any theological reason for being. To be even more specific, without *Dei Verbum's* confession that "the deepest truth about God and the salvation of humankind shines forth for us in Christ who is the Mediator and at the same time the fullness of all revelation" (2), there is no foundation upon which Christian theology may wisely build.[7]

As Pope Francis said in his homily to the cardinals the day after his election: without Christ and his cross at the center, the church would only be "a charitable NGO (non-governmental organization), but not the church, the bride of the Lord."[8]

The second implication of seeing theology as "faith seeking understanding" is that the faith is transmitted, handed on to the theologian by the church. Theologians reflect upon that which they have received. "We hand on to you what we also have received" (1 Cor 15:3). And the bearer of that tradition is, of course, the church in its kerygma, its liturgy, and its catechesis.

The *credo* of the believer is always derivative from the *credimus*: the faith of the church into which he or she has been baptized. Thus, if we take "faith seeking understanding" as a helpful approach to the task of theology, it highlights theology's ecclesial nature and responsibility. The faith the theologian seeks better to understand is the faith received from the Church; and the further understanding it seeks is to serve the Church and its mission.[9] The theologian is not an independent contractor.

2. As a second "riff" upon the theme that Hanvey sounded, let me pass the lead to the Apostle Peter. In the First Letter of Peter we find a verse often taken as justification for the theological task: "Reverence in your hearts Christ as Lord. Always be ready to make a defense to anyone who asks you for an account of the hope that is in you" (1 Pet 3:15). The word translated here as "account" is *logos*: thus, always be ready to speak a word, to give a reason for the hope that is in you. I've often been struck that the author does not say: give an account, speak a word about your faith, but instead says speak about your hope. One could thus play a variation of Anselm and say that theology is "hope seeking understanding."

Now what is the hope that Peter evokes? The response is clear from the letter's opening "benediction." "Blessed be the God and Father of the Lord Jesus Christ! By his great mercy we have been born anew to a living hope through the resurrection of Jesus Christ from the dead" (1:3). The ground of Christian hope, therefore, is the resurrection of Jesus from the dead. Indeed, this living hope extends the horizon of believers to a transcendent realm: "to an inheritance which is imperishable, undefiled, and unfading kept in heaven" (1:4).

In his fine book *The Spirit of Early Christian Thought* the patristics scholar Robert Wilken does not hesitate to say: "The Resurrection of Jesus is the central fact of Christian devotion and the ground of all Christian thinking."[10] He is only drawing out the implications of Paul's famous declaration in 1 Corinthians: "If Christ has not been raised, then our preaching is in vain and your faith is in vain" (1 Cor 15:14). And Peter would insist: "your hope is in vain." It would have no objective basis; it would be mere illusion and delusion. Indeed, Paul himself continues: "If for this life only we have hoped in Christ, we are of all men and women most to be pitied" (1 Cor 15:19).

This hope is not founded in the expectation of a general resurrection of the dead on the "last day." Its assurance is based upon the concrete and singular occurrence of the resurrection of the one who had been crucified. As Peter proclaimed in his Pentecostal kerygma reported in Acts: "This Jesus God raised up, and of that we are all witnesses ... God has made him both Lord and Christ, this Jesus whom you crucified" (Acts 2:32, 36).

David Bentley Hart draws out the implications of the narrative. He writes: "The crucifixion and resurrection of Jesus tell us nothing in the abstract about human dereliction or human hope.... [They] concern first what happened to Jesus of Nazareth, to whose particular truth and radiance all the general 'truths' of human experience must defer."[11] The scandal of particularity, indeed!

If, then, we approach the theological task as reflection upon Christian hope seeking understanding, the *novum* of the risen Christ will stand at the very center of our theological vision. Theology will ponder Jesus Christ, "the concrete universal" who fulfills all human yearning. In *Gaudium et Spes*, Vatican II strikingly proclaims that:

> the Word of God, through whom all things were made, was made flesh so that as perfectly human he would save all human beings and sum up all things. The Lord is the goal of human history, the point on which the desires of history and civilization turn, the center of the human race, the joy of all hearts and the fulfillment of all desires. (45)

3. I can now add a third voice to the chorus: the Beloved Disciple. In the wonderful "Epilogue" to the fourth gospel, John narrates

the encounter of the Risen Jesus with Peter. The famous threefold question. "Simon, son of John, do you love me?" evokes the heart-felt confession: "Yes, Lord, you know that I love you" (Jn 21:15).

We catch an echo of this scene at the very beginning of the First Letter of Peter. Peter tells the community: "Without having seen Jesus, you love him; though you do not now see him, you believe in him and rejoice with unutterable and exalted joy" (1 Pet 1:8). Robert Wilken says forthrightly:

> The church gave men and women a new love, Jesus Christ, a person who inspired their actions and held their affections. This was a love unlike others. For it was not only that Jesus was a wise teacher, or a compassionate human being who reached out to the sick and needy, or even that he patiently suffered abuse and calumny, and died a cruel death, but that after his death God had raised him from the dead to new life. He who once was dead now lives.[12]

Consequently, Christian existence is lived in intimate relation with the Risen Lord. The risen Jesus is not primarily a figure of the past, for "he always lives to make intercession for us" (Heb 7:25). Pope Benedict acknowledges the important contribution of the historical critical method to biblical study in his volume *Jesus of Nazareth*. But he discerns that, left to itself, it relegates Jesus to the distant past. Therefore, it must be complemented by a theological hermeneutic that mediates an encounter with the living Lord of the Church and nourishes a personal relationship with him.[13]

This love relationship to the living Jesus is at the heart of Christian discipleship. Christian theology, in service to the mystery of Christ and his church, is that love seeking understanding. We ever desire to know better the one whom we love.[14]

A Christocentric Turn

My purpose in this probing of the theological virtues as points of departure for Christian theology is to underscore that both theological education and handing on the faith are configured around the person of Jesus Christ. Christ is the fulfillment of the revelation that faith recognizes and affirms, his resurrection is the unique ground of Christian hope, a loving relationship with him is the distinctive mark of Christian discipleship. In the absence of this Christic center, things fall apart.[15]

Thus, though it is understandable that, for the sake of inter-religious dialogue, one often hears that there are three "religions of the Book"—Judaism, Christianity, and Islam—it is truer to the distinctiveness of Christianity to call it the "religion of the person," because of the uniqueness of its identity-defining relation to the person of Jesus Christ. In its recent document "Theology Today," the International Theological Commission writes: "The Church greatly venerates the Scriptures, but it is important to recognize that the Christian faith is not a 'religion of the book'; Christianity is the 'religion of the word of God,' not of 'a written and mute word, but of the incarnate and living Word.' "[16]

Hence, both for the sake of a fuller appropriation of its distinct identity and to elucidate better the connection between "teaching theology and handing on the faith," theology needs to recover and renew its Christocentric focus. Doing so will promote a deeper reception of the Second Vatican Council and will support and strengthen efforts toward the new evangelization.[17]

A "Christocentric turn" in theology will by no means negate the valid insights of the "anthropological turn" that Karl Rahner cogently thematized and that has characterized much of post-conciliar Catholic theology. But it will root the Christian vision of the human in the new Adam who both reveals and enables humanity's true dignity and transcendent destiny.[18]

I am convinced that Vatican II's singular, though sometimes ne-glected, accomplishment was its recovery of a robust and renewed Christocentricity.[19] The finest fruit of its program of *ressourcement* and *aggiornamento* was its "re-Source-ment": its faithful and creative return to the Source who is Jesus Christ himself.[20] The Council documents are Christologically saturated.

Taking up and developing Vatican II's teaching on the primacy of Jesus Christ also entails heeding the Council's call for a re-newal of theological education in this light. Here the Council only provides general orientations, but they are suggestive. Thus *Dei Verbum* declares that "the study of the Sacred Page is, as it were, the soul of sacred theology," and that theology should proceed "by investigating, in the light of faith, all the truth that is stored up [*conditam*] in the mystery of Christ" (24). Further, the Decree on Priestly Formation, *Optatam Totius*, asserts the need to renew theological disciplines "by livelier contact with the mystery of Christ" ["*vividior cum mysterii Christi contactus*"] (16).

These desiderata of the Council are still a work in progress.[21] Let me sketch two lines of thought worth pondering as we consider the meaning and implications of theology in the Catholic tradition. One might be called "epistemological," the other "ontological." The point of departure for these further reflections is the famous affirmation of Vatican II's Pastoral Constitution on the Church in the Modern World, *Gaudium et Spes*:

> In fact, it is only in the mystery of the incarnate Word that light is shed on the mystery of humankind. For Adam, the first human being, was a figure of Him who was to come, namely Christ the Lord. It is Christ, the final Adam [*novissimus Adam*], who fully discloses humankind to itself and manifests its sublime calling, by the revelation of the mystery of the Father and His love. It is not surprising, then, that in Christ all the truths stated here find their source and attain their fulfillment. (22)

Epistemological Implications

If the living Lord Jesus Christ stands at the center of Christianity's theological vision, then theology will engage a mode of knowing beyond the historical and empirical. It will also appeal to a more experiential, participative, and personalist mode of thought. It is this that Pascal alludes to when he speaks of "the reasons of the heart"—a more integral, incarnational form of human knowing.

Recall how Bernard Lonergan exegetes Pascal. Lonergan writes: "Besides the factual knowledge reached by experiencing, understanding, and verifying, there is another kind of knowledge reached through the discernment of value and the judgments of value of a person in love." And he goes on to speak of faith as "such further knowledge when the love is God's love flooding our hearts."[22]

For the Christian this experiential, affective knowledge of God's love is always mediated through Jesus Christ. As Saint Paul exults at the climax of the magnificent chapter 8 of Romans: "For I am sure that neither death, nor life, nor angels, nor principalities, nor things present, nor things to come, nor powers, nor height, nor depth, nor anything else in all creation, will be able to separate us from the love of God in Christ Jesus our Lord" (Rom 8:38-39). Paul's assurance of things hoped for is firmly rooted in his personal experience and knowledge of "the Lord Jesus, who loved me and gave himself for me" (Gal 2:20).

Such affective cognition also permeates the Johannine tradition. Here are two salient examples from the First Letter of John: "The one who does not love does not know God, for God is Love" (1 Jn 4:8); and "By this we know that we abide in him and he in us, because he has given us of his own Spirit" (1 Jn 4:13). Again, the Johannine tradition is clear that such knowing is always mediated through the Son, as Jesus himself states in his "High Priestly Prayer" in the Gospel: "that they may know you, the only true God, and Jesus Christ whom you have sent" (Jn 17:3).

I suggest, therefore, that such participatory "knowledge of the heart" introduces us to the mystical depth of theology. Gregory the Great summed up this persuasion in his well-known dictum: "*amor ipse notitia est*"—"love is itself knowledge."[23] If Christianity is, as affirmed above, preeminently the "religion of the person," then personal knowledge, the knowledge of persons in relation, must have a crucial place in theological reflection upon Christian faith.[24]

Let me draw out further consequences of this claim for our understanding of theology. The privileged locus for theology is the celebration of the liturgy, where knowledge born of love is both expressed and nurtured. In the liturgy the Bible becomes Scripture, *Sacra Pagina*.[25] Scripture studies, in the Catholic tradition, cannot prescind from this liturgical setting if they hope to avoid a reductionistic approach that leads to an ever more fragmented text. Gerhard Lohfink has recently reminded us that "the gospels, after all, are the church's texts and their true 'life situation' is the liturgy. There they are celebrated as the word of God. There they are proclaimed as Gospel and authentically interpreted."[26]

Tellingly, Lohfink goes on to assert that "faith is true knowledge, true recognition, but a recognition of a different kind from that which analyzes, that is, literally, 'dissolves.' " He goes on to speak of personal knowledge and its consequences: "Whoever wants to truly recognize another as a person must expect to encounter the unexpected and be led into a new world of which previously one had no idea—a world whose strangeness fascinates but also frightens."[27] If this is true of everyday human encounters, how much more is it true of the encounter with the person of Jesus Christ that is at the heart of Christian discipleship?

A further consequence is that the classics of spirituality, such as Augustine's *Confessions*, Dame Julian's *Revelations*, Teresa of Avila's *Interior Castle*, and Merton's *New Seeds of Contemplation*, become crucial theological sources, not merely "extracurricular reading," but intrinsic to the curriculum.[28] The Anglican theologian Sarah Coakley draws boldly upon these sources, especially the Greek fathers, to retrieve the notion of "the spiritual senses." She writes: "This tradition charts in some detail the proposed capacity of our gross physical senses to undergo profound transformative change, or sharpening in the Spirit." This entails "a very particular, and normally undiscussed, form of epistemic receptivity" that requires a dispossession of self, an "undoing of epistemic blockage."[29]

To lift up the classics of spirituality as important theological resources is to underscore that theology reflects upon revelation not as, in the first instance, providing information, but as issuing a summons to transformation. By placing "conversion" as the subject of the functional specialty, "Foundations," Bernard Lonergan argues that "One's interpretation of others is affected by one's understanding of oneself"; and he goes on to insist that "the converted have a self to understand that is quite different from the self that the unconverted have to understand."[30] The theologian enjoys no exemption from the Gospel's summons to ongoing conversion.

Thus what makes the classics of spirituality so important for theological education is their mapping of the logic of transformation from the truncated, in-turned self to the self liberated and renewed in Christ, the new Adam. This theme of the new self features prominently in the paranetic portions of the Letters to the Colossians and Ephesians. So Colossians: "You have put off the old self [*ton palaion anthropon*] with its practices and have put on the new self [*ton neon*], which is being renewed in knowledge, according to the image of the one who is creating" (Col 3:9 and 10). And Ephesians: "Put off your old nature [*ton palaion anthropon*] which belongs to your former manner of life and is corrupt through deceitful lusts, and be renewed [*ananeousthai*] in the spirit of your minds; and put on the new self [*ton kainon anthropon*] created according to God in true righteousness and holiness" (Eph 4:22–24).[31]

In this connection Sarah Coakley insists upon the importance of spiritual practices, a formation for transformation, if you will. She sees the need for "a cumulative tangle of practices—meditative, sacramental, but also moral—in order to sustain this paradoxical form of unknowing/knowing."[32] Besides contemplative and liturgical practices, Catholic theology promotes actions for the sake of justice that honor and serve Christ in his members, as Matthew 25 requires.

I do not necessarily advocate that the theological classrooms incorporate practices that may be more proper to the catechumenate—though certain practices may indeed be conducive to a more meditative climate, even in the classroom. But, in keeping with my stress on continuity rather than discontinuity between the two ecclesial undertakings, the teaching of theology ought at least to be sensitive to more affective modes of presentation of the Catholic theological vision, theological forms that speak to the heart as well as the head.

A final consequence, therefore, is the recognition that the study of theology bears special affinity to poetry, art, and music. I say this not to depreciate more conceptual modes of knowing, but to complement them for the sake of a more integral and integrated understanding of the human. Thereby, we seek to do some measure of justice not only to claims about truth and goodness, but about beauty as well. I confess to resonating deeply with David Bentley Hart's claim that "Bach is the greatest of Christian theologians, the most inspired witness to the *ordo amoris* in the fabric of being. . . . No one as compellingly demonstrates that the infinite is beauty and that beauty is infinite."[33] Reference to "the fabric of being" leads, then, to a reflection on some ontological implications of a theology centered on Christ.

Ontological Implications

What vision of reality emerges from reflection upon Christian existence that flows from conversion to Christ? It is the vision of a personal universe whose alpha and omega is the tri-personal God.

The Great Tradition of the church has pondered over the centuries the mystery of the three-fold Name that is at the heart of its liturgical celebrations. From baptism "in the Name of the Father, the Son, and the Holy Spirit," to the Eucharist offered to the Father through the Son in the Spirit, the reflection of the church has elucidated and explored the Trinitarian grammar of its confession.[34]

The dogmatic formulae of Nicaea and First Constantinople sought to provide an authentic reading of Christian experience as it is constituted and nourished by word and sacrament, to affirm and guide that experience, not to replace it. In the course of the centuries, theological giants like the Cappadocians and Augustine, Richard of Saint Victor and Thomas Aquinas, Karl Rahner and Joseph Ratzinger, have sought to provide some *intellectus fidei,* some understanding of the church's faith (and, of course, I would add: the church's hope and love).

With regard to the mystery of the most Holy Trinity, a fertile approach has been to think in two registers: substantive and relational. So the "persons" of the Trinity are understood in terms of the reciprocal subsistent relations among Father, Son, and Spirit. It is not my intention to investigate in any detail the sense and significance of the church's Trinitarian doctrine.[35] What I want to highlight is that, in the theological tradition, "person" is exegeted in a richly relational key.

If this offers some analogical access to a consideration of the mystery of the Trinity, it also entails consequences for theological anthropology, for a theological understanding of the human mystery. Man and woman themselves are called to relationality, to enter into personal relationship with one another and, inseparably, with the three-personed God. Indeed, such relationality is intrinsic to their becoming persons.

Hans Urs von Balthasar has suggestively distinguished the "individual" and the "person." The latter is preeminently a theological category rooting personal identity in the assumption of a dramatic role within a network of relations. He thus situates the emergence and enrichment of personhood within a relational context. We become more fully persons as we enter more deeply and richly into the field of life-giving relations that replicate the eternal rhythms, the relational fecundity and generosity that is the life of Father, Son, and Spirit.

The *telos* of these relations is *koinonia,* or communion.[36] Not the resolution of individuals into an undifferentiated unity, but the abiding of persons in peaceful and mutually enriching relational interaction. The vision of a personal universe, founded in belief in a three-personed God, supports the realization of a communion of persons in which "If one member of the body suffers, all suffer; if one is honored, all rejoice together" (1 Cor 12:27). It is the vision poetically painted at the end of Dante's *Paradiso*: the image of the White Rose, the communion of holy ones in the Triune God.

Lest we take this vision for granted, it is well to ponder the striking contrast that Nicholas Lash draws with another onto-logical vision—one all too prevalent in our culture. Lash writes:

> In the beginning, according to Nietzsche, there is violence, the struggle for mastery, the will to power. Christianity an-nounces and enacts another tale, according to which in the beginning, and in the end, is peace, pure donated peaceful-ness which, in the times between, makes its appearance in the endless uphill labor of transfigurative harmony.[37]

Lash's fine phrase, "the endless uphill labor of transfigurative harmony," well captures the situation of the Christian in the world. But it also points to what sustains the journey and the end to which it is directed. Christ's Resurrection and Ascension have brought to full realization humanity's vocation to transfiguration—not in some disembodied state, but precisely in his body transformed in the Spirit, what Paul calls the "*soma pneumatikon*" (1 Cor 15:44).

Thus we can take a further step in reflecting upon the ontologi-cal implications of Christian theology's Christological concentra-tion. I speak of it as the vision of a "Christological ontology" wherein the glorified and transfigured humanity of Jesus Christ reveals the depths of reality itself. Salvation, in the Christian un-derstanding, is participation in the very body of Christ. Jesus Christ does far more than show the way to salvation. He creates the way in his own body into which all believers become incorporated.

Indeed, the tradition speaks of the tri-form body of Christ. There is the glorified body of the risen Jesus Christ which still bears the signs of his passion; there is the ecclesial body of the Lord, encompassing both Head and members; there is the Eucharistic body which mediates new life from Head to members. Hence, the Christian vision of reality is radically and pervasively personal, corporeal, and communal. It counters all gnostic temptations to "excarnation." The new creation will bring embodied relationality to transfigured fulfillment.[38]

Robert Barron articulates something of what I have been suggesting in these pages. He writes:

> If, as the Prologue to the Gospel of John insists, Jesus Christ is the visible icon of the Logos through which God has made all things, and if, as the Letter to the Colossians makes clear, Jesus is the one in whom and for whom all things exist and through whom they are maintained, then Jesus is the interpretive lens through which reality is properly read. Jesus Christ is for Christians epistemically basic. . . . We Christians claim to know in a distinctive way, but this does not exclude us from the general human conversation, quite the contrary. It allows us to enter it more honestly, effectively, and creatively.[39]

And, I would add, to bring to that conversation Good News that is genuinely new. In the words of the Letter to the Colossians: "to make known the riches of the glory of the mystery, which is Christ in you, the hope of glory" (Col 1:27).

The Notional and the Real

I have sought in this presentation to indicate the intimate nexus between "Teaching Theology and Handing On the Faith." My strategy has been to make a case for an understanding of Catholic theology that is radically Christocentric. The teaching of theology in the Catholic tradition, whatever the audience to which it is directed, must honor this Christocentric originality. Doing so *ipso facto* entails "handing on the faith" by communicating what is most proper to it. I insist, however, that this does not mean engaging in the effort to "convert" the students taking the course, proselytizing in the invidious sense it has acquired.

Here Cardinal Newman's distinction between the "notional"

and the "real" may be of help. What I ask of students is that they exhibit a notional understanding of the distinctive claims and implications of the Catholic theological tradition, in whatever aspect or area it is presented to them. Whether this "notional apprehension" becomes a "real assent" is the work of their own discernment and conscience—and the Holy Spirit.

Some may wonder whether, in so focusing upon a Christocentric approach to theology, I have ventured perilously close to that dread disease labeled "Christomonism." It is too late in the presentation to offer more than a brief assurance that I do indeed affirm the Trinity and the Third Person! I would stress, however, that our only grounds for confessing a Triune God is the Incarnation of the Son in Jesus Christ. As Khaled Anatolios writes: "A Christological reconception of divine transcendence was foundational for the deep structure of the developing Trinitarian grammar of what came to be associated with 'Nicene' faith."[40]

Moreover, the Holy Spirit is ever sent from the Father through the Son. Pentecost is the fruit and gift of Christ's Paschal Mystery. As *Gaudium et Spes* professes: "The Holy Spirit . . . offers to everyone the possibility of being associated with [Christ's] paschal mystery" (22). I can hardly do better, in this matter, than make my own the conviction of Yves Congar: "The vigor of a lived pneumatology is to be found in Christology. There is only one body which the Spirit builds up and quickens and that is the body of Christ."[41]

Having extolled the indispensable place of poetry, music, and the arts in the Catholic theological tradition, let me close by invoking a contemporary poet who has written of the need for a "poetics of belief," that is, the need for "a language capacious enough to include a mystery that, ultimately, defeats it, and sufficiently intimate and inclusive to serve not only as individual expression but as communal need."[42]

The contemporary American poet Christian Wiman also pens these words which spur us forward toward convergence and challenge in Christ:

> Modern spiritual consciousness is predicated upon the fact
> that God is gone, and spiritual experience, for many of us,
> amounts mostly to an essential, deeply felt and necessary,

but ultimately inchoate and transitory feeling of oneness or unity with existence. It is mystical and valuable, but distant. Christ, though, is a shard of glass in your gut. Christ is God crying *I am here*, and here not only in what exalts and completes and uplifts you, but here in what appalls, offends, and degrades you, here in what activates and exacerbates all that you would call not-God. To walk through the fog of God toward the clarity of Christ is difficult because of how unlovely, how "ungodly" that clarity often turns out to be.[43]

Notes

[1]Michael Peppard, "Testing the Boundaries," *Commonweal*, April 12, 2013, 16.

[2]http://www.commonwealmagazine.org/blog/?p=26547#comments.

[3]The notion of "form" is key to the theological vision of Hans Urs von Balthasar. See Aidan Nichols, *A Key to Balthasar* (Grand Rapids, MI: Baker Academic, 2011), 12–48.

[4]In the exchange on the *Commonweal* blog, I raised the question: Is Joseph Ratzinger's *Introduction to Christianity* a work of catechetics or theology? In my view it is inseparably both.

[5]Karl Rahner, "Theology," in *Sacramentum Mundi: Encyclopedia of Theology*, vol. 6 (New York: Herder and Herder, 1970), 234.

[6]James Hanvey, "*Quo Vadis*: Reflections on the Shape of the Church to Come," *America*, March 18, 2013, 15.

[7]Ormond Rush makes a similar point in his article, "Towards a Comprehensive Interpretation of the Council and Its Documents," *Theological Studies*, 73, no. 3 (September 2012): 550: "The theological focus of *Dei Verbum* can function as a lens for interpreting the more ecclesiologically focused constitutions *Sacrosanctum concilium*, *Lumen gentium*, and *Gaudium et spes*."

[8]Pope Francis, "Mass with the Cardinal Electors" (March 14, 2013): http://www.vatican.va.

[9]I find myself, therefore, in substantial agreement with Avery Dulles's articulation of an "ecclesial/transformative" understanding of the theological enterprise. See his *The Craft of Theology: From Symbol to System* (New York: Crossroad, 1995), 18–21.

[10]Robert Louis Wilken, *The Spirit of Early Christian Thought: Seeking the Face of God* (New Haven: Yale University Press, 2003), xv.

[11]David Bentley Hart, *The Beauty of the Infinite: The Aesthetics of Christian Truth* (Grand Rapids, MI: Eerdmans, 2003), 27.

[12]Wilken, *The Spirit of Early Christian Thought*, xv.

[13]Joseph Ratzinger/Benedict XVI, *Jesus of Nazareth, Part Two: From the Entrance into Jerusalem to the Resurrection* (San Francisco: Ignatius, 2011), xiv–xvii.

[14]See the perhaps insufficiently appreciated essay by Karl Rahner, "What Does It Mean to Love Jesus?" in *The Love of Jesus and the Love of Neighbor*, trans. Robert Barr (New York: Crossroad, 1983), 9–61.

[15]For a scathing indictment of "Christological collapse" in the contemporary Catholic context, see Luke Timothy Johnson, "On Taking the Creed Seriously," in *Handing On the Faith: The Church's Mission and Challenge*, ed. Robert P. Imbelli (New York: Crossroad, 2006), 63–76. For an irenic, but incisive analysis of the "de-centering of Christ" in some contemporary theology, see Harold Wells, *The Christic Center* (Maryknoll, NY: Orbis Books, 2004), chapters 4 and 6.

[16]International Theological Commission, "Theology Today: Perspectives, Principles, and Criteria," chapter 1, no. 7: http://www.vatican.va.

[17]In his essay "The New Evangelization and Theological Renewal," Avery Dulles argues that a Christ-centered theology is essential for promoting the new evangelization. See Avery Cardinal Dulles, *Evangelization for the Third Millennium* (New York: Paulist, 2009), 78–89.

[18]One of Rahner's interpreters, Francis Schüssler Fiorenza, makes this insightful observation: "Rahner's method is such that he does not take a secular modern version of humanity and project it back to Christology, but rather makes the concrete existence of Jesus the norm for understanding Christian existence." See "Method in Theology" in Declan Marmion and Mary Hines, eds., *The Cambridge Companion to Karl Rahner* (Cambridge: Cambridge University Press, 2005), 70. In the article "Theology" Rahner says that "theology is and remains perpetually linked to the historical event of salvation which took place once and for all" (see 236n5).

[19]See Robert P. Imbelli, "Do This In Memory of Me: Vatican II's Renewed Realization of the Primacy of Christ," *America*, April 22, 2013, 18–20.

[20]Ormond Rush writes: "One of the most significant teachings of the Council is its retrieval of the nature of divine revelation as first and foremost God's loving, personal self-communication to humanity in Christ through the Spirit. . . . God's continuous revelatory and salvific presence and activity in human history in Jesus Christ through the Holy Spirit": Rush, "Towards a Comprehensive Interpretation," 564.

[21]Gerald O'Collins laments the scarce treatment of the resurrection of Christ in sacramental and moral theology. See *Believing in the Resurrection: The Meaning and Promise of the Risen Jesus* (New York: Paulist, 2012), chapter 8: "The Resurrection's Impact on Sacramental and Moral Theology."

[22]Bernard Lonergan, *Method in Theology* (New York: Herder and Herder, 1972), 115.

[23]Gregory's phrase regarding affective cognition is developed in the fine book of the English philosopher John Cottingham, *The Spiritual Dimension: Religion, Philosophy, and Human Value* (Cambridge: Cambridge University Press, 2005). It will come as no surprise that Cottingham, in this book, draws appreciatively on Pascal.

[24]Students of Lonergan like Robert Doran, S.J., and Patrick Byrne have creatively extended Lonergan's "intentionality analysis" to posit a "fifth level of intentional consciousness": the interpersonal dimension.

[25]In setting forth his understanding of an "ecclesial-transformative" approach to theology, Avery Dulles writes: "A privileged locus ... is the worship of the Church, in which the biblical and traditional symbols are proclaimed and 're-presented' in ways that call for active participation (at least in mind and heart) on the part of the congregation" (Dulles, *The Craft of Theology*, 19). It is noteworthy that in the expanded edition of *Craft* (1995), Dulles added a new chapter on "Theology and Worship."

[26]Gerhard Lohfink, *Jesus of Nazareth: What He Wanted, Who He Was*, trans. Linda M. Maloney (Collegeville, MN: Liturgical Press, 2012), 8.

[27]Ibid., 20.

[28]One of the achievements of Frans Jozef van Beeck is his masterful integration of the classics of spirituality into the fabric of systematic theology. See *God Encountered: A Contemporary Catholic Systematic Theology*, volume 1 of *Understanding the Christian Faith* (Collegeville, MN: Liturgical Press, 1989).

[29]Sarah Coakley, "The Identity of the Risen Jesus," in *Seeking the Identity of Jesus*, ed. Beverly Roberts Gaventa and Richard Hays (Grand Rapids: Eerdmans, 2008), 312n21 and 313.

[30]Lonergan, *Method in Theology*, 271.

[31]A recent and quite personal reflection on the shape of the old self and the new self in Christ is Miroslav Volf, *Free of Charge: Giving and Forgiving in a Culture Stripped of Grace* (Grand Rapids: Zondervan, 2005).

[32]Coakley, "The Identity of the Risen Jesus," 316.

[33]Hart, *The Beauty of the Infinite*, 282 and 283.

[34]A fine account is Khaled Anatolios, *Retrieving Nicaea: The Development and Meaning of Trinitarian Doctrine* (Grand Rapids: Baker Academic, 2011).

[35]A brief but substantial treatment is Joseph Ratzinger, *Introduction to Christianity* (San Francisco: Ignatius, 2000), 162-190. A recent fuller presentation is Luis Ladaria, *The Living and True God: The Mystery of the Trinity* (Miami, FL: Convivium, 2010).

[36]Following the hint in Second Corinthians regarding the "*koinonia* of the Spirit" (2 Cor 13:13), one can consider communion to be the distinctive *proprium* of the Spirit both in the economy of salvation and in the Godhead. See Robert P. Imbelli, "The New Adam and Life-Giving Spirit: The Paschal Pattern of Spirit Christology," *Communio* 25, no. 2 (Summer 1998). In the same issue note the important article of Joseph Ratzinger, "The Holy Spirit as *Communio*: Concerning the Relationship of Pneumatology and Spirituality in Augustine."

[37]Nicholas Lash, *The Beginning and the End of "Religion"* (Cambridge: Cambridge University Press, 1996), 232.

[38]A very stimulating article that probes this tri-form body of the risen and ascended Christ is Anthony Kelly, "The Body of Christ: Amen!: The Expanding Incarnation," *Theological Studies* 71 (2010): 792-816.

[39]Robert Barron, "The Metaphysics of Coinherence: A Meditation on the Essence of the Christian Message," in Imbelli, ed., 83-84.

[40]Anatolios, *Retrieving Nicaea*, 9.

[41]Yves M. J. Congar, *The Word and the Spirit*, trans. David Smith (San Francisco: Harper and Row, 1986), 6. See also Robert P. Imbelli, "The Holy

Spirit," in Joseph Komonchak, Mary Collins, Dermot Lane, ed., *The New Dictionary of Theology* (Wilmington, DE: Michael Glazier, 1987), 474-89.

[42]Christian Wiman, *My Bright Abyss: Meditation of a Modern Believer* (New York: Farrar, Straus and Giroux), 124.

[43]Ibid., 121.

Cardinal Dulles and the New Evangelization

Anne-Marie Kirmse, O.P.

Avery Dulles once described himself as a "fundamental theologian," that is, one working within foundational theological categories such as revelation and faith.[1] While he considered his book *Models of Revelation* (1983) to be his most important work, and *The Assurance of Things Hoped For* (1994) to be his contribution to the theology of faith in our country (as it is the only book of its kind in English), he is probably most remembered for his masterpiece of ecclesiology, *Models of the Church* (1974). Dulles's ecclesiology was not limited to the Catholic Church, however, as he was committed to the ecumenical agenda that followed Vatican II. In fact, his interest in the teaching of Vatican II and his probing into its documents was so strong that in 1988 he could confidently say in an interview with Peter Steinfels, "what I've been doing these last twenty, twenty-five years really centers around interpreting Vatican II."[2] The same statement could have been made at the time of his death in December 2008 just by changing the "twenty, twenty-five years" to "forty, forty-five years." All these interests—faith, revelation, ecclesiology, ecumenism, and Vatican II—coalesced in his interest in evangelization.

Although Paul VI is usually remembered for his encyclicals *Ecclesiam Suam* (1964) and *Humanae Vitae* (1968), Dulles maintained that the Pope's apostolic exhortation on evangelization, *Evangelii Nuntiandi* (1975), was one of this pope's greatest and most important contributions to the life of the Church in our time. Dulles's appreciation of the significance of *Evangelii Nuntiandi* deepened during his years as Laurence J. McGinley Professor at Fordham University. During those two decades spanning the years 1988 to 2008, he delivered twenty-three lectures, both in the United States and abroad, pertaining to some aspect of evangelization, and published eighteen articles on the topic. Some of these articles were translated into other languages. His book *Evangelization for the Third Millennium* was published posthumously in 2009.

What exactly is meant by the term "new evangelization"? Specifically, what is *new* about the new evangelization? The term was first used by the Latin American bishops (CELAM) in 1968, but was not used by Paul VI, who called for "a new period of evangelization" (*EN* 2). Blessed John Paul II envisioned a new era of evangelization to coincide with the 500th anniversary of arrival of missionaries in what was considered to be the "New World." John Paul II later combined the coming of the new millennium with the need for a new evangelization.

Following his penchant for organizing material into categories, Dulles sees the new evangelization as having ten characteristics. As Dulles explains it, the new evangelization is actually quite ancient, going back to apostolic times. *Evangelium* refers to the proclamation of the Gospel or Good News by Jesus himself, followed by the kerygma of the apostles. Therefore, first of all, the new evangelization must be centered in Jesus Christ. Paul VI boldly states, "There is no true evangelization if the name, the teaching, the life, the promises, the kingdom and the mystery of Jesus of Nazareth, the Son of God, are not proclaimed" (*EN* 22).

Centrality of Christ

Vatican II sometimes uses the term "evangelization" to signify the basic message to be proclaimed, but sometimes more broadly, meaning the fullness of revelation given in Jesus Christ. The Dogmatic Constitution on the Church, *Lumen Gentium*, begins with the statement: "Christ is the light of the nations." Although this constitution was written in 1964, this opening sentence can be seen as the leitmotif of the entire Council. And while the term "new evangelization" was not used as such, it is obvious that this was the thrust of the Council. Dulles points out that Vatican II usually used the term "evangelization" in a narrow sense as the proclamation of the Christian message to non-believers rather than the broader concept of bringing the totality of the Christian message to bear on daily life in our world.

Ecumenism and Interreligious Dialogue

At first glance, ecumenism and interreligious dialogue, Dulles's second and third headings, seem to be antithetical to evangelization. After all, ecumenism has the reunion of the Christian churches as its ultimate goal, and interreligious dialogue seems to be at odds with missionary endeavor. Yet Dulles sees no contradiction here. In both situations, that of dialogue with believers in the Christian message and dialogue with nonbelievers, evangelization demands that the proclamation of the Gospel be honest and straightforward. Nothing is to be gained by "watering down" the Gospel message to make it palatable to others. Dulles has always maintained that dialogue requires respectful listening to the positions of the other participants and a responsible presentation of one's own position. In an interview with *Zenit*, he was asked if interreligious dialogue and ecumenism preclude apologetics. Dulles replied:

> In interreligious and ecumenical dialogues the objective is to find or extend common ground rather than to convert the dialogue partner to one's own faith, which is the purpose of apologetics. But honesty requires us not to conceal our true convictions where they differ from those of the partner. It may be that in dialogue we have to explain why we cannot accept the positions of the other party. If so, dialogue will contain an ingredient of apologetics.[3]

Here Dulles is speaking with the voice of experience—experience which predates both Vatican II and *Evangelii Nuntiandi*. In 1962 he was appointed to the Baltimore Archdiocesan Commission on Christian Unity; he was a member of the Advisory Editorial Board for Ecumenism for *Concilium* from 1963 to 1992; and served for seven years as a consultor to the Papal Secretariat for Dialogue with Non-Believers from 1966 to 1973. The group with which he had the most interaction was the United States Lutheran/Catholic Dialogue, serving as a member for twenty years (1972-1992) and then serving on its Coordinating Committee from 1992 to 1996.

Religious Freedom

Dialogue does not mean "agreeing to disagree." Instead, it is a process clarifying toward consensus even when there is still serious divergence. Therefore, evangelizing dialogue is not coercion, which leads us to Dulles's fourth characteristic of the new evangelization: religious freedom. Dulles notes that the new evangelization "proposes full acceptance of Vatican II's Declaration on Religious Freedom, which taught that people should be encouraged to follow their free and responsible judgments without external pressure."[4] This conciliar statement was restated in *Evangelii Nuntiandi* in the words, "the Church should propose the truth of the gospel without seeking to impose anything on the consciences of the hearers" (*EN* 80). Thus ecumenism and interreligious dialogue are not proselytization but a proclamation of Jesus Christ.

Continuing Process

These first four characteristics seem to be directed toward evangelization *ad extra*, i.e., to those outside the boundaries of the Catholic Church. But the new evangelization has much more than an outward thrust. Dulles's fifth trait is continuing process. In *Evangelii Nuntiandi*, Paul VI set forth a wide concept of evangelization. Dulles quotes John Paul II as delineating this concept into three categories: evangelization to (1) those who have not yet heard the Gospel message, in other words, the missionary work of the Church per se, (2) those who have received the Gospel and wish to follow the teaching of Jesus Christ more fully, and (3) those who have heard the Gospel message but who have grown lukewarm or even fallen away and are in need of a re-evangelization. It is in this area of continuing process that the concept of new evangelization is most evident. For centuries, the proclamation of the Gospel or "first evangelization" or "primary evangelization" as it is sometimes called, was viewed as primarily the work of missionaries. However, first or primary evangelization also took place in the home, school, and religious education classes, as acknowledged in *Evangelii Nuntiandi*. Catechesis—the transmission of the faith—belongs in the second category listed above. For this reason, Dulles notes that "Catechesis is not wholly distinct from evangelization; indeed it may be called the second stage, following upon primary evangelization, in which the basic elements of the faith are presented."[5]

Evangelii Nuntiandi states that "A means of evangelization that must not be neglected is that of catechetical instruction" (*EN* 44). This leads to the question: How best does the Church catechize its members? The fact that Dulles did not have parish or pastoral experience and came into the Church as an adult convert long before the RCIA Program limits his view of catechesis, a fact he readily admits:

> I have never been personally involved in the work of catechesis or elementary religious education. My field of specialization is, and has been, theology, and as a teacher of theology I have conducted classes for seminarians and graduate students whose basic familiarity with and acceptance of the Christian message could be take for granted. All of my students would have been evangelized and catechized long before coming to my classes.[6]

Nevertheless, he continues:

> The catechetical process interests me and appears to me to be extremely important for the future of the Church in this country and all over the world. We face enormous difficulties in transmitting the Catholic faith to new generations in the present atmosphere of secularism, relativism, and postmodernism.[7]

After surveying the various approaches to catechesis, he examined the literature and proposed five models of catechesis. These models as he named them were: doctrinal, kerygmatic, liturgical, experiential, and praxis. As was his practice when dealing with models, Dulles presented the merits and liabilities of each one. He found the first four somewhat narrow in their approach, but he did find hope in his fifth model. Praxis is based loosely on liberation theology and the work of Paulo Freire. In this approach, prayerful reflection is made on the situation at hand with a critical eye. While theory is important, it leads to praxis, hopefully contributing to the building of the kingdom of God. Thomas Groome, the only religious educator whom Dulles praises, fits this model. In Dulles's judgment, Groome seems to integrate the necessity of magisterial teaching, the importance of salvation history, and the lived experience of the students, while insisting that such experience must be judged through theological reflection. The only deficit Dulles finds in Groome's presentation of praxis is not enough emphasis on liturgy.

Dulles felt that the answer to reviving religious education as a form of catechesis in the second level of continuing process in the new evangelization could be found in *The Catechism of the Catholic Church*. In his view, the Catechism's four foci of creed, sacramental worship, Christian life, and prayer provide the proper basis for catechesis, which can be and must be adapted to the background and age of the students. Unfortunately, Dulles did not address ongoing education of adult Catholics, nor did *Evangelii Nuntiandi*.

Social Teaching

Catechetical formation should lead to action following the example of Jesus, who described his own mission in the words of Isaiah, "The Spirit of the Lord is upon me, because he has anointed me to bring glad tidings to the poor. He has sent me to proclaim liberty to the captives, and the recovery of sight to the blind, to let the oppressed go free, and to proclaim a year acceptable to the Lord" (Lk 4:18-19). This brings us to Dulles's sixth characteristic of the new evangelization, that of emphasis on social teaching. True followers of Jesus must be concerned about the condition of their brothers and sisters in their local and global communities. They cannot be content to wait for a transformation of the world at the end-time, but must be concerned with transforming the world by working for peace and justice within contemporary society. True, the Church has always been involved in educational, health care, and pastoral initiatives, both in its own native lands and especially in missionary endeavors. But the new evangelization sees efforts on behalf of justice as part and parcel of its own agenda. In Paul VI's words, "Evangelization would not be complete if it did not take account of the unceasing interplay of the Gospel, and man's concrete life, both personal and social" (*EN* 29). However, this agenda can never be so focused on improving the human condition that it loses its vision of the kingdom as proclaimed by Jesus. The Pope cautions, "The Church links human liberation and salvation in Jesus Christ, but she never identifies them." Thus, the work for bringing about a more just society can never be reduced to mere material progress, no matter how well intentioned that may be. The "interplay of the Gospel," as stated by the Pope, is the primary agent of social reform. This primacy of the Church's spiritual aim is a topic that Dulles has addressed. With Paul VI, he does not believe that Vatican II intended that such service be oriented primarily to the betterment of the social order. In fact, Dulles's opinions are quite the contrary. He distinguishes between what is "proper" to the Church's mission and the repercussions which flow from this mission, defining the former as "that which is specific to the church and would remain undone unless the church existed."[8] In this category, he places preaching faith in Christ and administering the sacraments. Naturally, the living of an authentic faith relationship with Christ and the deepening of this graced relationship with him sacramentally will lead his followers to strive for justice for all persons. But that is a result of the Church's salvific activity, not its cause. Dulles makes a subtle distinction in claiming that while the erection of a just society is not proper to the Church, contributing to this society is.[9]

Evangelization of Culture

The social teaching of the Church and the social action which builds on this teaching take place within a context, situated within a particular culture. The evangelization of culture is Dulles's seventh category in the new evangelization. This topic was a favorite of John Paul II. Culture is a rather amorphous term, with many possible meanings. In Dulles's view, "culture is a system of meanings, historically transmitted, embodied in symbols, and installed in new members of the group so that they are inclined to think, judge, and act in characteristic ways."[10] Human beings live and grow within a particular culture. They are shaped by the traditions of that culture, share in the customs and celebrations of that culture, and live in harmony with other members of their cultural community. The preaching of the Gospel has had a profound influence on the countries of the culture in which it has been planted, and, in return, the various cultures have affected the proclamation of the Christian message. It is a reciprocal phenomenon; the Gospel and culture have a significant influence on each other. Dulles writes:

> Faith and culture exist in a kind of mutual interdependence. Culture stands to benefit from faith, which helps it discern what is rich and noble in any given human system and to correct what is deficient. Faith, conversely, benefits from culture, because it uses the resources of various cultures to probe the meaning of revelation and give it better liturgical and intellectual expression.[11]

Western civilization as a whole and Europe in particular have been shaped by this reciprocity. For approximately eighteen centuries, Christianity was acknowledged as the basis of its culture. But the situation has changed dramatically, with some leaders wishing to disclaim the importance of Christianity in the past and to deny its relevance in the present. Paul VI mentions the crisis of "dechristianization" in *Evangelii Nuntiandi*, and the concept was furthered by his successors. John Paul II pondered this reality in many writings, and Pope Emeritus Benedict XVI bemoaned the "Dechristianization of Europe." Dulles addressed the possibility of the "Dechristianization of America," first in general terms in his second McGinley Lecture in 1989 and later very specifically in a lecture on the topic in 2006.[12] His answer is "No." The United States has a very different history from that of Europe. A very important difference is that of the lack of a national religion. For all their problems with organized religion, our founding fathers had a religious background and an appreciation for the truths which religion sets forth. This appreciation is most evident in our Declaration of Independence. Then, too, American culture is a diverse and complex reality. It was created from the many cultures of the peoples who came to this country to live, bringing with them the traditions and customs of their native lands. While there is an increasing secularization ongoing in our country today, there are also many immigrants who still bring with them their culture and their religion. Dulles saw the church's tasks in culture to be evangelization, proclamation, and dialogue. It is in the last of these three components that the preaching of the Gospel and the culture are able to serve each other.

Use of Modern Communications

An important component in any culture is communication, leading us to Dulles's eighth characteristic of the new evangelization. In the past culture was transmitted through art, music, and the printed word. The past century saw the growth of mass media in radio, movies, and television. Vatican II saw the media as so important as to write one of its earliest decrees on the topic, and Paul VI included an appreciation of mass media in *Evangelii Nuntiandi*: "The Church would feel guilty before the Lord if she did not utilize these powerful means that human skill is daily rendering more perfect" (*EN* 45). Dulles was an avid reader and kept abreast of current events. He had a great love of art and literature, and valued the ability to receive news quickly. However, he realized the dangers inherent in the way news is presented in contemporary society. Nuanced ecclesial statements cannot be reduced to simplistic sentences, and when polling responses to ecclesiastical pronouncements, care must be taken to try to ascertain the faith commitment of the respondents. He states, "Radio, television, and computer technology must not be allowed to dictate the message, but must be prudently employed to open new avenues of access to the gospel."[13] Dulles died before the widespread use of social media, so one can only wonder what his views on this phenomenon might have been.

Involvement of All Christians

Regardless of his views on the media, Dulles realized that it was no substitute for personal contact. This leads to his next heading under characteristics of the new evangelization, that of involvement of all Christians. In the past, too often the task of evangelization was seen as missionary work best left to the priests and women and men religious who followed that calling. There were lay missionaries, but their number was very low in comparison with members of the religious orders. Vatican II once again emphasized the role of the laity in the life of the church. It is all the members of the church who participate in its mission by reason of their baptism. Ten years after the end of the Council, Paul VI reiterated its basic message, "It is the whole church that receives the mission to evangelize" (*EN* 15). All are called to spread the gospel message by their faithful adherence to it. The laity in particular have the distinct privilege and responsibility of living the Christian life within their vocations as spouses, parents, and single laymen and laywomen.

Dulles always had an appreciation for the witness of those who could be called "the people in the pew." When he was a young man searching for the true church at Harvard, he was impressed by his courses in Renaissance literature, art, and music. This academic search was aided by the people he saw attending Mass and other liturgical functions in Cambridge. He remembered them fondly:

> A further fact that entered into my process of conversion was the existence of popular Catholicism as I witnessed it in a city such as Cambridge, Massachusetts. The Catholic faith had an extraordinary hold on the minds and hearts of the common people, most of whom, in that region, were of Irish extraction. They were remarkably faithful in their religious observance. Their piety was governed by the same revelation that had inspired the great artists and poets of earlier centuries.[14]

He realized that something must be bringing these people together in all kinds of weather despite whatever else might be happening in their lives. The witness of these people helped him make the decision to become a Catholic in 1940. Yet they never knew how much good they had done.

The Primacy of the Holy Spirit

But this witness, as effective as it is, brings us to the last of Dulles's ten characteristics of the new evangelization, the primacy of the Holy Spirit. Evangelization does not in the first instance depend on human initiative. Rather, as Paul VI points out, "The Holy Spirit is the principal agent of evangelization: it is he who impels each individual to proclaim the gospel, and it is he who in the depths of consciences causes the word of salvation to be heard and understood" (*EN* 75). Dulles's last category therefore brings us back to the first, for it is the Spirit who enables the proclamation of the message of Jesus to be made, to be heard, and to be accepted.

If it can be said that the last days of a person's life demonstrate what that person considers most important, then evangelization was uppermost in Cardinal Dulles's mind. He had long been planning to write a book on evangelization, but his busy schedule of lecturing, teaching, and writing commitments delayed his opportunity to do so. When a fall necessitated his moving to Murray-Weigel Hall, the Jesuit infirmary, in February 2008, he seriously began his work on this project, so dear to his heart.

Cardinal Dulles labored over the details of preparing this manuscript. Despite his rapidly declining health, he wanted to be involved in it, every step along the way. Cardinal Dulles himself chose the ten writings which appear in the book. At first, he was able to edit the texts himself on his computer in the infirmary and to edit the manuscript by writing his changes in the margins. But soon after making these preliminary corrections, he was no longer able to write, type, or speak. He read the next version of the manuscript and indicated further corrections by crumpling the bottom right-hand side of the page. The pages that weren't smooth indicated that something on that page needed to be changed. Cardinal Dulles's work on *Evangelization for the Third Millennium*, his last book, was truly a labor of love.

Pope Paul VI wrote in the beginning of *Evangelii Nuntiandi* that his purpose "was to make the Church of the twentieth century ever better fitted for proclaiming the Gospel to the people of the twentieth century" (*EN* 2). It was Cardinal Dulles's hope that his book would play a role in revitalizing the subject of evangelization for the people of the new millennium, and for this reason he devoted the last days of his life to working on it. May the Cardinal's hope become a reality.

Notes

[1]Avery Dulles, "Introduction," *Models of Revelation* (Garden City, NY: Doubleday, 1983), vii-xi.
[2]Peter Steinfels, "Fordham's New Theologian: A Flair for Diplomacy," *New York Times*, October 2, 1988.
[3]"Cardinal Dulles on the History of Apologetics," interview with *Zenit*, September 14, 2005, http://www.zenit.org.
[4]Avery Dulles, *Evangelization for the Third Millennium* (Mahwah, NJ: Paulist Press, 2009), 33.
[5]Ibid., 101.
[6]Avery Dulles, "Historical Models of Catechesis," *Origins* 37 (November 8, 2007): 348.
[7]Ibid.
[8]Avery Dulles, "Vatican II and the Church's Purpose," *Theology Digest* 32 (1985): 345.
[9]Ibid., 349-50.
[10]Avery Dulles, *The Reshaping of Catholicism* (San Francisco: Harper & Row, 1988), 40.
[11]Avery Dulles, "The Impact of the Catholic Church on American Culture," lecture at John Paul II Cultural Center, November 13, 2001.
[12]Avery Dulles, "The Dechristianization of Europe—Is America Next?" lecture at Duquesne University, Pittsburgh, PA, April 20, 2006.
[13]Dulles, *Evangelization for the Third Millennium*, 37.
[14]Dulles, "The Impact of the Catholic Church."

Giving God the First Word

Spirituality as the Bridge between Catechesis and Theology

Christopher Collins, S.J.

In Flannery O'Connor's "The Enduring Chill," we meet Asbury, a young man who conceives of himself as a rather sophisticated, learned, and therefore misunderstood figure.[1] Having fled his rural southern roots, he goes to New York to become an artist and an intellectual. We meet him as he makes his return home to Timberboro, having contracted some mysterious disease that seems to be leading inexorably to his tragic death. He is exiled now to live with his utterly simple and overbearing mother and his unsympathetic sister, neither of whom understands his lofty vision. As his concerned mother continues to badger young Asbury to go and see their old family physician, Dr. Block, the young ailing man repeatedly and defiantly proclaims, "What's wrong with me is way beyond Block."

Having surrendered to the prospect of his own demise, the one hope he clings to is the possibility of thoughtful conversation about the nature of life and death and the meaninglessness of it all. He seeks to face his mortality with the heroism of a contemporary philosopher or artist who confronts the absurdity of life. While he is not a believer, he must surely have no fear, even of confronting the great religious questions posed to him in his current predicament. He calls on his mother to send for a Jesuit priest. O'Connor explains the desire of Asbury as a kind of last demand: "He would talk to a man of culture before he died—even in this desert!" This man of culture will be a suitable interlocutor for him in this unfolding drama. This character he invites is writing *about* himself, *for* himself, and *should* fit perfectly.

When the priest finally arrives at Asbury's home, the drama will not be proceeding according to his plan. Asbury begins by thanking Father Finn:

> "It's so nice to have you come," Asbury said. "This place is incredibly dreary. There's no one here an intelligent person can talk to. I wonder what you think of Joyce . . ."
>
> "Joyce? Joyce who?"
>
> "James Joyce . . ."
>
> The priest brushed his huge hand in the air as if he were bothered by gnats. "I haven't met him. . . . Now, do you say your morning and night prayers? . . . You don't eh? . . . Well you will never learn to be good unless you pray regularly. You cannot love Jesus unless you speak to Him. . . . Do you know your catechism?"[2]

Asbury wants to talk about the irony of his existentially profound situation. He wants to engage the priest, whom he had assumed would be learned in the finer points of the great questions of interest for contemporary intellectuals like himself. He wanted, in other words, to be able to step back and examine his life from the outside. He wanted "God" to be an interesting character within this drama to observe alongside the worldly priest. Together they could offer insightful commentary. But the rather dull Jesuit would not cooperate. In O'Connor's imagination, neither would God.

After the conversation with the distressingly pedestrian Jesuit, Asbury sinks further until he finally realizes that he is not dying, but rather merely suffering from a low-grade chronic illness. He will live, but now an even more distressing reality emerges. He will have to live with himself. In the absence of talking to Jesus as the priest suggested, he will be left with the tediousness of his own thoughts and of his own isolated self.

The Role of Spirituality in Theology

In framing the task of the 2013 convention, the College Theology Society described the role spirituality can play in the task of translation that is incumbent upon Christian theology, namely that spirituality provides an interpretive geography in which our rhetorical and conceptual models can be framed and communicated across a number of personal and communal boundaries. Flannery O'Connor gives compelling descriptions of this geography within which the reality of grace is encountered, always in grotesque, sometimes even violent ways, but nevertheless ever-fruitful ways. The human person living in the confines of a sterile, fallen condition is repeatedly forced into a new horizon of a converted vision of self, God, and the surrounding world. O'Connor's manner of "doing theology" in this regard allows new modes of listening and seeing, which can uniquely enrich the tasks of both catechists and theologians. Asbury serves as a potent image of the paralysis of the contemporary person who is trapped in his own self-importance and abstraction, who is unable to speak genuinely. Ultimately, he speaks only to himself. Interested in the *idea* of God, Asbury prefers to keep this idea in the third person, precisely as an "It." The sterility and even death-dealing nature of approaching the "question of God," not in the *I-Thou* framework urged by Martin Buber but in the attempted objectivity of the *I-It* structure in exploring theological inquiry, fails to meet the needs of such a task. Only when the reality of God in the second person presents itself, as the dull priest had so clumsily urged, does Asbury begin to have his world shaken and begin to be given a new vision that is at once much more terrifying and more beautiful than what he had settled into in his own isolation.

Asbury can be a helpful icon, it seems to me, for both the catechist and the theologian, the priest and the religious, indeed anyone who is in the business of reflecting on the nature of God and all the questions that flow from there as well as attempting to pass on the fruit of those reflections to new generations. The temptation is common for anyone in this world that comprises both catechesis and theology: as we professionalize and gain greater critical distance from the subject at hand, there is a trap that can present itself of a false "objectivity" that comes with the science of theology. In the absence of the possibility of speaking directly with God, one is left only speaking to himself or herself. I propose that as we explore the distinctions and relationship between catechesis and theology, we might first be aware of the common temptation for both: to speak to oneself and to end up in sterile and lifeless abstraction.

Common Ground Between Catechesis and Theology?

A lively exchange was sparked in *America Magazine* a couple of years ago with an essay by Michael Lawler and Todd Salzman entitled "Beyond Catechesis." In part of their argument they admit, "Theology may include catechesis, but it is also more than that. Theology uses scholarly principles not only to communicate the truths of faith but also to explore the meanings of those truths and contemporary ways of articulating them."[3] Thomas Rausch responded by elaborating on the nature of this mission of the theologian, agreeing that the task of the catechist is distinct from the theologian while asserting the basic claim that the *origin* of the mission of each is the same. He explains,

> They [theologians] speak not for the church, but from it. In their concern for the church's mission they need the freedom to question traditional expressions, even magisterial for-mulations, to free them from their historically conditioned limitations and make them intelligible in new contexts. Their role cannot be reduced to simply providing support for the teachings of the magisterium.[4]

The task, then, of the theologian is to critique the tradition as it is handed down with new historical perspectives in mind, but always to do so from the heart of the church and for the service of the church. The key is highlighting that the task of the theologian is one given from the heart of the church. While it needs to engage in historical translation and critique, the task begins with *listening*.

In the half century since the Second Vatican Council, the American cultural landscape has obviously changed drastically. The ever-growing reality of religious pluralism impresses itself upon us, and it elicits a variety of theological responses. This pluralism poses challenges to the articulation of the fundamental doctrines of the Christian tradition, perhaps especially the unicity of Christ and the Church in the economy of salvation. The uproar that ensued after the promulgation of *Dominus Iesus* in 2000 highlighted this fact of changing sensibilities around the once taken for granted assumptions of the Christian theological tradition.

On another theological front, the rapidly shifting moral norms in contemporary society open new horizons and questions for the task of Christian ethics. The new realities of technology available in the realm of health sciences force new questions for the church's moral teaching. Changes in family structures, constant mobility of younger generations, and the impact of new media create new data for ethical reflection. Contemporary *experience* seems to have taken perhaps the position of the primary source for theology.

Even among the variety of understandings of the Catholic tradition held by theologians and bishops, it seems most would agree, at least theoretically, that the sources for theology are scripture and tradition but the sources also include ever new data presented by fresh cultural and sociological *experience*. Human *reason*, then, is required to reflect upon these new data. But perhaps precisely because this new data is so rapidly presenting itself, we might have a tendency to let that reality of new *experience* take prominence in our theological reflection. We might let the standard sources of Catholic theology, namely scripture and tradition, be set in a place of secondary importance because, relative to all these new realities that contemporary *experience* is providing, we might have a tendency to presume that the traditional sources for theology do not shed as much light on our reflection. This judgment is not an absolute methodology that has taken over. Perhaps the shift has been so subtle that it was rather unnoticeable as it has taken place, especially in the last decades. The modest proposal I would like to offer here is this: We need to call to mind the new data of cultural experience as an important and even essential source for theology, but we also must remember it is imperative not to lose sight of first principles, namely that theology is first and foremost *fides quaerens intellectum*. The experience of *faith* as articulated in scripture and tradition is still primary. Furthermore, the mode of engaging that primary experience of faith remains necessary. This mode we might call "spirituality."

Spirituality Accessing the Common Source

As conflicts have arisen between theologians and bishops at different times in the last several years, it is frequently recalled that
theology is not catechesis and that bishops cannot expect theologians to simply parrot the teachings of the catechism in their college
and university classrooms. True enough. Most would agree these
two praxes have different objectives. Catechesis most immediately
prepares the faithful for the personal encounter of Christ within
the church through the reception of the sacraments. Theology cri-
tiques the living tradition that attempts to describe the experience
of faith as it has been handed down so that it can continue to be
appropriated anew in every new age and cultural context. But lest
the differentiating line between these two become too bright, it is
also necessary to ask if there is an inner unity that exists between
catechesis and theology. If so, what is the nature of the unity?

First, catechesis and theological reflection both draw upon the
same source, namely revelation of the Word of God spoken in an
unfolding manner in scripture and tradition. In this sense, the tasks
of both catechesis and theology are fundamentally *dialogical*. Each
attempts to extend the appropriation of divine revelation always
in a new age and in a new place by first *listening* to the Word of
God, and only then by responding to it. Revelation is not simply
a fixed set of data about God and the human condition that gets
transmitted through the magisterium of the church. Rather, as
Joseph Ratzinger put it when he reflected on what had happened
in the immediate wake of the Council, the church had made it
clear that "Revelation is essentially dialogue," that is, dialogue
between God and God's people.[5] Two parties are required for
revelation to be fulfilled.

This dialogue is always *asymmetrical*. It allows the first word to
God but nonetheless depends upon the second word of response
from humanity. The *Antwort* is required, but only in response to
the *Wort Gottes* that precedes it.[6] In this regard, it is taken for
granted that humanity's response always emerges from a context
of communal, ecclesial faith informed by the tradition that has
preceded it. The primary source for this tradition, of course, is
sacred scripture itself, and secondarily but just as important, the
manner in which that Word of God has been appropriated by

people of faith, living "in the Spirit" in the ages that precede us.

The role of the catechist is to attempt to hand on the Word of God as it has been received up to the present moment to the current generation, with the proximate aim being the open receptivity of the sacraments of the church. The theologian does not receive the Word of God as handed down in tradition with the same ease as the catechist might, because her task is to call into question how well the Word of God is being received in today's context. The eye of the theologian is to the future development of the church's appropriation of the Word. However, when each of the tasks is performed authentically, the tradition as it has been handed down up to that point is allowed the first word. Or, better, the Eternal Word spoken in scripture and tradition is "allowed the first word" in the dialogue that continues to be extended into every new historical epoch and cultural setting.

Trinitarian Relationship

Both catechists and theologians, then, must first of all be "hearers of the Word," as Karl Rahner put it. As such, spirituality can rightly be understood as the foundational starting point or disposition for the tasks of both theology and catechesis. Rick Gaillardetz recently came to Saint Louis University and spoke to aspiring young theologians of the need for "holy conversation" in the context of increasing polarization within the church.[7] The first principle that he pointed to for a more constructive conversation was that the whole church—left and right, clergy and lay, bishop and theologian—might appropriate more consciously and deeply the reality of the *Trinitarian* ecclesial framework laid out in the Second Vatican Council and to operate from that lived reality. While he warned against the ahistorical "fetishization" of doctrines that some on the right and perhaps some members of the hierarchy can be guilty of at times, he himself admits that if we are to move forward constructively into the future, the foundational *doctrine* of the Trinity is indispensable. Not the doctrine alone, obviously, but rather the reality that it points to: that the very essence of the God in whose image we are created is that of relationality, intimacy, and communion. Entry into this intimacy, into this multiplicity of relationships that is the *communio* of the church, which is the locus for encounter with Christ who leads humanity into the triune life of God—this is the spirituality that must be the foundation for the tasks of both the catechist and the theologian.

Encountering the Word

In order to maintain this grounding of spirituality for the task of theology, coming back repeatedly to first principles is essential. Perhaps one of Joseph Ratzinger's greatest theological contributions has been to highlight this question of the sources for theology in the twenty-first century. Citing the basic insight of the Dogmatic Constitution on Divine Revelation, to which he contributed as a *peritus*, "scripture is the soul of theology" (*Dei Verbum*, 24). In his own impressive theological career, from the earliest days in the seminary, in part due to renewed ecumenical sensibilities, he noted late in life, "Exegesis has always remained for me the center of my theological work."[8] Following the call of the Council, he thinks that in doing theology one must let the Word of God speak first. While scholars draw upon the discoveries and insights of various forms of critical exegetical methods in recent years, it remains necessary to maintain that *theological* framework for interpretation, fulfilled only when a hermeneutic of faith is employed. He later explains,

> The demand for a scientific method is not sacrificed when theological research is carried on in a religious spirit of listening to the Word of God. . . . Spirituality does not attenuate the work of scholarship, but rather supplies theological study with the correct method so that it can arrive at a coherent interpretation. Theology can develop only with prayer. . . . This is a road that is worth traveling to the very end.[9]

The other great source for a renewed theology, for Ratzinger and an increasing number of theologians today, is the liturgy itself. This liturgical emphasis for theology provides an important perspective on the issue of how spirituality can inform and enhance the projects of both theology and catechesis. If one accepts the reality of the liturgy as a source for theology, it becomes harder for the theologian to escape into abstraction, since the liturgy itself is an act of the faithful attempting that most intimate encounter and dialogue with the triune God made known through the sacrifice of Christ. Ratzinger sees the liturgy as an essential source for theology as well as catechesis, because it is in the context of the liturgy that the whole person is engaged. Exploring this reality, he cites a curious source in the midst of his own "spiritual christology."[10] In emphasizing the need for a simple and open heart as the prerequisite for authentically entering into the experience of the liturgy, he recalls the words of Antoine Saint-Exupéry's Little Prince, who asserts at one point, "You only see properly with the heart." Ratzinger goes on to explain, "The Little Prince can be taken as a symbol for that childlikeness which we must regain if we are to find our way back out of the clever foolishness of the adult and into man's true nature which is beyond mere reason."[11]

That journey beyond mere reason, into the mystery of meeting and speaking with the living God, is begun only at the end of the story I mentioned at the beginning of this essay. At the conclusion of Flannery O'Connor's "The Enduring Chill," Asbury makes the most crushing discovery of all. He is not indeed dying a tragic death. He is only plagued with a case of undulant fever that probably came with drinking some unpasteurized milk. Knowing that his future seems dreadfully worse now that he is stuck with his own isolated self, Asbury feels the beginning of something new unfolding.

I'd like to close with the conclusion of O'Connor's story, which is also a description of the *beginning* of Asbury's new life on the verge of a kind of violent breakthrough out of his isolation. It perhaps can also serve as a pointer toward the renewal of any forms of catechesis and theological reflection that have grown stale and lifeless:

> He glanced across the room at the small oval-framed dresser mirror. The eyes that stared back at him were the same that had returned his gaze every day from that mirror but it seemed to him that they were paler. They looked shocked clean as if they had been prepared for some awful vision about to come down on him. He shuddered and turned his head quickly and turned his head the other way and stared out the window. A blinding red-gold sun moved serenely from under a purple cloud. Below it the treeline was black against the crimson sky. It formed a brittle wall, standing as if it were the frail defense he had set up in his mind to protect him from what was coming. The boy fell back on his pillow and stared at the

ceiling. His limbs that had been racked for so many weeks by fever and chill were numb now. The old life in him was exhausted. He awaited the coming of new. It was then that he felt the beginning of a chill, a chill so peculiar, so light, that it was like a warm ripple across a deeper sea of cold. His breath came short. The fierce bird which through the years of his childhood and the days of his illness had been poised over his head, waiting mysteriously, appeared all at once to be in motion. Asbury blanched and the last film of illusion was torn as if by a whirlwind from his eyes. He saw that for the rest of his days, frail, racked, but enduring, he would live in the face of a purifying terror. A feeble cry, a last impossible protest escaped him. But the Holy Ghost, emblazoned in ice instead of fire, continued, implacable, to descend.[12]

Notes

[1]Flannery O'Connor, "The Enduring Chill," in *Everything That Rises Must Converge* (New York: Farrar, Straus and Giroux, 2000), 82-114.

[2]Ibid., 105-107.

[3]Michael G. Lawler and Todd A. Salzman, "Beyond Catechesis: What Is the Proper Role of Theology?" *America*, September 12, 2011.

[4]Thomas Rausch, "Theology and Catechesis: What's the Difference? Responses to Michael G. Lawler and Todd A. Salzman," *America*, online response added October 17, 2011. Available at http://americamagazine.org.

[5]Joseph Ratzinger, *Commentary on the Documents of Vatican II*, vol. 3 (New York: Herder and Herder, 1967), 171.

[6]Joseph Ratzinger, *The Nature and Mission of Theology: Essays to Orient Theology in Today's Debates* (San Francisco: Ignatius Press, 1995), 26.

[7]Richard Gaillardetz, "Becoming a Community of Holy Conversation," presented at Saint Louis University, April 18, 2013.

[8]Joseph Ratzinger, *Milestones: Memoirs: 1927-1977* (San Francisco: Ignatius Press, 1998), 52-53.

[9]Benedict XVI, "Message of His Holiness Pope Benedict XVI to the Participants in the International Convention on the Occasion of the Centenary of the Birth of the Swiss Theologian Hans Urs von Balthasar," October 6, 2005, available at www.vatican.va.

[10]Joseph Ratzinger, *Behold the Pierced One: An Approach to a Spiritual Christology* (San Francisco: Ignatius Press, 1986).

[11]Ibid, 55.

[12]O'Connor, *Everything That Rises*, 113-14.

Hans Urs von Balthasar as Source for Teaching Theology in North American Higher Education

Christopher Hadley, S.J.

Theologians who do research on Hans Urs von Balthasar could entertain reasonable doubts about whether North American undergraduates can be effectively taught with his texts. For Balthasar, a "trilogy" consists of fifteen volumes. His prose is a dense synthesis of heavily layered Western-canonical references. Luke Timothy Johnson's favorable review of Karen Kilby's *Balthasar: A (Very) Critical Introduction* in a recent issue of *Commonweal* expresses the ambivalence of many theologians concerning the favor he enjoys in some circles in academia and within the Vatican.[1] Yet Balthasar has had a significant influence on aspects of popular Catholicism via his influence on John Paul II, and he is at the height of his prominence twenty-five years after his death.

This essay is not a practical guide to using Balthasar in an undergraduate classroom, nor will it provide a complete educational theory based on Balthasar's theology. It is a thought experiment in which I suggest that Balthasar's fundamental orientation to the task of theology aligns significantly with North American college students' potentials to develop spiritually in their studies. Balthasar characterizes his work as "kneeling theology," a phrase born of his frustration with the rationalistic neoscholasticism ("sitting theology") he encountered in his own studies and his desire to reconcile theology with spirituality.[2] This approach to intellectual life in the church is potentially well-suited to students as a foundation for thinking critically and holistically as they appropriate their own education in the university. This is true in no small part because contemplation plays a central role in moral, intellectual, and theological development both for Balthasar and in the spiritual lives of students. A recent study conducted by the Higher Education Research Institute (HERI) at UCLA and published in the book *Cultivating the Spirit: How College Can Enhance Students' Inner Lives*[3] provides the relevant data for addressing questions of basic approaches to teaching theology that also cultivate faith and spirituality. Karen Kilby's new introduction to Balthasar serves as a guide to some of the critical issues in his work. In this essay I will make a connection between the cultivation of spiritual qualities in students noted in the HERI study and the contemplative dimensions of Balthasar's theology.

What responsibilities and advantages do teachers have who are sympathetic to Balthasar's theological project? The HERI study has identified trends in student life that suggest a great openness to spiritual development. The study was conducted with the hypothesis that the questions of meaning, purpose, and lifetime goals that students face in college are intimately related to their spiritual and religious development.[4] The seven-year study began with a pilot survey of 3,700 students in 2003. The main part of the study consisted of the creation of a longitudinal database with a survey of 112,000 college freshmen in 2004 from a wide variety of schools across the country, followed up by another survey of a sub-sample of 15,000 of these students as juniors in 2007. This quantitative material was supplemented by extensive interviews with both students and faculty on the role of spirituality and religion in higher education. The results strongly suggest that opportunities to develop spiritually enhance most other student outcomes.[5] While this spiritual development does not necessarily coincide with developing religiously in a particular tradition, neither does it categorically exclude it.[6]

A popular distinction between "spiritual" and "religious" has gained notoriety in recent decades, but the HERI study has given parameters for discussing it quite rigorously.[7] The five measures of spirituality in the study are (1) the *Spiritual Quest* for purpose and meaning; (2) *Equanimity*, which is a feeling of balance under stress, (3) an *Ethic of Caring*, (4) *Charitable Involvement*, and (5) an *Ecumenical Worldview* that sees the core roots of compassion and love in all major religious traditions. There are three measures of "religiousness": (1) *Religious Commitment*, a measure of certain attitudes and beliefs regarding core religious teachings such as the existence of a higher power; (2) *Religious Engagement*, an external behavioral measure of church attendance, meditational practices, and sacred reading habits; and (3) *Religious Conservatism*, measuring adherence or opposition to religious moral teachings about pre-marital sex, abortion, gay marriage, the need to pray for forgiveness of sins, the need to evangelize or proselytize, and the inclination to identify the divinity as a father figure. These three religious measures are highly correlated and do not change much during college, with the slight exception of the conservatism measure.[8] A general reduction in conservatism correlates with a general increase in the spiritual measures of equanimity and the ethic of caring as students progress through college.[9]

These spiritual measures are significantly affected by the willingness of faculty to discuss deeper questions of meaning with their students, but this encouragement does not take place universally among all institutions and populations in the HERI study.[10] The students whose professors did not encourage them to engage spiritual questions manifested the classic academic reluctance to get too close to religion, as they considered it too much of a mix of church and state and therefore inappropriate in the university.[11] This might suggest to some that the "kneeling" aspect of Balthasar's theology could be a liability. Nevertheless, spiritual development tends to enhance academic and other developmental outcomes in college, such as psychological wellbeing, a sense of satisfaction in learning, and academic performance.[12] Teachers of academic theology at the college level therefore have a responsibility along with teachers in other disciplines to participate in this general enhancement.

What I am suggesting is that, in light of the spiritual-religious distinction and in the interests of finding academically responsible ways to transmit Christian faith in the theology classroom, Balthasar could encourage the teacher to view her work and that of her students as a participation in a liturgy—not only in terms of what people do for God, but more fundamentally in terms of how God is working for, in, and through people. An early, pre-Vatican II essay on the vital connection between ancient Christian liturgical patrimony and the inchoate, existential hopes of humankind gives us his basic outlook:

What is most important in the Christian perspective is that each person is so much more than he or she imagines. And so the ontological and liturgical element of patristic piety only gets a different coloring in the modern principle, for now the great liturgical action is no longer being acted out, as it were, away from the world and in another divine realm beyond this one (one might think here of the complete transcendence of the art of icons), but is being enacted by God in the world.[13]

Balthasar's work thus contextualizes the spiritual measures of the HERI study in such a way that yields a more deeply symbolic and inclusive sense of religious engagement, not merely in terms of how often students attend liturgical services or even of how often they engage themselves intentionally in prayer. In looking at the theological task in Balthasar's way, the teacher must trust that the form of what she is teaching will reveal itself in its beauty. Balthasar believes he is responding to what is "out there" in revelation, and that the form of his response is dictated by the form and content of revelation.[14] The theology teacher's method models a trust in the form of her own theological knowledge and corresponds to what this form demands in terms of readings, writing exercises, and opportunities for students to respond in class. In this approach to teaching, students must be given the time and support to think in more than a merely task-oriented way, and to read more attentively and reflectively.

The processing of academic material in this mode is a contemplative exercise, if we understand contemplation in terms of §§230-37 of St. Ignatius Loyola's *Spiritual Exercises* as a beholding of a "live" event that is inclusive of the beholder.[15] The activity of theological thought is a participation in the event, as Balthasar sees it through his own Ignatian identity and orientation as a former Jesuit. According to the HERI study, "*contemplative practices are among the most powerful tools at our disposal for enhancing students' spiritual development.*"[16] The extent to which professors encourage this activity and engage their students on questions of spiritual import both in and out of class has a proportionate effect on their equanimity, their ethic of caring, and on their ecumenical worldview. These results in turn have an effect on their motivation in their academic careers, their intellectual self-confidence, their active citizenship in the world, and their grades.[17] Theology must become more than busy work for students, or it will be neither true to itself nor effective in promoting intellectual clarity in our students.[18]

Since many students come to expect and hope for some kind of spiritual growth either before or after they arrive at college,[19] their theology professors have an opportunity to invite them to consider how God works in this world in ways they had not previously imagined. The challenge for Catholic and many other Christian universities, according to many of their institutional mission statements, is to form young people who can think theologically about the world's problems both within their own tradition and with respect to other traditions. But for Balthasar, contemplative activity is entirely and almost exclusively *Christian* activity. This indicates the importance of putting him into conversation with *Gaudium et Spes* and his own principles of thinking about universal salvation,[20] augmented by the work of theologians who engage the challenges of pluralism more positively. Both Balthasar's and the Council's principles are explicitly Christocentric, but the ecumenical worldview that students tend to acquire as they develop spiritually in college could be an opportunity to help them make key distinctions that will increase their religious literacy in addition to making them more compassionate, even if they choose not to become more religiously engaged in church attendance and religious group membership.

Balthasar never taught at a university, before or after he left the Jesuits. In fact, one of his earliest Jesuit assignments was as a university chaplain, an assignment that he requested. He was also an avid leader of retreats throughout his career.[21] The HERI study finds that there are risks involved in stirring up the spiritual lives of students with religious and non-sectarian spiritual activities; the more prayer services, meditation sessions, retreats, and masses there are on a campus, the more prevalent religious struggle is among students.[22] Students in the state of religious struggle experience "distance" from God and anxiety over the meaning of evil and death in the world.[23] Can theological studies be an opportunity for the student to seek intellectual integration of existential struggles? The following passage from Balthasar's short book *Heart of the World* is intended as an articulation of his vision, rather than as a nugget of pastoral wisdom to dole out to students in their moments of doubt:

> This is a new mystery, inconceivable to mere creatures: that even distance from God and the coolness of reverence are an image and likeness of God and of divine life. What is most incomprehensible is, in fact, the truest reality: precisely by not being God do you resemble God. And precisely by being outside of God are you in God. For to be over against God is itself a divine thing. As a person who is incomparable you reflect the uniqueness of your God. For in God's unity, too, there are found distance and reflection and eternal mission: Father and Son over against one another and yet one in the Spirit and in the nature that seals the Three of them together.[24]

The passage represents the conscious location of Balthasar's thought in relation to the relational God, even "within" the relational God. He expands on the eschatological, and therefore unfinished, dimension of this viewpoint in volumes IV and V of the *Theo-Drama*. The distance mentioned in the passage is not one of loss, alienation, or sin, but there is an unavoidable time of experiencing it that way in the process of spiritual growth. Balthasar's point is that God is the prime actor in a Trinitarian play in which all of these experiences of "distance" from God are being re-envisioned, re-evaluated, and redeemed. The theological trick is to facilitate the process by which students come to their own place of doing theology.

Facilitating this learning process could include the activity of organizing doctrinal concepts that are proposed to students. For the Christian students, this theological exercise would result in catechesis—a formation that is taking place in them, an "informing" of their lives of faith. The non-Christians in the class would be engaging in the study of religion. But the activity can and ideally would be contemplative in either case. Balthasar harmonizes all of his doctrinal conceptualizations with biblical narrative, and with the existential dimensions of human life. His Trinitarian theology of the processions and missions of the Word and Spirit is characterized by an outward movement: being sent out characterizes divine Personhood in the economy of salvation, as well as ecclesial Christian personhood.[25] There is a "distance" in the progression from pre-theological experience in the world outside the classroom or outside the faith to the theological reflection on that experience in the classroom or in Christian life. Balthasar sees a similar kind of distance that he learns from his reading of Gregory of Nyssa, namely that progress in the life of grace occurs within a salvific Trinitarian and pneumatological framework.[26] There is here a conceptual theological overlap with the formative influence of service learning on the spiritual and intellectual lives of students, which could perhaps be a privileged way to capitalize on these benefits while teaching categories of thought.[27] Intellectual growth is part of spiritual progress in Christian life: just as the Spirit reveals the Personhood of Father and Son in relation with each other, so does the Spirit facilitate and accompany us as we grow in knowledge, spiritual freedom, and more meaningful relationships. What Balthasar can offer is a solid Trinitarian-theological context for thinking about the very process of learning.

In her critical introduction, Karen Kilby concludes that Balthasar's way of being a theologian is irresponsible in our current university contexts.[28] While I would not entirely concur, one obvious difficulty she notes is the nature of his writing, which relies on an erudition vis-à-vis the totality of Western culture that is virtually impossible to require of theologians who teach, much less of undergraduate students (even very well catechized ones). Balthasar's authorial tone of supreme confidence in his subject matter is a legitimate concern, as it could over-awe some undergraduates and render him immune to a more critical reading.[29] For other students, this same quality in his tone could also squander any credibility he might have with them, causing them to write him off altogether. Either extreme would be a shame.

In addition to these practical problems with using his texts with undergraduates, there are some serious professional concerns with his theology. In spite of his contemplative, negative-theological method, Balthasar does have a tendency to project absolutized gender categories into God and then read them back into flesh-and-blood gendered life on earth in ways that are quite disturbing, and even "loony," as Luke Timothy Johnson says.[30] However, the very concern that Balthasar has gone too far in his theology of gender could initiate a critical discussion with advanced theology majors who have read him carefully alongside other theologians. Gender is not primarily a theological topic, and while there is a legitimate concern regarding the level of catechesis in many classrooms with respect to theological texts, some students bring considerable interdisciplinary skills and intellectual patience with them that could compensate for a lack of catechetical knowledge. Interdisciplinary courses of study are shown to be helpful for students' grades, educational aspirations, and intellectual self-esteem.[31] This is something that those of us who deplore the crisis in catechesis among young people need to trust and capitalize on, even in core-required theology courses that are not cross-listed in other departments. Balthasar's gender issues touch on ecclesiology and the theology of revelation, and there is an interdisciplinary orientation of Balthasar's theology as a whole vis-à-vis literary criticism and philosophy. This could offer a productive chal-lenges and opportunities for some students to think at a higher theological level.[32]

Balthasar insists that the theologian has a role in the "Trini-tarian drama" of the redemption and salvation of this world.[33] One could ask him if this means that absolutely everyone is a potential theologian in light of this paradigm of Christian spiritual experience. According to this view, the teacher's task would be to find what kinds of texts and discussions would allow students to participate in the Trinitarian "event" of theology. The research briefly surveyed above tells us that students naturally yearn for the contemplative dimensions of their college experience, including their academic experience. It would be irresponsible of me not to note in closing that I have merely gestured in the general direction of some serious practical problems, if in fact I and Balthasar are "on to something." Asking how to make the practice of academic theology and the academic lives of undergraduates more contem-plative involves asking some disturbing questions about the way our institutional lives are organized on our campuses and in our guilds. Balthasar chose to extract himself from these problems altogether. But, in addition to raising some critical questions about how appropriate Balthasar is for theological education, it is worthwhile to ask questions of how we might recover or keep some of what he offered, and nourish it in ourselves, in each other, and in our students.

Notes

[1]Luke Timothy Johnson, "God's Eye View," *Commonweal,* April 12, 2013, 32-34.

[2]Karen Kilby, *Balthasar: A (Very) Critical Introduction* (Grand Rapids: Eerdmans, 2012), 153.

[3]Alexander W. Astin, Helen S. Astin, and Jennifer A. Lindholm, *Cultivating the Spirit: How College Can Enhance Students' Inner Lives* (San Francisco: Jossey-Bass, 2011).

[4]Ibid., 1.

[5]Ibid., 9-10.

[6]Ibid., 95-98; levels of religious engagement are affected most of all by students' exposure to peer groups: if their peers are religiously engaged, so will they be.

[7]Ibid., 18-23.

[8]Ibid., 84-85.

[9]Ibid., 92.

[10]Ibid., 60, 74.

[11]Ibid., 37-38.

[12]Ibid., 10.

[13]Hans Urs von Balthasar, "The Fathers, the Scholastics and Ourselves," trans. Edward T. Oakes, S.J., *Communio: International Catholic Review* 24 (1997): 392. What Balthasar means by "the modern principle" is that the liturgical view of reality can no longer be relegated exclusively to the realm of transcendence, as it tended to be in the patristic age, but must be seen as enacted in earthly history as well.

[14]Kilby, *Critical Introduction*, 44-45, 59.

[15]St. Ignatius Loyola, *The Spiritual Exercises of Saint Ignatius: A Translation and Commentary*, ed. and trans. George E. Ganss (St. Louis: Institute of Jesuit Sources, 1992), 94-95.

[16]Astin et al., *Cultivating the Spirit*, 148.

[17]Ibid., 134-35.

[18]Ibid., 46.

[19]Ibid., 3.

[20]See Balthasar's short volume, *Dare We Hope: "That All Men Be Saved"? With a Short Discourse on Hell* (San Francisco: Ignatius Press, 1988).

[21]Kilby, *Critical Introduction*, 161.

[22]Astin et al., *Cultivating the Spirit*, 105.

[23]Ibid., 103.

[24]Balthasar, *Heart of the World*, trans. Erasmo S. Leiva (San Francisco: Ignatius Press, 1979), 35.

[25]Kilby, *Critical Introduction*, 96-98.

[26]Balthasar, *Presence and Thought: An Essay on the Religious Philosophy*

of Gregory of Nyssa, trans. Marc Sebanc (San Francisco: Ignatius, 1995), 163-64; this appropriation of Trinitarian revelation comes to Gregory via pneumatology: the Spirit who knows, plumbs, traverses, and speaks of the mutual love of Father and Son to the human spirit. In *Presence and Thought* and throughout all his works, Balthasar makes Gregory's Trinitarian theology of in-dwelling his own: "The revelation of the Presence, that is to say, the depths, of Divine Being is in concrete terms nothing other than the revelation of the Trinity by the Trinity."

[27]Astin et al., *Cultivating the Spirit*, 40.

[28]Kilby, *Critical Introduction*, 167; she agrees that a "charitable" reading of Balthasar as a work-in-progress is quite possible, but she emphasizes the dangers in his method that just as often suggest an "all-or-nothing" approach to his subject matter and to his conclusions that too often presumes arguments rather than making them. My purpose here is not to mount a defense of Balthasar from accusations, such as Kilby's, that he does not hold himself "accountable to Scripture, tradition, or [his] readers, but somehow soars above them all"; ibid., 40.

[29]Ibid., 55-56.

[30]Johnson, "God's Eye View," 33.

[31]Astin et al., *Cultivating the Spirit*, 128.

[32]Kilby, *Critical Introduction*, 128-29.

[33]Ibid., 60.

No More Time for Nostalgia

Millennial Morality and a Catholic Tradition Mash-Up

Maureen H. O'Connell

In the third installment of his longitudinal study of the religious identities and spiritual lives of Millennials (1980-2000) over the past ten years, Notre Dame sociologist of religion Christian Smith identifies some troubling developments: many of our students have difficulties identifying moral dilemmas, are morally adrift in a myopic worldview tainted by individual relativism and constrained by political correctness, and have a limited sense of the common good and a weak personal commitment to it.[1] Smith notes that "many emerging adults segregate 'moral' matters off to the side, as part of a narrowly defined set of issues or problems. . . . And that produces a moral myopia that in turn undermines the ability for robust moral reasoning."[2] This leaves most emerging adults ill-equipped to identify and respond to unprecedented dilemmas that shape their formative college years, from identity formation in an age of social media and the physical and emotional dangers of a hookup culture, to the expectations of self-sufficiency in the midst of an economic recession, and to the challenges of autonomy in the midst of financial and emotional dependence on their parents.

Although studies of the Millennial generation have become a cottage industry,[3] some of which illuminate Smith's pessimistic portrayal of this age cohort,[4] normative Christian ethics has only just begun to assist American college students with the moral dilemmas they face *in this particular stage of their moral formation.*[5] "Millennial morality" remains a peripheral concern despite the fact that the vast majority of Christian ethics professors teach Millennials.

Perhaps our relative silence reflects the fact that those of us engaged in Christian ethics are wrestling with our own generational issues, perhaps nostalgically longing for the heady bygone times of post-Vatican II moral theology, undergraduates, and moral dilemmas, or maybe straddling the chasm between the pedagogical expectations of our students for profound spiritual awakenings and those of our more senior colleagues for rigorous critical thinking.[6] Either way, these are serious silences, since contemporary collegiate culture potentially launches our students on a treacherous trajectory that extends long beyond their early twenties.

Attention to the particularities of Millennial anthropology, however, might "remix" the Catholic moral tradition in our classrooms, so that we can use it to see more accurately our students' needs for moral formation and empower them to be moral agents in the critical period of emerging adulthood. Doing so not only shakes us out of our own generational comfort zones on the dance floor of the moral life, but also makes the tradition viable to a generation increasingly disinclined to dance at all, much less to a Catholic playlist.

Millennial I-thropology

Theological anthropology provides the building blocks for any method of Christian ethics. Today's "*i-thropology*" eviscerates the foundational imperatives associated with each of the three dimensions of traditional theological anthropology—the person as *relational,* and thereby constituted by and for embodied encounters with others; the person as *made in the image and likeness of God*, and imbued with sacred creativity and animated by a deep concern for justice; and the person as endowed with the distinctive *capacity of reason* to discern and incarnate the vision and values of one's individual and communal life. I contend that it is not so much that our students do not understand these components of the person, but rather that they *mean something quite different to them* and therefore function differently, as a kind of "i-thropology" that reflects coming of age in a world of social media and push technology. "I-thropology" is an approach to what it means to be human characterized by restless multitasking and narcissism, an insatiable and private obsession with happiness, and the need for public and yet disembodied manifestations of having achieved it. This i-thropology affects each of the three fundamental components of theological anthropology.

Relationality as Connectivity

Millennial i-thropology revolves around a notion of relationality perhaps best understood in terms of the connectivity, tethering, or constant availability that smart technology supports and social media platforms provide. Relationality increasingly means staying connected to hundreds of other people via truncated nonverbal communication on one's smart device, "friending" others on Facebook, or "following" them via Twitter. Common denominators here are *constant* disembodied availability, the virtual omnipresence of others in our students' lives and their omnipresence in the lives of others, strategic posturing via public broadcasts, and equally public feedback strongly influenced by the virtual social body.

However, while our students may be constantly *relating* to others, they may not necessarily be in life-giving or just *relationships*. Researchers note that these technological and virtual forms of relationality actually deplete capabilities needed for relationships in real time, such as empathy, vulnerability, resilience, and solitude. Consider the fact that rates of empathy have reached their lowest numbers among college students—down 34 percent on "perspective taking" and 48 percent on empathetic concern—since these dispositions where first tracked in 1980.[7] The YOLO culture (You Only Live Once) that seems to motivate much of our students' decision making reveals that public posturing in online profiles leaves little space for acknowledging personal vulnerabilities or failures, and fosters instead what Stephen Marche describes as a compulsion to assert one's own happiness or one's own fulfillment. "Not only must we contend with the social bounty of others," he notes, "we must [also] foster the appearance of our own social bounty. Being happy all of the time, pretending to be happy, actually attempting to be happy—it's exhausting."[8]

Stephen Marche notes students' constant connectivity gives rise to what psychologists call "super-connected loneliness" heightened by the "illusion of intimacy" provided by social media platforms such as Facebook. William Deresiewicz observes that friendship has become a verb, "friending," which functions primarily as an "elective affinity" or expression of preference or choice.[9] Not only do relationships of preference reinforce already congealing lifestyle enclaves of similarity, but also friending does not forge "ties that bind" us in real time, suggests Marche, but rather "ties that preoccupy us" with the tasks of constantly observing others and superficially interjecting from a safe virtual distance.[10] MIT professor of the social studies of science and technology Sherry Turkle notes that the demands of this 24/7 posting and monitoring contributes to what she calls the "alone together" phenomenon, an anxiety that comes with always having to be available to others at the expense of periods and practices of solitude.[11] Scientists are just now discovering the literal depth of this anxiety in the human physiology in terms of its effects on our cells, the expression of certain genes, and the shape of neuro-pathways, particularly those connecting the brain and the heart.[12] Says University of North Carolina psychologist Barbara Frederickson, "If you don't regularly exercise your ability to connect face to face, you'll eventually find yourself lacking some of the basic biological capacity to do so."[13]

Constant connectivity presents a variety of challenges to fundamental components of the moral life, particularly conscience. Richard Gula's now-classic definition of conscience, "me coming to a decision"[14] for myself but not by myself, is quite helpful in terms of helping students move beyond the dictatorial direction of the "shoulds" of their lives, rooted in various external sources, toward the invitational orientation of their deepest wants. However, many of our students actually have a hard time discerning their wants in the midst of the cacophony of constant connectivity and weakened embodied relational bonds with those who assist them in forming their consciences. Marche notes: "We are now left thinking about who we are all the time, without ever really thinking about who we are."[15] Moreover, our students might have trouble coming to a decision for themselves, since Turkle notes that they are not necessarily conditioned to being alone, being solitary, being quiet. "We've created situations where people cannot think by themselves or feel by themselves," she notes, "and so then we depend on other people sometimes for the wrong reasons."[16]

The Image and "Like"-ness of God

Who or what we understand God to be shapes our understanding of what it means to be human. Christian Smith has identified some of the characteristics of the Millennial God, which in turn shape their "i-thropology." Two creedal statements about this God emerging from his recently coined term "moralistic therapeutic deism" are of interest to me here: "God wants people to be good, nice, and fair to each other," and "God does not need to be particularly involved in one's life except when God is needed to resolve a problem."[17] I suspect that these conditions have only been calcified by the dispositions and practices of our mediatized society that foster a shallow sense of happiness and make distanced observation and sporadic interjection into the lives of others the normative way of relating. Moreover, the thumbs-up symbol, the central icon that unites the 1.1 billion citizens of "Facebookistan,"[18] only reinforces a connection between liking and being created in *imago dei*.

Many of our students may indeed understand God as one who "likes" rather than as one who loves, since according to Smith, "God is something like a combination Divine Butler and Cosmic Therapist: he is always on call, takes care of any problems that arise… and does not become too personally involved in the process."[19] To be made in the image and "like"-ness of a liking God is to function quite differently in the world. To "like" is to be politically correct and polite, to avoid imposing one's values on another, and thus to be perceived by others as "nice." To "like" is to avoid conflict and to sidestep the messy vulnerability that comes with truly loving one's self or others, or the unpredictability of passionate commitment to people or things or issues. Smith summarizes it this way: "Being moral in this faith [that of moralistic therapeutic deism] means being the kind of person that other people will like, fulfilling one's personal potential, and not being socially disruptive or interpersonally obnoxious."[20]

But to "like" is to be paralyzed by fear: of failure, of rejection by the social body, of struggle, or of not having it all. Certainly there is nothing new about these fears, but the ways many of our students face them, or actually choose not to face them, are new. Students are increasingly paralyzed by a FOMO culture (Fear Of Missing Out) that fuels a manic and superficial engagement with life—relationships, courses, extra-curricular activities, religious traditions—at the expense of deeper and potentially riskier explorations. It busies them with observing something happening to someone else somewhere else with little expectation for involvement or personal commitment at the expense of being present to the present or developing one's deepest passions so as to live out of them.[21] Ultimately, "liking, in general, is commercial culture's substitute for loving," observes novelist Jonathan Franzen.[22] He notes a person consumed with the desire to be liked is ultimately a narcissist "who can't tolerate the tarnishing of his or her self-image that not being liked represents, and who therefore either withdraws from human contact or goes to extreme, integrity-sacrificing lengths to be likable."[23]

Reason as an Emotion-Seeking Feedback Loop

Ultimately, reason is the cognitive capability we rely on to evaluate critically the cultural constructions of "the right" and to illuminate the contours of the more fundamental and ephemeral "good." Reason allows us to discern and commit ourselves to a set of values or a vision we have of ourselves and others. But this capacity has also been shaped by Millennial "i-thropology."

Smith notes that many Millennials orient themselves in the public and political landscape by the constellation of individual moral relativism. By this, he means that Millennials "say that there are no real standards of right or wrong, that morality changes over history, that morality is merely a social construction, that morality is merely subjective beliefs."[24] While this sounds fairly typical of relativism, Millennial relativism is a bit different, largely because it is organized around the bright and yet misguiding north star of personal happiness, understood by Millennials (through their parents) as the absence of struggle or pain or failure. Journalist Lori Gottlieb observes that "nowadays, it's not enough to be happy—if you can be even happier. The American Dream and the pursuit of happiness have morphed from a quest for general contentment to the idea that you must be happy at all times and in every way."[25]

Individual moral relativism animated by happiness shapes our students' capacity of reason. Turkle observes that constant communicative connectivity weakens if not silences many of our students' internal editors, limits their abilities to engage with contradiction or ambiguity, and facilitates reactive and ideological stances to the given or non-negotiable circumstances of their lives.[26] Perhaps more importantly, she also notes that social media undercuts the emotive component of reason *and* enhances the impassibility of conventionality. For example, young people increasingly don't experience emotions unless they are publicly shared in tweets or status updates and then validated by others through "likes," "comments," and re-tweets. This constant feedback loop motivated by a need for affirmation is fast becoming a new step in creating a sense of the good, one that sidesteps emotional reasoning so integral for disrupting the conventional wisdom of the status quo that denies mortality, vulnerability, and interdependence.[27] Moreover, "clicktivism" or "slacktivism"—expressions for activism supported by a variety of social media and internet platforms—suggest social consciousness or concern is best exercised virtually. Social media cultivates what political philosopher Iris Marion Young calls the "liability model of justice" so ingrained in Eurocentric ways of reasoning and social relationships—characterized by self-sufficiency, merit and desert, and *noblesse oblige*—at the expense of the social connection model of justice rooted in mutuality, cooperation, and reciprocity.[28] Even among our students engaged in regular community service, Millennial reason oriented by personal happiness and constant feedback from the virtual social body perpetuates both the cycle of charity that fails to examine the structures of social injustice sustained by the consumerist framework on which social media hang, and an inflated idea of their moral goodness and innocence in the eyes of that same social body.

A Catholic Moral Theology Remix

While the "status update" of i-thropology "posted" here seems bleak, it offers an invitation for "comment" from Christian ethicists rather than a distancing "unlike" or "untag" strategy. I think we can "remix"—as opposed to the more Millennial "mash up" approach—at least three ideas in the tradition to address some of these concerns. Feminist ethicist and musician Rachel Bundang suggests that while the mash up "is a Frankenstein-[ish] subgenre of the remix in which the vocal track from one song is laid over the music track of another to create an entirely new work," the remix is far more participatory and "provides the space for imagination to transform [existing ideas] and reinvigorate their meaning for transmission and adoption into a new context."[29]

From Virtual Connectivity to Embodied Encounter

In order to remix embodied encounters into our students' "i-thropology," we need to do more than teach the wisdom of Christian spirituality in our ethics classes. We must incorporate actual spiritual practices into ethics classrooms. We have to do more than contribute to students' construction of mental or intellectual frameworks; we have to help them reconnect with their bodies and the bodies of other people. I have found organizing this embodied learning around Sandra Schneiders' definition of spirituality—a lifelong integrating project of reaching out beyond the self in love—deepens students' somewhat limited understanding of spirituality.[30] Following the example of a variety of colleagues interested in these pedagogical innovations,[31] students in my courses participate in embodied learning: Facebook or texting fasts, real-time dating, and meditating for ten minutes a day for ten days. We pay attention to what they notice happening in their bodies in these tactile experiences to tease out the difference between individualism and individuality, between profile and identity, between bodies and embodiment, between objectivity and subjectivity.

From Like to Self-Love

We can remix a little self-love in order to transform FOMO and YOLO culture by emphasizing self-love and not simply self-*like*. Jesuit ethicist Edward Vacek links dimensions of self-love with agapic love, which is far more demanding and risky than merely "liking," noting that "through an agapic self-love, we affirm and delight in our power to enact and develop our many natural and learned inclinations and capacities."[32] Integrating self-love into conscience requires a willingness to create opportunities to come face to face with one's deepest and multi-dimensional self, and not merely to take advantage of opportunities to project one's face in one-dimensional profiles. It requires taking a risk to acknowledge that students may not really know themselves and the patience to enter into an ongoing process of self-disclosure.

I begin each of my courses with five minutes of silence.[33] Sometimes students provide an image or a quote for reflection, but more often than not we simply sit quietly together for five minutes. Students report that this process of settling into the classroom space and into themselves has offered a chance to get comfortable with the restlessness or longings that lie beneath the manic energy created by their constant connectivity or the noise of the social body that drowns out their own inner voice. This silence also helps them understand Margaret Farley's distinction between relativism and subjectivity, namely that "our subjectivity is embodied consciousness and conscious embodiment."[34] An appreciation of the depth of embodied subjectivity allows them to extend their connections to others, to heighten their vulnerability, and to deepen their sense of the mystery of themselves and others. In other words, subjectivity is not the same as simply liking something or someone else, but rather the liberating process of "becoming" by tapping into the deep reserves of the embodied self.

From Emotional Crowd Sourcing to Subsidiarity

In her recent assessment of the living significance of *Quadragesimo Anno*, Meghan Clark summarizes subsidiarity this way: *decisions should be made at the lowest level possible and the highest level necessary.*[35] Why can't teaching theologians apply this principle to cultivate our students' agency in the midst of the millennial culture in the unique context of higher education? The hierarchical structures of colleges and universities, with their vertical accountability in the name of economic viability or excellence or prestige, too often trumps horizontal accountability to the members of the community who comprise it. This presents real challenges for our students' flourishing, particularly for members of marginalized groups.

Remixing subsidiarity in the context of American higher education helps students to see that ethics is something that is required in the everyday. Incarnating the principle of subsidiarity among our students might foster a commitment to the common good by virtue of developing a commitment to "the commons" on campus—the residence hall, athletic field, classroom. It might cultivate face-to-face encounters among estranged or mutually suspicious campus groups such as "students for life" and "students for justice," leaders in student government and those further from the center of institutional power, students of color and white students. Developing subsidiarity as part of campus culture can counter our students' flailing ability to detect moral dilemmas and empower them to identify appropriate responses among themselves or the immediate community.

I attempt to cultivate subsidiarity through a semester-long project with working groups of no more than five students with shared concerns about campus life or culture—hookup culture, addiction, relationships between residents and commuters, the relationship between spiritual health and mental health, preparedness for life after college, and more. Groups do the work of descriptive and normative ethics: describing as accurately as possible the dimensions of the issue or problem of their choosing and identifying principles that might be effective in addressing it. They then develop a five-part strategic plan, complete with assessment and goals projection, which they present to the class and to administrators in student life at the end of the semester.

As teaching theologians, we engage with 30 to 110 Millennial students each semester. Designating their experiences of their generational culture as the focal point of theological investigation not only opens up new insights into the tradition, but also invites students to use the tradition to tap into the distinctive gifts and perspectives of their generation. Identifying campus cultures as a focal point of ethical reflection can help students to name the ways in which they themselves are both drivers and byproducts of these sets of meanings and values that inform the life of their collegiate community. It also makes it possible for students to employ remixed Christian symbols, practices, values and beliefs into the process of reconstructing alternatives as they emerge into adulthood.

Notes

1 I am grateful for sustained conversation among members of my Wabash Center for Teaching and Learning in Theology and Religion pre-tenure work-

shop cohort—Whitney Bauman, Joseph Marchal, Karline McLain and Sara Patterson—which helped to surface insights here.

[2]Christian Smith et al., *Lost in Transition: The Dark Side of Emerging Adulthood* (New York: Oxford University Press, 2011), 66. Smith's is not the only assessment of Millennials, but I find his study most helpful for three reasons: (1) the longitudinal breadth of his National Study of Youth and Religion (http://www.youthandreligion.org/), (2) his focus on the religious and spiritual dimension of Millennial identity and generational experience in the midst of cultural conditions beyond their control, and (3) the implicit pedagogical challenges he identifies.

[3]Mark Bauerlein, *The Dumbest Generation: How the Digital Age Stupefies Young Americans and Jeopardizes Our Future (or, Don't Trust Anyone under 30)* (New York: Tarcher/Penguin, 2008); Jean Twenge, *Generation Me: Why Today's Young Americans Are More Confident, Assertive, Entitled—and More Miserable than Ever Before* (New York: Free Press, 2006). John Palfrey and Urs Gasser, *Born Digital: Understanding the First Generation of Digital Natives* (New York: Basic, 2008).

[4]For a more positive assessment, see Neil Howe and William Strauss, *Millennials Rising: The Next Great Generation* (New York: Vintage, 2000); Eric Greenberg, *Generation We: How Millennial Youth Are Taking Over America and Changing Our World Forever* (Emeryville, CA: Pachatusan, 2008); and Don Tapscott, *Growing Up Digital: The Rise of the Net Generation* (New York: McGraw-Hill, 1998).

[5]Jennifer Beste, "Empowering College Students to Integrate Ignatian Spirituality within Their Sexual and Relational Lives," *Association of Jesuit Colleges and Universities Connections E-Newsletter* (February, 2011); Donna Freitas, *Sex and the Soul: Juggling Sexuality and Spirituality, Romance and Religion on College Campuses* (New York: Oxford University Press, 2008), and *The End of Sex: How Hookup Culture is Leaving a Generation Unhappy, Sexually Unfulfilled, and Confused about Intimacy* (New York: Oxford University Press, 2013); Jason King, "A Theology of Dating for a Culture of Abuse," in *Leaving and Coming Home: New Wineskins for Catholic Sexual Ethics,* ed. David Cloutier (Eugene, OR: Cascade Books, 2010); William Mattison, *Introducing Moral Theology: True Happiness and the Virtues* (Grand Rapids: Brazos Press, 2008); and Kari-Shane Davis Zimmerman: "Hooking Up: Sex, Theology, and Today's 'Unhooked' Dating Practices," *Horizons: The Journal of the College Theology Society* 37, no.1 (2010): 72-91.

[6]Barbara Walvoord, *Teaching and Learning in College Introductory Religion Courses* (Hoboken, NJ: Wiley-Blackwell, 2007); Maureen H. O'Connell, "A Response to James D. Davidson," in *CTSA Proceedings* 63 (2008), 18-27.

[7]Paul Anderson and Sara Konrath, "Why Should We Care? What to Do about Declining Student Empathy," *The Chronicle of Higher Education,* July 31, 2012, http://chronicle.com.

[8]Stephen Marche, "Is Facebook Making Us Lonely?" *The Atlantic,* May 2012, http://www.theatlantic.com.

[9]William Deresiewicz, "Faux Friendship," *The Chronicle of Higher Education,* December 6, 2009, http://chronicle.com.

[10]Marche, "Is Facebook Making Us Lonely?"

[11]Sherry Turkle, *Alone Together: Why We Expect More from Technology and Less From Each Other* (New York: Basic Books, 2011).

[12]Marche, "Is Facebook Making Us Lonely?"

[13]Barbara Frederickson, "Your Phone vs. Your Heart," *The New York Times*, March 23, 2013, http://www.nytimes.com.

[14]Richard Gula, *Reason Informed by Faith: The Foundations of Catholic Morality* (New York: Paulist Press, 1989), 131.

[15]Marche, "Is Facebook Making Us Lonely?"

[16]Krista Tippett, American Public Media on Being podcast, "Alive Enough? Reflecting on Our Technology with Sherry Turkle," November 15, 2012, http://www.onbeing.org.

[17]Christian Smith, *Soul Searching: The Religious and Spiritual Lives of American Teenagers* (New York: Oxford University Press, 2005), 162-63.

[18]American Public Media's "On the Media" podcast, "The Facebook Show," http://www.onthemedia.org.

[19]Smith, *Soul Searching*, 165.

[20]Ibid., 163.

[21]Marche, "Is Facebook Making Us Lonely?"

[22]Jonathan Franzen, "Liking Is for Cowards. Go for What Hurts," *The New York Times*, May 28, 2011, http://www.nytimes.com.

[23]Ibid.

[24]Smith, *Lost in Transition*, 27-28.

[25]Gottlieb, "How to Land Your Kid in Therapy," *The Atlantic*, June 7, 2011.

[26]Tippett, On Being podcast, November 15, 2012.

[27]Martha Nussbaum, *Upheavals of Emotion: The Intelligence of Emotions* (New York: Cambridge University Press, 2003).

[28]Iris Marion Young, *Global Challenges: War, Self-Determination, and Responsibility for Justice* (New York: Polity, 2006), 157-85.

[29]Rachel Bundang, "The Mixtape as Secret Syllabus," presentation at the College Theology Society Annual Convention, Omaha, NE, June 2, 2013.

[30]Sandra Schneiders, "Religion vs. Spirituality: A Contemporary Conundrum," *Spiritus* 3, no. 2 (2003): 163-85.

[31]Most notably Laurie Cassidy at Marywood University, Kari-Shane Davis Zimmerman at St. John's University/College of St. Benedict, and Karen Peterson-Iyer at Santa Clara University.

[32]Edward Vacek, *Love, Human and Divine: The Heart of Christian Ethics* (Washington, DC: Georgetown University Press, 1996), 259.

[33]I am grateful to Laurie Cassidy at Marywood University for reflecting with me on the pedagogical significance of this practice.

[34]Margaret Farley, *Just Love: A Framework for Christian Sexual Ethics* (New York: Continuum, 2006), 130.

[35]Meghan Clark, "Subsidiarity Is a Two-Sided Coin," http://catholicmoraltheology.com.

PART II

TEACHING THEOLOGY

"For I Handed On to You as of First Importance What I Myself Had Received"

Theologians and Handing On the Faith

Aurelie A. Hagstrom

I am an associate professor of theology at Providence College, where I am finishing up my term as chair of the department. I have been at Providence College for ten years, before which I taught for eleven years at the University of St. Francis in Joliet, Illinois. I have, therefore, over twenty years of experience in the undergraduate college classroom to bring to bear on our topic of teaching theology and handing on the faith.

Let me begin by noting that although the rough-and-tumble of undergraduate theological education can be very challenging and even frustrating at times, my overwhelming experience has been that it is intellectually energizing and even spiritually edifying. I love teaching and I love to be in the classroom. It is much better than sitting in my office doing administrative paperwork! Teaching theology to the eighteen-to-twenty-one-year-old crowd is not easy when most of them are taking one's course as a requirement for graduation rather than as a class they have freely chosen because of their own religious interest. Add to that challenge the philosophical and cultural factors of a postmodern and, many would argue, post-Christian society, and the professor is faced with a sometimes daunting task. Nevertheless, I consider teaching undergraduate theology one of the best jobs in the world.

My experience at Providence College is that my students fall into one of three very general categories. I teach a small number of students who are active Catholics, most of whom have gone to

Catholic schools their whole lives. I also teach inactive Catholics, some would say cultural Catholics. They have been sacramentalized, but not evangelized. I would say these are the majority of the students in my classroom. The third group of students belongs to other religious traditions or might not self-identify with any religion. This third group is also smaller in number. The majority of my students are Catholics who have received the sacraments but who are perhaps better characterized as cultural Catholics rather than intentional Catholics.

This makeup of the classroom, of course, influences my teaching. Somehow I have to adapt the content of my course to the diverse backgrounds, needs, training, and formation of my students. It takes hard work, patience, and scholarly creativity. All this is simply to note that context is important. If I am trying to help students to understand the Catholic faith, I need to consider the students sitting in front of me. And here is where, in my experience, the interplay between theology and catechesis comes in.

I teach theology, but on a regular basis I find myself also having to do catechesis. That is, because of the diverse backgrounds of my students, there are times when I have to switch to a very fundamental and catechetical approach to the faith. This usually happens as a result of a student question in class. These questions often call for a change in modality. Instead of an academic theological answer, I switch to a more basic catechetical explanation. I don't find that this is a disruptive experience in the lecture. In fact, I try to integrate the question and the answer back into the flow of the lecture and in so doing, I find that this can generate even more basic questions that students might have but were reluctant to ask. Thus, the interplay between theology and catechesis, in my experience, can add energy to the classroom rather than drain it away. In both modalities, I am trying to present the faith of the church in a way that is engaging, joyful, convincing, and mature.

Matthew's gospel speaks of the scribe of the kingdom as one who brings out of the storehouse treasures that are both old and new. It seems to me that this is the challenge that the undergraduate classroom brings to a college theology professor. The fact that students have quite diverse backgrounds in religious training offers an opportunity to think about how the faith is best expressed and explained. After all, we know that the deposit of faith is one thing, and how we express and explain it to a new age, a new context, embracing new questions, is another.

If one were to ask me, "Do you teach theology or do you do catechesis?" I would say, "Yes!" And in so doing, I am not reluctant to speak about my own faith commitment. I am comfortable using the first person singular when I grapple with the faith of the church. I want my students to see that I am both a serious academic and a serious believer. But this doesn't mean that I am preaching a homily, or running an RCIA session, or offering a retreat talk in class. No, I am teaching theology. I'm not a catechist. But, as I've explained, I don't see a huge disconnect between theology and catechesis when I'm trying to explain fundamental teachings of the church to students who have very little background in religious instruction. So, for me it's not an either/ or proposition.

So far, so good? But now comes the hard part. What about the question of intentionally handing on the faith? Another way of asking this is, what about the theologian's role in what has been called "the new evangelization"?

How are we to think about theology and handing on the faith in the classroom in light of the new evangelization? To be honest, this is a more difficult question for me. Vatican II taught that evangelization is a divine mandate. According to *Dignitatis Humanae* 13, "There rests, by divine mandate, the duty of going out to the whole world and preaching the gospel to every creature."[1] *Ad Gentes* 35 states: "The whole Church is missionary, and the work of evangelization is a basic duty of the People of God."[2]

After the Council, Pope Paul VI wrote the 1975 apostolic exhortation *Evangelii Nuntiandi,* in which he unpacked this evangelization mandate in very concrete terms. One of the most famous passages from this text is Section 14, where it states that the church "exists to evangelize."[3] It continues, "Evangelizing is in fact the grace and vocation proper to the Church, her deepest identity." The other passage quoted most often from *Evangelii Nuntiandi* is Section 22, which states in part: "There is no true evangelization if the name, the teaching, the life, the promises, the kingdom, and the mystery of Jesus of Nazareth, the Son of God, are not proclaimed."[4]

Indeed, this conciliar and papal teaching on evangelization is beautiful, bold, and powerful. As we know, both Pope John Paul

II and Pope Benedict XVI took up this challenge and coined it "the New Evangelization." But what does the New Evangelization have to do with what we do in the undergraduate theology classroom?

In 2012, the Synod of Bishops had as its theme "The New Evangelization for the Transmission of the Christian Faith."[5] After preparatory work, the Synod submitted fifty-eight propositions to the Pope. Proposition Number 30 states, in part: "Theology as the science of faith has an importance for the New Evangelization."[6] It continues: "Theologians are called to carry out this service as a part of the salvific mission of the Church."[7] According to the Synod, then, theologians are supposed to be "agents of the New Evangelization."

And here, in my opinion, is where the problems begin. The plain truth is that most theologians in the Catholic academy here in the United States are uncomfortable with this language. Many of us bristle when we hear statements that suggest theologians are to be the agents of the New Evangelization. Most of us in the Catholic theological academy would frankly not self-identify that way. We don't use this language on job ads, curricula vitae, or authors' biographies on the backs of our books. Why?

My personal theory is that most of us did not have an ecclesial formation during graduate school which would equip us to absorb language like this. Synod Proposition 30 goes on to say: "It is necessary that they (theologians) think and feel with the Church."[8] Most of us went to graduate school and completed our doctorates in academic environments that did not shape us to "think and feel with the Church (*sentire cum Ecclesia*)." Most of us went to top-notch programs with high academic standards and elite faculty doing critical research on cutting-edge topics. We completed a rigorous Ph.D. program, but not an ecclesial formation. Thus, this rhetoric of the New Evangelization is foreign to us. The rhetoric of theologians being agents of the New Evangelization is not something that resonates with most of us. It's simply not our formation.

It is true that in the past most of the members of our theological professional societies were clergy, and so had a formation that went beyond just the academic. But now most of us are lay theologians, and have not had that sort of experience of the church during our graduate school years. And when we got our teaching jobs, we were usually not asked in the job interview these sorts of questions about catechesis and theology in the classroom and how we might see ourselves being evangelizers. Our student evaluations at the end of the semester do not include questions about whether or not students were converted through our teaching, or whether our teaching was effective for their faith life. When we apply for promotion and tenure, we are not evaluated on "thinking and feeling with the Church," to be absolutely honest.

So, when asked by our bishops how we engage in the salvific mission of the church, we bristle. But we react not because we just want to be confrontational or contrary or troublemakers (maybe some of us want to be troublemakers, but not all of us!). I think the bristling arises because this is a rhetoric we are not used to, and it makes us nervous. In fact, to be honest, we are even fearful of what might be behind it.

I think at this point some basic questions emerge: Is teaching theology an ecclesial vocation? Do we see ourselves as part of the salvific mission of the church? These are serious questions that go deeply into our self-identity and our sense of vocation. Who are we and what do we do?

On May 24, 1990, the Congregation for the Doctrine of the Faith issued an Instruction entitled "*Donum Veritatis:* On the Ecclesial Vocation of the Theologian."[9] It caused quite a stir. The Instruction began by stating that "The service of doctrine, implying as it does the believer's search for an understanding of the faith, that is, theology, is therefore something indispensable for the Church."[10] The Instruction also stated that it wanted to "describe the role of theologians and shed light on the mission of Theology in the Church."[11] Obviously, then, the Magisterium understands theology as part of the mission of the church.

Donum Veritatis goes further in describing the role of theologians using the language of vocation.[12] One of the vocations that the Spirit awakens in the church is that of the theologian. The role of this vocation is to "pursue in a particular way an ever deeper understanding of the Word of God found in the inspired Scriptures and handed on by the living Tradition of the church. The theologian does this in communion with the Magisterium which has been charged with the responsibility of preserving the deposit of faith."[13] This 1990 Instruction from the CDF, then, gives an explanation of theology and the work of theologians in the language of vocation and mission. Being a theologian is a vocation that gives service to the ecclesial community.

The last element of *Donum Veritatis* that I want to highlight is its assumption that personal faith and love for the church is at the heart of this vocation and mission. That is, the Instruction understands theology as an activity of faith. It states: "The right conscience of the Catholic theologian presumes not only faith in the Word of God whose riches he must explore, but also love for the Church from whom he receives his mission, and respect for her divinely assisted Magisterium."[14] It also states that "the theologian is called to deepen his own life of faith and continuously unite his scientific research with prayer."[15]

It seems to me that most of us did not get this sort of formation in graduate school. How many of us were told to unite our scientific research with prayer? How many of us were formed to think of the job of teaching theology as a vocation? How many graduate programs have questions on their comprehensive exams about loving the church and respecting the divinely assisted Magisterium? How many of our thesis directors told us that theology was an activity of faith? Or that, as theologians, we were supposed to think and feel with the church? Sometimes, then, I think there can be a disconnect with how the Magisterial teaching understands who we are and what we do and with how many of us (not all) perceive our identity and role.

This disconnect affects how we understand what we should be doing in the classroom. Should we be handing on the faith in the classroom? Are we agents of the New Evangelization? It seems to me that how we answer those questions has a lot to do with how we have been formed in our craft. An ecclesial formation brings with it an ecclesial language, a sense of vocation, and a perception of mission and spirituality. But most of those who teach theology in Catholic higher education in the U.S. have not had this sort of experience.

When we pose the question of teaching theology and handing on the faith, it exposes another disconnect. That is, I think we have another issue to grapple with in our understanding of theology itself. And it is a basic one. Is theology an activity of faith? Another way of asking it would be: Is faith a necessary prerequisite for doing theology? Do you have to be a person of faith to engage in theology?

Certainly the Magisterial teaching would be that faith is the indispensable spiritual milieu that an authentic theological culture needs. Without faith, theology would be defective. But if one were trained in a pluralist, constructive, revisionist tradition of theology, as many American Catholic theologians were, then one would probably not hold for the necessity of faith as a prerequisite for theology. How we think about the science of theology itself obviously influences how we perceive what we do in the classroom.

So, what *do* we do in the classroom? And what about handing on the faith? A few New Testament passages use this language of "handing on." The first is from St. Paul in 1 Corinthians, reminding the Corinthians of what he taught them when he was in Corinth. In chapter 11 of 1 Corinthians, he is instructing them about abuses in their celebration of the Eucharist. He reminds them of a formula he had taught them: the words of Jesus at the Last Supper, what we call the words of institution:

> For I received from the Lord what I also handed on to you, that the Lord Jesus on the night when he was betrayed took a loaf of bread, and when he had given thanks, he broke it, and said, "This is my body that is for you. Do this in remembrance of me." In the same way he took the cup also, after supper, saying, "This cup is the new covenant in my blood. Do this, as often as you drink it, in remembrance of me." (1 Cor 11:23-25)

The words of verse 23 contain a formula. The formula of "handing on" is a technical term for transmitting an oral tradition. We know that the English word "tradition" comes from the Latin *tradere,* literally meaning: to transmit, to hand over, to give for safekeeping, and to hand on. Tradition is a handing on of the faith. Paul had received it, and he hands it on to the Corinthian church.

1 Corinthians 11 is a good example of an apostolic tradition. Paul is handing on a teaching about the Eucharist. He is handing on the Christian faith about the bread and wine ritual at the center of their worship life. Paul himself is dependent upon the apostolic tradition of the early church—its kerygma, its liturgy, its

hymns, its confessional formulas, and its theological terminology. Paul is explicitly calling attention to the fact that he is handing down (Greek = *paradidomi*) what he himself had received (Greek = *paralambano*).

Later, in 1 Corinthians 15, he uses the same technical vocabulary of tradition. In chapter 15, Paul is teaching them about the *kerygma*, the gospel, the dying and rising of Jesus. In this chapter we have the earliest literary fragment of the kerygma. And, as we know, this kerygma later on becomes the basis for the Apostles Creed:

> Now I would remind you, brothers and sisters, of the good news that I proclaimed to you, which you in turn received, in which also you stand, through which also you are being saved, if you hold firmly to the message that I proclaimed to you—unless you have come to believe in vain. For I handed on to you as of first importance what I in turn had received: that Christ died for our sins in accordance with the scriptures. (1 Cor 15:1-3)

Notice in verse 3, the last sentence above, the use of this formula of "handing on." Here is another example of apostolic teaching being handed on. Paul is handing on the gospel message, the kerygma, to the Corinthians in the context of his instruction on the resurrection of Christ.

This is one New Testament tradition of the handing on of the faith. It is apostolic in origin and it follows a formal process. Technical language is used to describe the transmission of oral teaching—handing on the faith.

There is, however, *another way* of thinking about handing on the faith in the New Testament. This second way of handing on the faith is in the family. And it is by and large a familial, often feminine activity. After all, how many of us learned the faith from our mothers and grandmothers? This second approach can be found in Paul's Second Letter to Timothy: "I am reminded of your sincere faith, a faith that dwelt first in your grandmother Lois and your mother Eunice and now, I am sure, dwells in you" (2 Tim 1:5). Notice how the Deutero-Pauline author speaks about Timothy's Christianity. The faith lived in his grandmother Lois, it lived in his mother, Eunice, and now it lives in Timothy. This is a living faith that is passed down by the maternal line in Timothy's family. This intimate, familial transmission of the faith is different from that found in 1 Corinthians. This familial transmission of faith is different from the formal apostolic "handing on."

The Deutero-Pauline author does not use the technical terminology of "handing on." Instead, the author speaks of a living, interior, personal faith that is communicated in the family. Lois, then Eunice, and now Timothy have this sincere faith. Timothy learned his faith from his mother and his grandmother.

Apparently, there is more than one way to pass on the faith. There are different modalities for communicating the truths of the kerygma. There are different approaches in the New Testament to spreading the gospel to others. As we have seen in these New Testament passages, there is the formal apostolic handing on of teaching, and there is the more informal, familial way of sharing and witnessing to the Good News of Jesus Christ.

If we turn to the liturgy, we find these diverse ways of passing on the faith confirmed. We hear in the First Eucharistic Prayer, for example, that there are more ways of teaching the faith than just by the office of bishop. It is not only the episcopal office that teaches the faith, although they certainly are the principal teachers in any diocese. But the First Eucharistic Prayer has a petition for "all those who hold and teach the Catholic faith that comes to us from the Apostles."[16] "All who hold and teach the Catholic faith" must mean catechists and bishops, of course, but also mothers, fathers, grandparents and Lois and Eunice. By the way, I have used the old translation here. The new translation of the First Eucharistic Prayer is that we pray for: "all those who, holding to the truth, hand on the catholic and apostolic faith."[17] But I think the effect is the same. There is more than one way to communicate the faith.

This brings me back to our question: What about theologians and the handing on of the faith? Are we included in this petition of the First Eucharistic Prayer? Or not? Do we understand our task as including being a witness to the faith—academically and personally? Is that our charge as theologians? Or not? Do we perceive theology as an activity of faith? And if we did—what would that look like?

Is being an agent of the New Evangelization and sharing in the salvific mission of the church attractive or not? Realistic or hopelessly naïve?

Obviously, I raise these open-ended questions to promote conversation and dialogue. The organizers of the College Theology Society annual conference obviously wanted us to grapple with these issues. And so I am trying to put them in bold relief for us.

If we don't work in the campus ministry office, if we are not catechists or retreat leaders, if we are not running RCIA programs out of our theology departments, or using our classroom podiums to preach sermons to our classes, then what would it mean for theologians to "hand on the faith"?

If we are not St. Paul, handing on the kerygma in a formal apostolic and magisterial way, and if we are not Lois and Eunice, then might there be a third way, in our role as theologians in the classroom? A third way of "holding and teaching the Catholic faith that comes to us from the Apostles"?

I think the answer is yes, there is a third way. We can turn to Vatican II to find this third way. If we look at *Dei Verbum*, on divine revelation, I think there is an opening of a space for us as theologians in the classroom and handing on the faith. Chapter 2 of *Dei Verbum* talks about the "Transmission of Divine Revelation." Paragraph 8 in that chapter speaks of the apostolic tradition of the church progressing with the help of the Holy Spirit. The Council says that there is a growth of insight into the realities and words that are being passed on. This growth of insight comes about in various ways:

> This tradition which comes from the Apostles develops in the Church with the help of the Holy Spirit. For there is a growth in the understanding of the realities and the words which have been handed down. This happens through the contemplation and study made by believers, who treasure [or ponder] these things in their hearts (see Lk 2:19, 51) through a penetrating understanding of the spiritual realities which they experience, and through the preaching of those who have received through Episcopal succession the sure gift of truth. For as the centuries succeed one another, the Church constantly moves forward toward the fullness

of divine truth until the words of God reach their complete fulfillment in her.[18]

What are some of the ways that greater insight and understanding of the apostolic tradition come about? In this quote from *Dei Verbum* 8, there are two ways. The first is the contemplation and study of believers, who ponder the Word in their hearts. The second is the preaching of those in the episcopate. I want to focus on the first way that growth of insight and understanding happens: "the contemplation and study of believers who ponder these things in their hearts." It seems to me that this sentence can be an opening for a *third way* of handing on the faith done by those who contemplate and study the Word—that is, theologians. Isn't part of our task to study the Word and come to deeper and deeper understandings of it—and then pass it on to others? It seems to me that *Dei Verbum* 8 is saying that our study is a vital part of how the church's understanding of tradition grows.

In this paragraph, the phrase "pondering of the word" comes from the Lucan infancy narrative. After the phrase "the study of believers who ponder these things in their hearts," the citation is Luke 2:19 and 2:51. The way that Mary pondered all these things in her heart? The study of believers is to do the same thing.

I am claiming that *Dei Verbum* 8 can be applied to the work of theologians because this is exactly how the *Catechism* interprets it. The *Catechism* treats the work of theologians in Part 1 "Profession of Faith." In the section on the transmission of divine revelation, it relies heavily on *Dei Verbum*. In Section 94, it quotes *Dei Verbum* 8 about the Holy Spirit assisting the church to grow in its understanding of the realities and words of the heritage of faith.[19] Then it talks about how this growth takes place. The first way the *Catechism* lists is right from *Dei Verbum* 8: "through the contemplation and study of believers who ponder these things in their hearts."

But in 94 the *Catechism* goes further. It adds these lines: "It is in particular *theological research* which deepens knowledge of revealed truth."[20] Here the *Catechism* is relying on conciliar teaching as well. The footnote references *Gaudium et Spes*, sections 44 and 62.[21] Both citations mention the work of theologians as critical in the ongoing tasks of penetrating, understanding, and presenting the revealed truth of God. The *Catechism* weaves together a few conciliar references in stating that "in particular," our research as theologians deepens knowledge of revealed truth. Might another way of saying this be "passing on the faith"?

Catechism 94 points the reader to one more cross-reference. This time it is no. 2651 of the same *Catechism,* in the section "Christian Prayer,"[22] which states that faith takes shape and grows through prayer. Then it says that faith also takes shape through "the contemplation and study of believers who treasure in their hearts the events and words of the economy of salvation, and through their profound grasp of the spiritual realities they experience."[23] Once again, I think the implication is that through our *theological study,* faith can take shape. Through the work of theologians, the faith takes shape and grows. The faith of the church is enriched through our work. Is this not a third way?

It seems to me that these passages from the Council and the *Catechism* open up a space for understanding how theologians hand on the faith. Not in the formal, apostolic way of St. Paul, nor in the intimate, familial way of Lois and Eunice. But a third way, through pondering and studying the Word. Neither in formal magisterial pronouncements nor in the domestic catechesis of the family, but rather through study and teaching, the theologian passes on the faith to the students in the classroom. It seems to me that this is a way for the enterprise of theology to be integrated into the overall mission of the Church to transmit the gospel of Jesus Christ.

I want to end by going back to the phrase used by the Council and the *Catechism* concerning the work of the Holy Spirit in the study of believers and the unpacking of the faith. The phrase used was "the contemplation and study of believers who ponder these things in their hearts."[24] As stated earlier, this is a reference to Luke's gospel and his portrait of Mary. Mary is the one who ponders the word, stores up all these treasures in her heart.

Mary herself models how theology should be done. If she is indeed the archetype of the church, then her contemplative practice of "pondering the word" in her heart shows us what theology should be. Theology is an activity of faith, a pondering in the heart of the mysteries of our faith.

In Luke 1:29, she is perplexed by the words of Gabriel at the

Annunciation, and she "pondered what sort of greeting this might be." The word that Luke uses here in the Greek for "ponder" or "consider" comes from the Greek root for "dialogue." That is, Mary enters *into an interior dialogue with the Word*. She ponders, she carries on an inner dialogue with the Word that has been given her. In Luke 1:29, Mary shows us what we are to do as theologians—have an ongoing inner dialogue with the Word that has been given to us. Here Mary shows us what it means to make space, to welcome the word, to allow it to penetrate our thoughts, words, and intentions of the heart.

At the birth event in Luke 2:19, after the arrival of the shepherds, Luke says, "Mary treasured all these words and pondered them in her heart." In the Greek, Luke says that Mary "kept," "held together," and "placed together" these words in her heart. Luke shows Mary in a kind of insightful, meditative remembrance. Mary brings these words into her heart—into that interior dimension of understanding where sense and spirit, reason and feeling, thoughts and emotions, come together. Mary integrates the Word into her life.

And, lastly, at the finding of the child Jesus in the Temple, Luke tells us that "Mary treasured all these things in her heart" (Lk 2:51). But the word that Luke uses here in the Greek is not precisely the same as the one he used after the scene with the shepherds. The word here more accurately connotes "holding fast," "carrying it through," "carrying the word to term." Mary doesn't understand in this scene, but she accepts the mystery of Jesus' word with humility, and in patience receives it interiorly, and carries it to term. She stores up the word in her heart. I think we should maybe add another line in the litany of titles for Mary. "Mary as theologian," pondering the Word, may she pray for us!

On the feast of the Visitation, May 31, we remember the beautiful Lucan scene where Mary, after the Annunciation, makes haste to visit Elizabeth, who is already six months into her pregnancy of John the Baptist. The scene of this visit, this encounter, can model what theology can be. Mary and Elizabeth are revealing the mystery of the Incarnation in this Lucan passage. Apparently, this isn't just a "homey scene." Luke wants us to see something deeply salvific.

The Visitation scene contains two beautiful Canticles on the lips of Elizabeth and Mary. These Canticles of salvation proclaim the power of God to raise up, empower, and save. The Canticles testify to God's action in their own lives, and consequently in the lives of their people. God has a plan to save his people, and these two women are his instruments, his channels, his agents of salvation. God uses these poor and lowly women, these *anawim*, to bring about his plan of salvation.

I think this scene can model for us how theology can be done in handing on the faith. First, the Visitation is one of the Joyful Mysteries. Our enterprise should be *joyful*! Elizabeth says that the baby leapt in her womb at the sound of Mary's greeting. John the Baptist leaps for joy in the womb of Elizabeth. Second, the Lucan Visitation scene models *relationship*. We engage in our theological endeavor in relationship, not in isolation. Mary and Elizabeth are cousins, but they are also related as daughters of Israel, sisters in the faith, women of Zion. And lastly, this Visitation scene shows us a *dialogue*. There is a dialogue of salvation going on between these two women. Their interaction is a revelation of the mystery of salvation. And it seems to me that dialogue is a critical component in our theological enterprise. Dialogue in the academy, dialogue in the church, dialogue in the classroom.

Joy, relationship, and dialogue—it seems to me that theologians *are* called to hand on the faith. A faith that is mature, convincing, self-critical, and joyful.

Mary, Mother of God, and Elizabeth, mother of the Baptist— pray for us.

Notes

[1]Second Vatican Council, *Dignitatis Humanae*, December 7, 1965, paragraph 13.

[2]Second Vatican Council, *Ad Gentes*, December 7, 1965, paragraph 35.

[3]Pope Paul VI, *Evangelii Nuntiandi*, December 8, 1975, paragraph 14.

[4]Ibid., paragraph 22.

[5]Synod of Bishops, "The New Evangelization for the Transmission of the Christian Faith," June 19, 2012.

[6]Synod of Bishops, "*Synodus Episcoporum* Bulletin," October 7-28, 2012, from the Holy See Press Office, Proposition 30.

[7]Ibid.

[8]Ibid.

[9]Congregation for the Doctrine of the Faith, *Donum Veritatis* (On the Ecclesial Vocation of the Theologian), May 24, 1990.

[10]Ibid., paragraph 1.

[11]Ibid.

[12]Ibid., paragraph 6.

[13]Ibid.

[14]Ibid., paragraph 38.

[15]Ibid., paragraph 8.

[16]"Eucharistic Prayer I," *Roman Missal*, 3rd ed., (Totowa, NJ: Catholic Book Publishing Corporation, 2011).

[17]Ibid.

[18]Second Vatican Council, *Dei Verbum*, November 18, 1965, paragraph 8.

[19]*Catechism of the Catholic Church* (New York: Doubleday, 1995), paragraph 94.

[20]Ibid.

[21]Second Vatican Council, *Gaudium et Spes*, December 7, 1965.

[22]*Catechism*, paragraph 2651.

[23]Ibid.

[24]*Dei Verbum*, paragraph 8.

Teaching Theology and Handing On the Faith

One Institutional Perspective

David Gentry-Akin

I am entering my twentieth year of teaching at Saint Mary's College of California. Saint Mary's is a Catholic liberal arts college founded by the first archbishop of San Francisco, Joseph Alemany, OP, in 1863, and sponsored by the De La Salle Christian Brothers since 1868. Saint Mary's is an institution of almost 2,900 "traditional" undergraduates, by which is meant young people between the ages of eighteen and twenty-two who are enrolled in a full-time, day program, about 1,700 of whom are residential students living on campus. The College has been coeducational since about 1970, and today women make up more than 60 percent of the student body. College enrollment is increasingly diverse ethnically, with more than 40 percent of the student body consisting of people from historically underrepresented ethnic communities, many of whom are the first in their families to pursue a college education. About 65 percent of the students would claim at least a nominal identification with the Catholic faith tradition. On the faculty side, we have a declining number of religious Brothers (currently ten to twelve Brothers involved in the day-to-day life of the College, but many of them are semi-retired and thus serve only part-time, so the full-time equivalent is closer to five or six). The full-time faculty of the College is almost two hundred, with, by my estimate, fewer than 10 percent of that number being scholars who would make any claim to expertise in the Catholic intellectual tradition.

Teaching at Saint Mary's, located as it is in the culturally diverse and politically progressive environment of Northern California, can be challenging. There is a significant and growing gap between the aggressively secular milieu of the geographic region and the truth claims of the Roman Catholic Church. Misunderstanding and mistrust abound on all sides. Even though located in a rather bucolic and isolated suburban community, the College is deeply affected by the cultural milieu that surrounds it. This is seen in the ethnic diversity of the student body, in the ideological diversity of the faculty, and in the highly secularized rhetoric of "diversity" and "social justice," a rhetoric that has effectively replaced the earlier narrative of Catholic faith and culture, and one that now pervades the ethos of the campus.

An Unambiguous Commitment to the Catholic Faith and Intellectual Tradition

My own stance in this context is that I clearly and unapologetically understand myself to be a Roman Catholic theologian, deeply committed to my faith tradition and desirous of sharing the intellectual, moral, and aesthetic riches of the tradition with my students. If our exploration of the Catholic intellectual tradition should open new doors for students—helping them to reaffirm a faith tradition they thought they had left behind, or perhaps opening them to the possibility of embracing a new faith tradition because it speaks to the deepest longings of their hearts—I would be (and have been) thrilled. So, in that sense, my work is clearly evangelical, and I see myself, as a Catholic intellectual, participating fully in the evangelical mission of the Church.

Note, however, that I wrote that I want to *share* the riches of the Catholic intellectual tradition with my students, not *impose* them. I am highly cognizant of the tremendous power that I have in the classroom. Because I am perceived as the "expert," or because students are keenly aware that I am the dispenser of grades—grades which affect GPAs and which can affect a person's future in terms of career and graduate school—students may feel undue pressure to adopt my perspective or agree with my opinions, or at least give me the impression that they have done so. Therefore, I want to do everything humanly possible to create an atmosphere of open intellectual inquiry in my classroom, an atmosphere in which each person feels free to share her doubts, questions, or disagreements with whatever subject matter is under exploration.

Students who attend Saint Mary's for all four years of their undergraduate education are required to take two courses in theology
and religious studies, the first of which is a foundational course in
the Bible. Students often avoid taking the course, postponing it for
as long as they can, because of their misgivings about the content
or the process they perceive to be used in the course. Some fear
being "proselytized"; others have heard from friends that some of
the instructors of the course teach it from such a highly specialized
and technical perspective that it is impossible to do well in it. My
goal in teaching this course is to assuage their fears and to help
them to see that to study the Bible and theology generally is to
embark on a challenging and rewarding intellectual journey that
can help each student—regardless of their faith stance—to find
greater meaning and purpose in their lives. I want to help them
to find a *love* for the study of the Bible and of theology. I want
to help liberate my students from their fears, disabusing them of
false ideas about the Bible and religion, so that this field of study
can bring them to a deeper, richer, and fuller experience of the
abundant life that God wants for all of us.

To What Extent Is the Work of a Theologian an Evangelical One?

I do not see a contradiction between authentic evangelization
and freedom of intellectual inquiry. Every faculty member in every
discipline is, in fact, an evangelist of sorts. All of us are enthusi-
astic about our respective disciplines. We love the fields to which
we have chosen to devote our lives, and we believe that they are
worth sharing with others. While we strive to conduct our teaching
and research according to the accepted canons of our discipline
and its respect for method and objectivity, we are thrilled when a
student discovers a love for our discipline and chooses to devote
his or her life to its further study and cultivation.

It seems to me that, just as God leaves each of us absolutely
free to respond to divine initiatives in our own way and time,
so authentic evangelization consists in sharing the kerygma enthusiastically, but also with complete and utter respect for the
freedom of the person to have doubts, questions, and disagree-

ments, and ultimately to choose to reject the message if that is what she feels compelled to do at any point in her journey. Each person's relationship with God is sacred and inviolable, and it is therefore essential that I approach each person with the utmost respect for them and for the mysterious workings of God's grace in their lives.

I make no apologies about being a Catholic theologian or designing my classes around Catholic themes, ideas, beliefs, and values. This is a Catholic institution, and a constitutive dimension of its mission is the cultivation and handing on of the *Catholic* faith. I am here *because* I am a Catholic theologian, and my role is to make the study and understanding of the Catholic faith tradition available to students, Catholic and non-Catholic alike.

Along with my unapologetic stance about being a Catholic theologian and doing Catholic theology, however, I am highly intentional about creating an atmosphere of unconditional hospitality, welcome, and inclusion for *all* of the students in my classroom—catechized and uncatechized, Catholics and members of other traditions and of no faith tradition at all. I believe that God has brought them to this institution, and that we have something important to offer them on their life journey. I must seek to recognize God in each of them and to affirm the best of who they are and who they can become.

Is "Diversity" a Trojan Horse?

When it comes to trying to cultivate and hand on a tradition—and in this case the Catholic tradition—I must say that I find the current "diversity" rhetoric so prevalent on college campuses to be extremely unhelpful. Certainly, welcoming people of diverse ethnicities and cultures onto a college campus can create a vibrant environment for learning from one another's unique background and life experience. And, in this sense, no movement or institution on Earth is more diverse than the Roman Catholic Church. However, my experience is that the current "diversity" rhetoric has come, really, to be a code term for the very "dictatorship of relativism" about which Pope Emeritus Benedict XVI has written. It has come to mean, in practice, that the highest value is to be accorded to the creation of a neutral space in which all belief systems are considered equally valid. My fear is that this rhetoric has come to be the "Trojan Horse" inside the house, denying any normative status for the very tradition that was the motivation for the building of the house in the first place.

A tradition, however, is like a garden. It requires gardeners who are drawn to the beauty of its plants and flowers, and who are willing to commit themselves to the tilling of its soil in the hope of keeping its beauty alive and of bringing even greater beauty into being. There is diversity in any garden, but diversity is not an absolute value. If it were, the garden would soon devolve into nothing more than a bed of weeds. Diversity is welcomed, but only insofar as it contributes something to the beauty of the whole. Just as with a garden, a tradition does not survive and thrive if it is not nurtured and cultivated and given a safe and hospitable environment in which to do so.

The Catholic intellectual, moral, and aesthetic tradition must be privileged on our campuses. Especially in the highly secularized and increasingly polarized milieu of the United States, with its growing antagonism toward the Catholic tradition, it is essential that the tradition enjoy a "safe zone" in which its exploration and cultivation is the highest value. That is why these institutions were founded, and it is a purpose that they should seek to recover before it is too late. Students, regardless of religious affiliation or lack thereof, have freely chosen to come to a Catholic institution. For a student to expect that they will be able to progress through a Catholic institution without having to engage the Catholic tradition is unjustifiable, and reduces the role of the institution in their lives to the purely instrumental role of just another "delivery system" in our consumerist culture, the only difference being that the "product" in this case is an educational credential rather than a new car or a household appliance.

To be welcoming of diverse peoples and perspectives is one thing; to be so overwhelmed by "diversity" that the core identity and mission of a place is eclipsed is quite another. "We" cannot be welcoming of "other" peoples and perspectives if, in fact, the institution has become so pluralistic that it has devolved into a collection of mere interest groups, each competing for the conquest of their point of view in the marketplace of ideas. In that case there really is no "We" that might hope to welcome anyone.

Teaching Methodology

I teach by raising important questions and witnessing to the ways in which the Catholic intellectual tradition has helped me to negotiate those important questions. I "evangelize" *not* by imposing anything, but by seeking to witness—sometimes quite silently—to how the Catholic Christian faith has been deeply salvific for me personally.

In my classroom, I seek to emphasize learning as a *collaborative* rather than a *competitive* process. I encourage students to move away from "disagreement" as a method of discourse and to emphasize what I have come to call "sympathetic engagement" with an idea or a belief. To what extent does this idea or belief make sense? Where is it coming from? Can we understand why someone might embrace it, even if we personally chose not to do so? So often, in our highly polarized culture, we rush to the evaluative level to assert our "disagreement" with something that has been asserted by another, when in fact *we do not really understand* the position or how a person or a culture came to it. I find it much more helpful to probe whether we really understand what has been asserted, and to leave "disagreement" for a later stage.

I seek to articulate Catholic teaching clearly, but at the same time to create a climate of openness in the classroom whereby questions, criticisms, and divergent points of view are welcomed and engaged. Especially in classes that are populated by students of other faiths or of no faith, I always ask, "How does this idea, concept, or teaching strike you? In what ways does it converge with or diverge from your own tradition or worldview? If it converges, how and why? If it diverges, how and why?" I strive to look for the commonalities that we can all affirm, even while not shying away from a frank and open discussion of the differences.

It is utterly essential that students know that there is going to be no coercion in the classroom, that their intellectual freedom will absolutely be respected, and that their progress in the course will be based on clearly stated, objective criteria in the syllabus for the course, and *not* on the extent to which they share my faith commitment or philosophical worldview. Further, I make sure that students know, on Day One, the approach that I will take, so that if a student is "turned off" by my approach, he or she has ample opportunity to drop my class and add another one.

Prayer: Creating a Space for Mystery and the Transcendent

I open my classes with a moment for prayer and reflection. My goal is to be very intentional about creating a space for the transcendent, one that *invites* students, in a non-coercive way, to acknowledge God's mysterious presence and to ground themselves in that presence. We are seeking to do theology in my classroom, and theology, by Anselm's classic definition, is "faith seeking understanding." My classroom, therefore, must be a place in which both faith and reason are welcomed and understood to be important ways of knowing. Both must be welcomed and respected. One does not cancel the other out.

When I pray with students, silence is an important element. The prayer acknowledges that life is sacred, that each of us is sacred, that deepening our understanding of reality is something that requires that we be open to both faith and reason as sources of knowledge and wisdom, and that my classroom is a "safe zone" for the asking of deep fundamental questions, the "God" questions. I very much like to use a beautiful excerpt from Pope Emeritus Benedict XVI's homily at his inaugural Mass in 2005: "Each of us is the result of a thought of God. Each of us is loved. Each of us is willed. Each of us is necessary."[1] This text calls us back to our mysterious origins in God's ineffable design, and to our equal dignity as daughters and sons of God without regard to distinctions of ethnicity, gender, socioeconomic class, and even religious affiliation.

A Critical Juncture

I believe that we are at a critical juncture in the future of Catholic higher education. We must find a way of bringing the Catholic intellectual tradition back to the heart of the educational endeavor in these institutions, or they will, in a very few years, cease to be Catholic institutions in any meaningful way. It is time to reassert the distinctiveness of Catholic higher education. We must be less ashamed of what we have to offer. We must seek to be deeply rooted in the Tradition, but also seek to create a space of openness and hospitality for all women and men of good will who want to come and engage in the search for Truth with us.

Finally, we must strive to raise up another generation of Catholic intellectuals in all fields, Catholic thinkers who can help all of us to tease out the implications—in the arts, in literature, and in the natural and social sciences—of the Catholic way of looking at the world. Philosophy and theology are at the very heart of the Catholic intellectual tradition, but in themselves they are not nearly enough to sustain an entire intellectual, moral, and aesthetic tradition and worldview. The "Catholic Thing," the Catholic faith tradition and intellectual tradition, must also be understood as a project. Certainly it has a past, and that past deserves to be studied. But it also has a future. It is a project worth doing and sharing. It is time for a vigorous and unapologetic reaffirmation of the role of the Catholic tradition in historically Catholic institutions of higher education. It is time to rededicate, in very intentional ways, the resources of these institutions toward the cultivation, development, exploration, and handing on of the tradition which has been their very lifeblood and reason for being from the beginning.

Notes

[1]Pope Benedict XVI, "Homily of His Holiness Benedict XVI," April 24, 2005.

Handing On the Faith as a Guest and Teaching Theology When You're Not Teaching Theology

Andrew D. Black

As part of the "Evangelical Catholics and Catholic Evangelicals" session at the College Theology Society annual meeting in 2013, I was asked to reflect on the question, "How do I teach theology and pass on the faith, in my particular institutional context?" I assumed that the conveners were envisioning a panel featuring two Catholics and two evangelicals (most likely Baptists, given the traditional composition of this group), and all of the panelists would be teaching theology in institutions affiliated with their respective ecclesial communities. Representatives from each group would then reflect on their pedagogical experiences in such a way as to illuminate the particular shape of their institutional roles, their distinctive theological emphases, and some characteristic differences in the textures of the respective faith traditions[1] that they are seeking to hand on (for instance, the very word "tradition" will register in radically different ways among Catholics and Baptists—important differences within those traditions notwithstanding). At the same time, partly because the panelists would all be teaching theology in *these* times, but especially because the panelists are, to some degree, willing to be identified as *evangelical* Catholics and *catholic* Evangelicals (or Baptists), there would likely be some noteworthy convergences among the presentations.

With these assumptions about the panel in view, I found myself wondering if I was really the right person to speak. This is because I do not fit the template I just described. I have deep Baptist roots— my Canadian-born great-great-grandfather was a Baptist missionary to Indian Territory [Oklahoma] and I have two relatives who wrote gospel songs now included in the Baptist Hymnal—and I remain an active member of a Baptist congregation. But for nearly six years now I've been teaching at a Catholic, Marianist institution (the University of Dayton). And I've done this while studying—and occasionally praying and worshipping—with Catholic colleagues and their families. For the past year I have also been commuting to teach at Capital University in Columbus, Ohio—a historically Lutheran institution. So as I bring my own ecclesial formation to the task of teaching in these various locations, the matter of just what faith I am passing on—and to whom—has not been a simple one.

Thus, I am not easily able to play either of the roles I sketched above (i.e., I am not a Baptist teaching at a Baptist institution, nor have I been primarily tasked with handing on the faith). What I *can* offer are some reflections on what it has been like to teach as a guest—a Baptist teaching at a Catholic institution, in classes filled mostly with Catholics—and a few comments about what I have learned, as a theologian, while teaching in classes that were not formally theological.

The Blessings and Burdens of Being a Catholic Evangelical

First, the existential part: what has it meant to teach theology and hand on the faith as a Baptist at a Catholic institution? My group of incoming doctoral students in theology was evenly split between Catholics and Protestants. We had former Catholic Workers and Jesuit Volunteers, together with a cadre of ("big-B") Baptists, mostly from the south and southwest, and other free-church Protestants. Though they might offer a few qualifications, I think that my peers would agree that our doctoral cohort at the University of Dayton was characterized by a remarkable degree of intellectual and spiritual community. In abstract and less explicitly theological terms, I think it fair to say that we had in common a desire for a substantive, even radical, "center" in the midst of a struggle with soul-wearying political and ecclesiological polarization.

We acknowledged and joked about particular differences in our backgrounds, of course. One of my new Catholic friends gave me a scapular after I was so fascinated and amused to learn that they were still a part of some Catholics' devotional practice. I also have a vivid memory of an afternoon during which I was preparing to teach a few class sessions introducing my students to the Bible. I created a matching exercise in which groups would look up texts that contained famous passages or illustrated general points about scripture that I would want to make later in the class.

I have to confess the secret pride I felt when my Catholic officemate was simply amazed to watch me pull all this together in less than half an hour, as I zoomed back and forth through the text. All those years spent in Bible-drill exercises as a youngster had paid off! I facetiously responded to her: "But why *shouldn't* we Christians know our way around this book? It's our *home . . .* right?" Of course, her home—in that sense—was the Mass, along with a host of other prayers and gestures, steeped in scripture and ancient Christian example, that she had been praying and doing throughout her life.

Again, I believe I am on fairly solid ground in claiming that, despite our disparate ecclesial formations, there was a profound sense among this group that we were participating in a profound unity. We were friends in the best sense, as we discovered a common love of Christ and the church (or *in* Christ and the church). Of course, it's the second of those loves that made things interesting and challenging, both existentially and theologically: which church? We were all ostensibly committed to a theological vision that made it crucial that we see and make organic connections between our theological work and the life of actual, concrete churches. But there remained the awkward fact that the actual, concrete churches that had formed us—and that continued to feature prominently in our thinking—were not ultimately in communion (a fact made both painfully and helpfully clear whenever I attend Mass). It is surely fair to say that none of us knew how to talk about this well.

In the second year of the doctoral program, together with other first-time instructors, I began teaching undergraduates who selected the "Catholic Option" (or who had it selected for them by their parents) for their required general education religion course at the University of Dayton. That year, we used William Portier's *Tradition and Incarnation: Foundations of Christian Theology* as our primary text. It would be inappropriate to call it merely a ("small-c") catholic book, as the numerous sources and illustrations were consistently Roman Catholic. In other words, what we were presenting was not exactly the kind of "mere Christianity," a Christianity from nowhere. Yet the focus was on a kind of reflective, broadly ecumenical approach to the classic foundations of Christian thought that I could easily embrace, given the sort of Baptist I was and am. During the two semesters I taught that course, I did not tell my students that I was not personally a Catholic, and it never became an issue.

Our task was not one of catechesis in any facile sense. Yet I now wish that I had done more to help those students make connections between what we might call "thinking Christianly," and their participation in a living, communal tradition that extends beyond the classroom, and that has to do with much more than the space between their ears. Later iterations of that particular course, after I was no longer teaching it, have done just this sort of thing by, e.g., tying the presentation of basic Christian teaching to the order and practices of the Mass. To be clear: it was a joy to teach those first two courses. I was teaching out of the heart of the Christian intellectual tradition and in ways that were fresh and appealing to me as a Baptist. It is difficult for me to communicate to cradle Catholics the way in which "tradition" can serve as a highly creative, even provocative and subversive, theological and pedagogical resource for someone coming from a context such as my own. This was virtually the same joy I knew while experiencing such substantial unity among my fellow doctoral students during those first years in Dayton. I had the privilege of tasting and sharing from an inexhaustible fountain of wisdom alongside saints past and present who would ensure that I felt neither alone nor too comfortable.

What sent my thoughts in this direction as I was preparing these remarks is the fact that I recently read an interview with George Lindbeck in which he described the marvelous sense of real communion he experienced while in Rome as an official Lutheran observer during the Second Vatican Council.[2] As he interacted with various Catholics at different levels of the hierarchy, he received something much more than generic hospitality, but not quite a homecoming either. On a less historically momentous scale, of course, I have experienced a similar, but perhaps more extended, form of hospitality during my time in Dayton.

Yet following Lindbeck's "mountaintop experience"—as my tradition usually names such episodes of intense spiritual consolation—the path toward realizing in a lasting, visible way the unity in Christ he experienced at Vatican II has been difficult. Indeed, it may at times appear as if the path itself has actually been lost. The modern ecumenical movement, at least in its classic form of high-level dialogues between distinct and divided ecclesial bodies, is now widely seen as a spent project.

Therefore, what I most want to say about teaching *theology* as a guest in someone else's ecclesial home is that I have had to locate my own teaching, as a Catholic-Baptist theologian, in something like this interpretation Lindbeck recently offered, in the twilight of his career:

> What the good God is doing to the church, it seems to me, is destroying us bit by bit. I think that God wants us to be united. And destroying each denomination's identity is precisely the way in which eventually we'll have to be united. But, nevertheless, if you are going to be really ecumenical, you are going to have to know your own tradition and love it to its depths.[3]

What does it mean to know and love a tradition and love it to its depths, even if God is intent on destroying that very tradition, this communal identity, as it is now constituted? What does it mean to be really ecumenical, in that way, as a teacher of Christian theology? Again, such questions matter when you are engaged in handing on the faith to particular students in particular universities. These students all come from somewhere, and they are all going somewhere—but where?

Vincent Miller's *Consuming Religion: Christian Faith and Practice in a Consumer Culture* is the product of a theologian who has thought at great length and with substantial depth about the challenges of handing on the faith today. Miller presents consumer culture as not merely a particular set of ideologies—that is, consumer*ism*. As pernicious as that may be, his focus is on consumer culture as "a way of relating to beliefs—a set of habits of interpretation and use—that renders the 'content' of beliefs and values [and their intrinsic connection to other beliefs] less important."[4] The bulk of the book is a discerning discussion of consumer culture and of religious agency within it.

I continue to learn from and wrestle with Miller's analysis. One of my initial concerns with *Consuming Religion* was the fact that in the final chapter, when he takes up a discussion of specific tactical responses to consumer culture, Miller focuses on resources available to Catholics—that is, members of the Roman Catholic Church. Clearly, I understand and share his reasons for focusing not simply on "Christianity," but on an actual ecclesial community and living historical tradition. Yet I was concerned with what seemed to be his lack of acknowledgment of the ways in which consumer culture reinforces the theological scandal of Christian division—that is, in the way that American-style denominationalism also fuels a desire to focus on particular ecclesial identities— and primarily for "branding" purposes. I certainly did not have a straightforward plan for addressing the dilemma, and I have since come to realize that Miller is far from insensitive to my concerns. Drawing on the work of Michel de Certeau, he concluded in *Consuming Religion* that, given the fact that consumer culture essentially holds the field and is fiendishly successful at blunting or even co-opting nearly all forms of critique, what Christians have available to them are tactics, the "art of the weak." Perhaps we could call what we heard in the quotation from Lindbeck above a tactical approach to the question of Christian unity, as it leaves matters of ultimate strategy in God's hands. It is a lesson I have come to know more profoundly while teaching theology to and with Catholics as one of their estranged siblings.

Nothing Is More Practical Than Finding God with Others

After two semesters teaching the foundations of Christian theology, I have spent most of the last few years teaching the "general option" of the introductory religion course at UD—an introduction to the study of "religion" and a comparative survey of major world religious traditions. I have also been doing something very similar more recently at Capital University. Without explicit intention, the approach I and others have taken to teaching these non-theological general education classes is consonant with Miller's diagnosis and prescription in *Consuming Religion*:

The fundamental problem with the commodification of culture is that it trains believers to abstract religious doctrines, symbols, and practices from the traditional and communal contexts that give them meaning and connect them to a form of life. Such shallow retrieval of doctrines, prayers, symbols, and practices can be countered by tactically emphasizing their embeddedness in an ongoing, historical tradition. As with commodities in general, the more they are associated with their particular origins, the less susceptible they are to abstraction and shallow engagement.[5]

In formal terms, Miller's counsel articulates what I have found to be the best approach for teaching these kinds of religious studies courses at this time.

As I am usually teaching first-year undergraduates, I try to avoid getting bogged down in too much explicit theoretical work deconstructing the term "religion." However, I do offer the thesis that any beliefs worth studying are the kinds that give enduring shape to the lives of communities and the persons within them—what they read, whom they associate with, what they do habitually, how they order their time. I reinforce this by sharing with them a copy of the well-known poem attributed to Pedro Arrupe, S.J., which begins by affirming, "Nothing is more *practical* than finding God."[6]

When designing these courses, I have drawn upon, without making explicit reference to, Baptist theologian James Wm. McClendon, Jr.'s definition of theology as a "science of convictions," with a "conviction" defined as "a persistent belief such that if X (a person or community) has a conviction, it will not be given up easily, and it cannot be given up without making X a significantly different person (or community) than before."[7] Since convictions are displayed over time, I assign students narratives that feature characters from particular religious traditions (I tend to focus on the Abrahamic traditions). I always enjoy assigning Chaim Potok's classic novel *The Chosen*. As I teach it, I am certainly striving to teach students things about Judaism in general and about various Jewish responses to modernity in particular. But I'm also hoping to *show* them that, as I regularly put it, "Part of what it means to be a Jew is to be in an argument with at least some other Jews about what it means to be a Jew"—and that this arguing takes place in and through such practices as the study of Torah and Talmud.

I almost always ask students the following meaningless question, sometimes as the prompt for an essay assignment: which of the two fathers at the heart of *The Chosen* is "more religious"—the imposing Hasidic *tzaddik*, Reb Saunders, or the modern Orthodox scholar and Zionist, David Malter? The point is not that it is patently unjust to make such judgments in the subjective realm of "religion" (that's what many of them will want to say). Rather, I hope that they will come to see that the modifier, "religious," can't be made to do that kind of evaluative work without smuggling in criteria from somewhere else.

These examples illustrate the direction I'm generally trying to move in these classes—always trying to *show* people and communities with specific convictions that are lived out through a variety of practices. It's simply a fact that to take such an approach to "religion" is to swim against a great cultural tide—though I avoid making frontal assaults on consumeristic spirituality that are sure to alienate. I strive to provide material that is vivid and compelling and that helps me to instruct and, in appropriate ways, entertain students. But given the nature of such classes, it is only through indirect, tactical ways that I can attempt to delight or allure them with the prospect of a less commodified and more complex participation in the Christian faith most of them still claim in at least some form.

These are challenging times to teach theology, wherever and whenever we do it. But as one of my dissertation readers had to remind me, though I should have known better: at what point in at least the past five hundred years have people *not* felt that their world was changing faster than they could come to terms with? When I graduated from a Baptist seminary a decade ago, I would never have thought that in the coming years I would be teaching theology to Catholic students or teaching a host of world religions/ religious studies courses.

In the end, the greatest challenge I've faced as a teacher of theology has not been a matter of mastering and presenting course content, or of dealing with perplexities about the specific nature of my instructional role. As someone formed in Christian faith and piety by Baptists and evangelicals, my greatest challenge has been dealing with an instinctual pressure to remain haunted by the possibility that, especially when teaching required general education courses, what my students receive in the classroom may be "the only Jesus they'll ever see."

That is, of course, too much responsibility for anyone to bear, and certainly too much to bear alone. Teaching is sufficiently demanding work on its own. Thus, I am deeply grateful for the opportunities the College Theology Society provides for us to reflect more explicitly on these kinds of questions and, more basically, to be renewed for the pedagogical task by (re)discovering friends who *know* the griefs and the anxieties, the joys and the hopes of teaching theology and handing on the faith.

Notes

[1] I do not particularly care for this locution (i.e., "faith tradition"), but it is less problematic than referring to Catholics and (E)vangelicals as handing on different "faiths." Another alternative would be to talk about "ecclesial traditions," but it is far from clear in what way "evangelicals" (according to most ways of using this notoriously difficult term) represent a distinct "ecclesial tradition," rather than an un-ecclesial or even anti-ecclesial tradition. The option works better if we are trying to refer to Catholics and Baptists, rather than "evangelicals" per se.

[2] John Wright, ed., *Postliberal Theology and the Church Catholic: Conversations with George Lindbeck, David Burrell, and Stanley Hauerwas* (Grand Rapids: Baker Academic, 2012).

[3] Ibid., 18.

[4] Vincent J. Miller, *Consuming Religion: Christian Faith and Practice in a Consumer Culture* (New York: Continuum, 2005), 1. The bracketed phrase is my own.

[5] Ibid., 195.

[6] Of course, I add qualifications when necessary (e.g., for non-theistic "religions" such as Theravada Buddhism). The poem attributed to Arrupe is available online at http://www.ignatianspirituality.com, and can also be found in *Finding God in All Things: A Marquette Prayer Book* (Milwaukee: Marquette University Press, 2009).

[7] This definition comes from the book McClendon co-wrote with agnostic philosopher James M. Smith, *Convictions: Defusing Religious Relativism*, rev. ed. (Valley Forge, PA: Trinity Press International, 1995), 5. They define theology (or, if one prefers, "theoretics") as a "science of convictions" which is tasked with "the discovery, understanding or interpretation, and transformation of the convictions of a convictional community, including the discovery and critical revision of their relation to one another and to whatever else there is" (184).

"Turn, Turn, Turn"

Considering Conversion in the Theology Classroom

Katherine G. Schmidt

I am currently a doctoral student in theology in the Department of Religious Studies at the University of Dayton, a Catholic university operated by the Society of Mary, or Marianists. I have the pleasure of teaching the mandatory introductory course for the department, which can be a complicated task on its own, given that the course is intended to introduce students to both religious studies and theology. I will, however, largely bypass this particular complication in this essay and focus instead on the challenges of what it means to hand on the faith in the college classroom. In thinking about this theme, I considered not only my experiences as a young teacher of theology, but also the way I've gone about narrating them. I have, on several occasions, found myself on an airplane explaining my vocation to a veritable stranger. There is almost always something I include when discussing my teaching life, something that I've chosen to focus on for my reflection here. I must confess that after trying to describe what I teach, I tell my conversation partner, "But I don't try to convert my students. That's not my goal." I refer to this comment and the feelings behind it as the "conversion caveat." Though I don't say it, you could almost add a "so don't worry" to this very loaded statement, as I try to anticipate and then assuage the probably nonexistent concerns of the poor soul who ended up next to a graduate student on her flight.

I want people to know that my primary focus is not to proselytize, especially since my classroom audience is most assuredly captive. I usually describe the desired outcome of my course as something like religious literacy. I want my students to be able to hold their own in religious conversations, specifically ones about Catholicism or Christianity in general. As such, this does not seem to require any personal commitment or confession on their parts. Likewise, my class does not require any conversion or recommitment to the faith of Jesus Christ for my students to do well. I say as much in the first moments of the course, and in emails to non-Catholic students who are concerned that their lack or disparity of faith will adversely affect their chances for success.

It may be helpful to say more about why I feel the need to convince people that I'm not out to convert my students. Luckily, I have the eloquence of Thomas Merton for help. I recently wandered into an old bookstore in Bardstown, Kentucky, which had the biggest Merton book section I'll probably ever see, given that the store was only about twelve miles from Merton's hermitage at the Abbey of Gethsemani. There I found an out of print collection of Merton's essays on violence in the twentieth century. One of the essays is entitled "Apologies to an Unbeliever," and is an apology in the more conventional sense of the word. Quite simply, Merton is apologizing to a person who does not share his faith in God. He writes, "So I am apologizing to you for the inadequacy and impertinence of so much that has been inflicted on you in the name of religion, not only because it has embarrassed me, and others like me, but because it seems to me to be a falsification of religious truth."[1] My "conversion caveat" is a kind of mini-apology à la Merton, my small attempt to exempt myself from the inflictions of religion that dominate our political and cultural discourse at present. I want to represent the academic study of religion and make perfectly clear that I have little interest in being another cultural warrior. But I latched on to Merton's essay because he is able to write such an apology from within his religious vocation and not in spite of it. So, too, would be my goal as a teacher of theology.

The problem is that I actually see what I'm doing in the classroom as part of my own baptism, as my vocation, as my participation in the life of the Church and in the mystery of Revelation. As genuine as I am when I assure worried students that the course is not really about personal faith, I myself am teaching it as a very extension of my own. "Handing on the faith" sounds like such a simple idea, but the more I reflect on it, the more problems I encounter within myself: I am being honest in my conviction about my vocation to present the faith of the Church in a way that is creative and accurate and ultimately does not do harm to the faith lives of my students, as well as when I am careful to describe the aims of my course as only incidentally concerned with the state of my students' souls. For that reason, I want to reflect on my experiences at the University of Dayton in the context of the tension within my own life as a person of faith who teaches theology, and as someone who insists to strangers, friends, and herself that she is not out to convert her students.

As I mentioned, the University of Dayton is run by the Marianists, a small order of brothers, sisters, and priests who do not share the notoriety of their Jesuit brothers in the realm of Catholic academia, but nonetheless have a robust understanding of their charism with regard to the education of young people. Admittedly, the Marianist character of the university is one of the details I leave out when narrating my experiences to people outside of theology, yet I do consider it to be an important factor when I prepare courses for University of Dayton students. The founder of the Marianists, Fr. William Joseph Chaminade, presents the first challenge to my "conversion caveat." In a letter to retreat masters from 1839, Fr. Chaminade pens the following rather convicting lines: "It is for you to impress on the teachers what a great mistake they would be making if they were to limit their endeavors to instruction in human learning, if they were to put all their care and pride into making scholars and not into making Christians, or into gaining a worldly reputation."[2] It seems Fr. Chaminade wants me, an instructor at a Marianist institution, to make Christians, but this appears among no course or student learning objectives. Indeed, if my "conversation caveat" shows us anything, it's probably that I would be rather uncomfortable if it was. But I do have my students read Chaminade's words, mostly to get us all thinking about what exactly it means to be at a Marianist institution. Each time I have read his letter with students, it has caused me to reflect on my own role in Chaminade's vision, as well as the deep sympathies I have with his desire for students to be successful in more than just school and work. And yet, the "conversion caveat" looms.

Teaching at a Catholic university appears to a have a very

specific meaning in the teaching of the Church. I find no less challenging words than Chaminade's in Pope John Paul II's *Ex Corde Ecclesiae*. He offers four "essential characteristics" of the Catholic university:

1. a Christian inspiration not only of individuals but of the university community as such;
2. a continuing reflection in the light of the Catholic faith upon the growing treasury of human knowledge, to which it seeks to contribute by its own research;
3. fidelity to the Christian message as it comes to us through the Church;
4. an institutional commitment to the service of the people of God and of the human family in their pilgrimage to the transcendent goal which gives meaning to life.[3]

With regard to the tension I've described above, the Pope writes: "By its very nature, each Catholic University makes an important contribution to the church's work of evangelization. It is a living institutional witness to Christ and his message, so vitally important in cultures marked by secularism, or where Christ and his message are still virtually unknown."[4] Thus he challenges me in no uncertain terms that part of my job is to evangelize, to spread the Gospel, or as we might prefer to express it here, to "hand on the faith." And yet the Pope is also clear that the Catholic university as a university "is an academic community which, in a rigorous and critical fashion, assists in the protection and advancement of human dignity and of a cultural heritage through research, teaching and various services offered to the local, national and international communities."[5] "Rigorous" and "critical" are specific and important adjectives for theology as an academic discipline, and in a nutshell, this is really what my introductory course is introducing. I want my students to discover that one can think about God in a way that is rigorous and critical. But I also want them to know that such rigor and critique need not mean that one eschews faith. Indeed, I want them to see that the best theology is often done from within the tradition itself, in a posture of persistent unease with quick answers and simplistic explanations of the divine mystery. Indeed, I want to introduce them, in admittedly indirect ways, to what the world looks like through the eyes of the saints and to people who are trying to get there.

And so we have come to my second confession: I actually might want to convert my students after all. Here I've found Bernard Lonergan's preoccupation with conversion to be somewhat helpful. Without the philosophical chops to take Lonergan on in a comprehensive way, I only want to reflect on one of his categories, one that I've found helpful in sorting out this question of handing on the faith in the classroom. Lonergan writes that conversion is really a change in horizons. By horizon he means "the boundary of one's field of vision…what lies beyond one's horizon is simply outside the range of one's interests and knowledge: one knows nothing about it and one cares less. And what lies within one's horizon is in some measure, great or small, an object of interest and of knowledge."[6] It is important to note that simply learning more about a subject in which one already has some level of interest does not mark a conversion, but simply an expansion of one's horizon. For Lonergan, conversion is marked by being in love: "It is a state reached through the exercise of vertical liberty, the liberty that chooses, not among objects within a horizon but between different horizons, different mentalities, different outlooks."[7]

Any teacher knows that students come into the classroom with what we could describe as different horizons, to use Lonergan's preferred category. It seems to me that there are three important horizons that one must consider when teaching theology: a horizon that does not include interest in religion or faith at all, a horizon that includes at least a preliminary interest in religion or faith, and lastly, a horizon that is marked by the otherworldly love Lonergan says is the horizon of the person of faith. It is tempting to rank these three horizons in ascending order as I've presented them, especially for people of faith who see the third as the horizon of ultimate truth. However, out of respect for my students and colleagues who do not share my faith, it may be more appropriate to imagine them side by side. This will also prove helpful as I extend the analogy into teaching.

I propose that teaching theology is like sailing a boat into many horizons at once. To be an effective teacher, I have to be sensitive to the various horizons that make up my classroom, as well as the horizon that inflects the pedagogy and content of my course.

Admittedly, I cannot help but teach as a person whose horizon is the third, as a person of faith who has committed herself to the rigorous and critical study of theology. But I cannot and should not assume that my students are sailing with that same horizon in view. In fact, I would venture to guess that most of my students have different horizons from mine. For some, religion is simply not within the bounds of their fields of vision, although I imagine that this is actually a very small portion of students. For those for whom religion may be within the bounds of their fields of vision, there is much diversity to consider here as well. Some are interested because of their childhoods; others in a defensive or aggressive way; some are interested because of purely academic reasons; and some for very personal reasons. It is within this plurality of horizons that any instructor teaches day in and day out.

Let us finally return to the primary question: what does it mean to "hand on the faith" when I teach? And for me personally, to what extent am I concerned with bringing my students into the third horizon? As a Christian, I am of course committed to the truth and beauty of my horizon, a commitment that inevitably stirs a desire for all to know God through the Incarnation. As a teacher, I am given the difficult and invigorating *task* of teaching people with different horizons all at once. Ultimately, I do want my students to shift horizons. I want them to be interested in religion, but I also want them to turn themselves toward rigorous and critical thinking about religious ideas. At the very least, I want students in the first horizon to shift to the second, and students in the second to expand their knowledge and nuance their questions. I want all of my students to think more critically, write more clearly, speak more articulately, and act more compassionately. But how I envision the success of my course with these goals is inherently tied to my own horizon, to my own theology, to my own picture of God. As a teacher of theology, I must affirm for my students and for others that the thoughtful questioning, clear writing, eloquent speech, and charitable behavior that are the true goals of my course are genuine ways of participating in the divine. If I actually believe this, then I have to admit that such successes are small but integral steps on the way to conversion for students who are yet to turn to God. I also have to admit that my courses may actually find ways for students who do have faith in Christ to delve ever deeper into their faith in new and critical ways.

I noted earlier that I want to introduce my students to what the world looks like to the saints and to people trying to get there. The whole idea of the communion of saints is to have witnesses, a sort of cache of people who model what God calls us all to be. Helping my students shift to or expand that second horizon requires something very specific, something that I think is demanded by my own horizon. It is my job to model rigorous, critical, and faithful engagement with theological ideas for my students, a job which I do better on some days than others. But it is also crucially important to perform that fourth goal, acting with charity and compassion. In the end, I should focus on this above all else, for if I do it as well as I am able by grace, I have faith that it will give my students the space to "turn."

Notes

[1]Thomas Merton, *Faith and Violence: Christian Teaching and Christian Practice* (Notre Dame, IN: University of Notre Dame Press, 1968), 205-206.

[2]William Joseph Chaminade, "Letter to the Retreat Masters of 1839," trans. Lawrence J. Cada, SM (Dayton: Cincinnati Province of the Society of Mary, 1989), 10.

[3]Pope John Paul II, *Ex Corde Ecclesiae*, August 15, 1990, paragraph 13.

[4]Ibid., paragraph 49.

[5]Ibid., paragraph 12.

[6]Bernard Lonergan, "Horizons," *Philosophical and Theological Papers 1965-1980*, in *Collected Works of Bernard Lonergan*, ed. Robert C. Croken and Robert M. Doran (Toronto: University of Toronto Press, 2004), 10-11.

[7]Ibid., 20.

Nurturing Aesthetic Sensibility, Religious Imagination, and the Use of Analogy in the Academic Life of Contemporary College Students

Mary-Paula Cancienne, R.S.M.

Students enroll in college-level theology, religious studies, and spirituality courses with a range of experiences concerning the Christian tradition. While many enter with significant understanding and background, there seems to be an increasing number of students who have little experience or basic knowledge of Christianity or of any religious tradition. In some instances, students' theological understandings as perceived by professors may seem oddly frozen at a more youthful stage. Students' ideas about religion and spirituality can seem like an amalgamation of disparate thoughts and sentiments that can be comforting for students, but may not challenge adherents mentally or morally.

More so, limited understandings or misinformation can result in severe prejudice against religious practices and beliefs and their practitioners, as well as in a limited ability to analyze or critique religious traditions. Professors who teach material related to the Christian tradition, specifically, whether in the classroom or online, know from experience that there is a great need for good theological education.

Today's students often fall into three main groups: (1) those who simply accept their faith tradition as they understood it in their youth; (2) students who are now practicing a kind of personal-spiritual-syncretism that is heavily influenced by contemporary relativism and the need to be very inclusive of differences, but often without appropriate discrimination or consideration for degrees of value, or input or challenge by a broader community; and (3) students who have dismissed the subject of religion, and any of its associated disciplines such as theology and spirituality, because it no longer makes sense or it no longer helps them to make sense of their lives and the world.

Obstacles and difficulties arise when students desire to engage religious questions of meaning but do not know where to begin, or when they need to understand a situation where religious practices and beliefs are central, but they lack the necessary background information and understanding to do so. Students may feel drawn to religious practices. Upon engagement they find that they do not understand them or feel these traditions and practices really do not have much to offer.

Students may reflect age-level maturity in every other facet of their lives and have a desire for dialogue around questions related to religion, theology, and spirituality. Yet their capacity for such dialogue is underdeveloped. What may be lacking are not just religious content, knowledge, and a general framework of such, but some degree of fluency with analogy and symbol, and an aesthetic sensibility that can lead to a more nuanced sense of wonder, paradox, and curiosity. Along with solid theological and religious content, such facility can assist us with the discovery of meaningful interpretations of life experiences and the construction of probing questions about life, death, and purpose, as well as aid us in preparing for civil interreligious and political discourse. However, to have knowledge of religion or to be able to navigate the waters of life's meaningful theological questions does not necessarily mean a student needs to be a *believer.*

This chapter will argue that in order for today's students to learn or to "catch" what Christianity is about, even in a very general sense, it is helpful for them to have a basic competence with certain skills and for professors to include exercises in their course work for the development of those skills. Such skills include *aesthetic sensibility, religious imagination,* and the use of *complex analogy.* Without rudimentary development in these areas, how does one begin to even intuit the sacramental depth and meaning of the Christian journey personally and as part of a larger community?

Christianity, specifically Catholicism, is rooted in ritual, symbol, and interpretation.

Attention to the development of aesthetic sensibility, religious imagination, and the use of complex analogy can be helpful in terms of introducing students to a richer dimension of Christianity and in terms of engendering a richer appreciation for what the tradition is generally, and Catholicism is particularly. The development of these skills does not preclude covering necessary content, but can take place in conjunction with subject content.

According to David Tracy, the church "re-presents the Christ event paradigmatically in word and sacrament and keeps alive the dangerous memory of this Jesus who is the Christ."[1] How students view, interpret, and connect present realities through or alongside this "dangerous memory" requires that they use their imagination.[2]

By assisting students in their development of a lively and creative use of imagination and analogy regarding religious material, teachers may enable students to question the boundaries of their vision of human purpose and the purpose of creation. Indeed, so challenged, they might imagine what an experience of the revelation of Divine Mystery, God, even a unique incarnation of the Holy could mean. By attending to the development of these three skills with our students, we assist students in connecting their experiences with the poetic language of Christian faith and practice. This approach gives students a lived experience, a sort of rung to grab hold of, a few words in a different kind of language as they begin their work of understanding the Christian journey, especially in cases where there has been very little prior foundation.

Aesthetic Sensibility

Presently, we cannot afford to view the world as a bundle of fragmented parts. We are already reaping the consequences of overly compartmentalized thinking, specifically with regards to the environment. At least to some degree, we see how this kind of thinking, working, and living is leading to catastrophe. However, this ongoing struggle is the contemporary reality of our students. This fragmentation is the contextual experience that the Christian tradition must help students to make sense of and, more so, in which we must help them to discover meaning and purpose.

The chronicle of life's relationships, at all levels of creation, is bursting with ongoing stories, major plots and subplots, more overwhelming than science can fully discover or describe and more complex than economics can measure. However, at some point, we want to help students do more than perceive the connectedness of all of creation, visible and invisible. Rather, we want to help them recognize the quality of those relationships, as well as assist them in developing their ability to ponder, explore, and appreciate those relationships on many levels. Further, an aesthetic sensibility rooted in the Christian tradition encourages us to ponder those dimensions and relationships and calls us to question what those relationships and connections demand of us as moral creatures.

As theologians who are educators, we help our students perceive reality through a Christian lens or narrative, if only as an educational experience. Still, at some point in a semester, professors begin to notice those students who do not know how to recognize the poetic dimensions of life, or who do not know how to make sense of reality beyond a common sense level of experience, which makes it difficult to grasp a sense of the sacramental.

Ironically, poetic and aesthetic sensibility regarding religious subject matter does not necessarily begin with awe-inspiring experiences or lovely articulations, but sometimes with a simple meditation involving a biblical story where students sense a large but subtle world inside themselves. Shockingly, for some, this is a new experience.

The following are a few exercises that have been helpful with students regarding the nurturing of aesthetic sensibility:

1. Begin the class with three to five minutes of stillness and silence, but close with a brief reflection or prayer that brings the world and their lives into the present moment. Weave into the prayer some connection to a theological element, such as grace. In the beginning of the semester this can be difficult for most students. A simple acknowledgment of the fact that all present might not need this time of quiet and reflection, but that some do, usually encourages the group to settle down. The professor needs to be trusted that he or she can hold the quiet, or a meditative environment will not develop over the semester. Students

have commented that they look forward to these times and that they never knew it was so powerful. These kinds of experiences also indicate to students that what comes next in class is something that is significant. This routine helps prepare students for experiences with *lectio divina* later in the semester.

2.   Include awareness exercises of all kinds, especially those that use many of the senses. These can be in-class, on-campus, or off-campus experiences, and are modifiable for online classes. For example, exercises can include trips to sites from the tragedies of 9/11/2001, old cemeteries, parks, the ocean shore or a river, a hospital nursery, subway, inner city street corner, or a kayaking trip where students leave all of their cell phones at the dock. In this case, the professor took photos and used them in the following class to discuss the dynamic presence of the Holy in nature, of which humans are a part. One can construct theological reflection questions that engage and help students to penetrate the isolated event and to recognize connections with a larger reality. Use of biblical passages aids in this exercise.

3.   Divide students into teams and give them the assignment of writing a psalm that attends to the spirit of the tradition, but in contemporary time. They then have to sing or chant it in class, as well as teach it to the class. This exercise gets them into active and creative modes, sharing with others, while also engaging with the tradition. Reflection papers on their new psalm and the experience of writing and sharing it further deepen the assignment.

4.   Have students attend a Christian worship service. Give them a list of suggested questions to guide their awareness of the experience, but the questions are not to provide an outline for their essay assignment. Rather, their essay should concern how the physical environment, the participants, and the service ritualize the Christian story. How does it point to a greater reality, break open the meaning of the Christian story, and call its members to do good in the world? The essay may conclude with some degree of personal reflection on the experience.

Religious Imagination

Since students often perceive religion as lame, old-fashioned, flat, and static, the use of *religious imagination* sounds impossible or oxymoronic. However, when pushed to *imagine* a world with no God, no life beyond the sensate world, and no purpose of any kind, most students pause and think more deeply. The following exercises are used to stir students' religious imaginations:

1. Have students describe narrow and confining images of God that are too small for a living tradition. Acknowledge how these images have served in terms of the good that they have provided, as well as what theology has been borne by them. Next, explore how these images, depictions, or descriptions of God have served to keep "God" in a box, or to limit our imagination about who the Divine is in our lives. Perform some kind of ritual that buries the box with the too-small images of "God."

2. Role-playing helps to crack molds and lets students know that it is all right to imagine things differently. When examining biblical texts or stories, the use of role-playing, especially with improvisation, encourages students to engage the text using their imaginations, voices, bodies, and decision-making abilities. For example, they may have to decide how they will portray the serpent in Genesis. Pausing to dialogue, even doing the same scene several times and using multiple interpretations, gives students a chance to discover meaning differently, and to come to a sense of the meaning that is not black and white.

3. Assign to students a project where students must interview someone over the age of twenty-five who is practicing the Christian tradition. This project stirs their imaginations because it makes them wonder about the deeper life of the other person. Many students interview someone close to them, but not all will. Inevitably, they are surprised at the prayer life of the interviewee and at how important God or Jesus is for that person.

4. Have students name and briefly explain fifty names for

God, and then prioritize them according to their preferences; then ask why. This project can move students to wonder and ponder who and what "God" is or is not. Even if a student claims to be an atheist, the exercise can help the student to have greater understanding of the possibilities for God, Jesus, and the Spirit by those who are believers.

Complex Analogy

One important way that humans attempt to explore and understand creation and humanity's roles and relationships in and with creation is through the use of analogy. Using analogy in a vibrant, lively way can help students to experience the Christian narrative as active and not static, demonstrating that the Christian narrative is in relation with other ideas, stories, and events.

The use of complex analogy around the Christian narrative layers our experiences and deepens the story of our experiences alongside other stories, further giving rise to meaning and to questions. We envision our relatedness through analogy, and further envision deeper relatedness, as well as additional questions, through more complex analogies. The following examples go beyond familiar analogies that we often hear and rapidly dismiss. Rerouting the path into the material through the use of different and complex analogies can be productive. Consider the following examples:

1. God is Mystery versus God is Question.
2. God is the world versus God is the living, breathing world of creation and is constantly moving, ever inviting us beyond how we know ourselves presently to be.
3. God is love versus God is love incarnate who dies embarrassingly on a cross.
4. The Church is the Kingdom of God, Reign of God, or People of God versus the Church with all of its human flaws that is at its core an ongoing, evolving sacrament, constantly given to us by a dynamic, creative, and loving God, who calls and challenges us to give shape to it for healing, wholeness, creativity, joy, mercy, justice, and peace.

Conclusion

As teachers of theology, we hope students will grasp that within Christianity there is an invitation to lean into the "more" of life and death. Through the eyes of Christianity, we describe this more as *grace,* a kind of relational call and response that gives shape to our hearts and minds and lives. Through this *grace,* each and all of us participate in the ongoing holy drama called life, especially when we open to the needs of others, participating in the *dangerous memory* that is, paradoxically and wonderfully, ever alive and unfolding.

Further development of aesthetic sensibility, religious imagination, and the use of complex analogy can invite, support, and challenge students in terms of their growing understanding of the *dangerous memory* today. More particularly, the Christian community engages in three main activities I name below,[3] and development of our skill set can assist students in greater understanding of the nature of these activities as core elements of the tradition.

First, there is the invitation to relationship with the Divine or the Transcendent. We attend to this call in many ways, such as how we worship and pray, personally and communally, including, for Catholics, through the centrality of the Eucharist. Aesthetic sensibility, religious imagination, and the use of complex analogy are important in the planning of these events and actions, in how we participate in them, and in how we interpret and integrate these experiences.

Second, there is the activity of sharing the journey with fellow companions and with others in the world. Separately and together, we develop ways of seeing and understanding the world through a Christological aesthetic lens, as well as in discerning our actions in that world. As community we reflect, examine, and contemplate how we perceive and experience the Spirit of God through the Book of Scripture, the Book of Nature, and in the midst of ongoing culture and society. We share our insights and stories of faith, theology, and spirituality in many forms, including through the simple and intentional act of the gift of presence. Aesthetic sensibility makes us pause and notice the world around us and in us. Religious imagination invites us to wonder not only about what we perceive, but also about what we do not seem to know or know clearly.

Third, as church, as community, we are to act in service and charity in the world, not so much out of duty as out of love. The use of complex analogy and symbol, as in the Holy Thursday ritual of the washing of the feet, helps us to draw connections between abstract values and concrete enactment of those values. Without a broader and deeper understanding of our service in the world, our contributions are susceptible to reductionist views of labor, rather than fold into a larger vision of purpose and meaning, even if our particular focus and service be ever so humble and simple.

Students' understandings of Christianity benefit when they experience the dynamism of the Christian drama not as a metanarrative *per se*, but as ongoing discovery of the presence of wholeness/ Holiness that is part of their lives. Further development of aesthetic sensibility, religious imagination, and the use of complex analogy can help to prepare students for dialogue on the topics of religion, church, and the spiritual life within the Christian tradition, across traditions, and in society. With the assistance and development of these skills, students may begin to perceive and tell their own stories with greater nuance and depth, and with greater sensitivity to religious and theological questions.

Notes

[1]David Tracy, *The Analogical Imagination: Christian Theology and the Culture of Pluralism* (New York: Crossroad, 1981), 329.

[2]The phrase "dangerous memory" is a key phrase found in the works of Johann Baptist Metz's political theology when referring to Jesus Christ and the Eucharist.

[3]Second Vatican Council, *Lumen Gentium*, paragraphs 9, 12, and 48; *Gaudium et Spes*, paragraph 45.

Beyond Sunday School

Affirming Faith, Challenging Knowledge in the College Classroom

Emily Dykman, Michael Lopez-Kaley, and Laura Nettles

The Catholic liberal arts university is given the task of educating students in the area of theology, among other liberal arts subjects. However, many Catholic liberal arts universities do not have a homogenous population and, in fact, may have populations that are not even primarily Catholic. The diversity of such populations presents the opportunity to reconsider how courses such as "Introduction to Theology" will be taught. Is evangelization proper in the college classroom? We will consider evangelization more closely later, but as a basic definition, we understand evangelization to be the sharing of the Gospel through word and action.

It is our belief that a well-constructed theology or religious studies course at a Catholic university need not be a tool for proselytizing. On the other hand, the course need not be so watered down that Christianity is presented as nothing more than another philosophy by which one may choose to live. A well-constructed course can challenge believers to look more deeply into the foundations of their faith, while challenging non-believers to understand better why Christians believe what they believe, and why it makes a difference. Our experience has shown us that believers and non-believers alike are challenged in such courses to take a new look at what they thought about Christianity and the basic beliefs of the Christian tradition.

This chapter has four main parts. First, we will summarize the differing purposes for religious education in a parish setting and religious studies in the university setting. Second, we will consider the contrasting roles of the religious studies professor and university campus ministry experiences in the life of the student. Third, we will focus on the specific case of Viterbo University, showing how the format for Viterbo's "Introduction to Christian Theology" course links the Viterbo University mission with the religious studies department mission and the outcomes for the introductory course. Finally, we will define what we mean by Franciscan evangelization, and what role that kind of evangelization plays in the classroom.

The Purpose of the Catholic University

As we begin, it is important that we are reminded of the purpose of the Catholic university, as expressed in Pope John Paul II's apostolic constitution *Ex Corde Ecclesiae*. In this document, Pope John Paul II describes that purpose as "the ardent search for truth and its unselfish transmission to youth and to all those learning to think rigorously, so as to act rightly and to serve humanity better."[1] It is this search for truth that defines the unique nature of the Catholic university, as the university holds at its core a commitment to the dignity of the human person and the common good.[2] The designation of a university as Catholic recognizes that there is a particular relationship to the Church. *Ex Corde Ecclesiae* notes that this relationship has both local and universal implications.[3] Fidelity, or faithfulness, becomes the focus of this relationship on an institutional level, for both Catholic and non-Catholic members of the community. At a basic level, this faithfulness requires respect for and adherence to the teaching authority of the Church.

Theodore Hesburgh, president emeritus of the University of Notre Dame, considered the tension this faithfulness causes when brought into relationship with academic freedom. He edited a collection of essays entitled *The Challenge and Promise of a Catholic University*, published in 1994. Hesburgh describes the Catholic university, stating, "It is not the church teaching, but a place—the only place—in which Catholics and others, on the highest level of intellectual inquiry, seek out the relevance of the Christian message to all of the problems and opportunities that face us and our complex world."[4]

Catherine Mowry LaCugna deepens this discussion of inquiry, noting that the very nature of the Catholic university is "shaped by the religious and intellectual traditions of Catholicism; committed to the dialogue between reason and faith; concerned for the ethical dimensions of knowledge; diligent in the teaching of students; active in dialogue with all cultures and with other religious traditions; and concerned about the formation of the whole person."[5]

Faith Formation—Theology

How, then, is the purpose of the university theology classroom different from the learning that takes place in parish faith formation and/or campus ministry at a university? First, in considering the role of faith formation, one must note that there is a sacramental character at the core of the parish program. Also, faith formation expects and develops the ability for a faith response from those who are learning. In "To Teach as Jesus Did: A Pastoral Message on Catholic Education," the USCCB regards catechesis as a lifelong process that is at the core of the church's mission. The document regards this mission as "integrated ministry embracing three interlocking dimensions: the message revealed by God (*didache*) which the Church proclaims; fellowship in the life of the Holy Spirit (*koinonia*); and service to the Christian community and the entire human community (*diakonia*)."[6] The response of the learner in the faith formation setting is intended to be some form of faith response. This response may take the form of service or evangelization, or it may be a sacramental commitment to one's belonging to the Church.

"To Teach as Jesus Did" continues with a consideration of the role colleges and universities have in relationship to this mission. The document notes that colleges and universities "serve it by deep and thorough study of Catholic beliefs in an atmosphere of intellectual freedom and according to canons of intellectual criticism which should govern all pursuit of truth."[7] Through intellectual criticism, we offer our students an opportunity to ask probing questions about the faith that has been passed on to them from their parents, grandparents, and faith community. These questions are not intended to erode faith, but to assist students in developing a clearer understanding, an adult understanding, of the beliefs handed down. The impact of these questions within the theology classroom, the document notes, "encourages students to confront religious questions and explore beyond the limits of a narrow vision of life which excludes the religious dimension."[8]

Evangelization within the context of the parish faith formation program exists in a homogenous system of believers. In this type of system, a very direct approach can be utilized, as the intention of the faith formation is to draw the young person into a deeper faith and commitment to the Roman Catholic Church, often culminating in the sacrament of confirmation. The sharing of the gospel occurs in a variety of ways within the parish faith formation program (liturgy, Bible study, retreats, and more), and the intention is to offer the young person a way to express his or her faith in some intentional way. Parish faith formation often leads a young person to seek out a Catholic college or university in hopes of continuing one's lifelong faith journey. These young people often find a home within the campus ministry program on the campus.

Campus Ministry

Campus ministry also emerges as unique in its purpose on the college or university campus. The USCCB document "Empowered by the Spirit" notes the goals of campus ministry as threefold: sustaining a Christian community through pastoral care and liturgical worship; integration of apostolic ministry; and service.[9] Campus ministry is defined as "a public presence and service through which properly prepared baptized persons are empowered by the Spirit to use their talents and gifts on behalf of the Church in order to be sign and instrument of the kingdom in the academic world."[10] This definition is very limited, as it refers to those who are baptized and properly prepared for adult life in the Church. On the typical Catholic university campus, the population that fits this description is often not the majority of students. At the same time, it defines a place in which the Catholic college student can continue to find some like-minded individuals who have a similar commitment to faith formation.

Campus ministry often mimics the activity and engagement that existed in the parish faith formation program. While there is an aspect of campus ministry that continues to be focused on learning, there are six specific aspects, as articulated in "Empowered by the Spirit," which define the ideal campus ministry program. These aspects include: forming community; appropriating faith; forming conscience; educating for peace and justice; personal development; and developing leaders for the future.[11] Within the typical campus ministry program, those involved tend to be a relatively homogenous group with regard to faith. This is not always the case in the theology classroom.

What, then, is the impact of the diversity of religious faith (and non-faith) on evangelization on the Catholic college/university campus? While faculty and campus ministers can work together, their goals and outcomes are not necessary identical. "Empowered by the Spirit" notes, "The distinctive task of campus ministry on Catholic campuses is to call the total institution to spread the Gospel and to preserve and enrich its religious traditions."[12] The theology classroom typically focuses on application, analysis, and demonstration of knowledge of various beliefs, concepts, and vocabulary. Application, analysis, and demonstration are articulated in a systematic, historical, exegetical, and practical manner by introducing students to the development of the faith as it exists today.

Higher education as a whole is held in great esteem in the same document, which notes, "Higher education benefits the human family through its research, which expands our common pool of knowledge. By teaching people to think critically and to search for the truth, colleges and universities help to humanize the world."[13] Working collaboratively, campus ministry and the theology department at a university can achieve the education of the whole person, which is the ultimate goal of lifelong faith formation. There is a need, however, to take different approaches in method when presenting theology in the classroom.

The Role of the Religious Studies Professor

Evangelization in the religious studies classroom takes its lead from the words of Pope Paul VI. In his 1975 apostolic exhortation *Evangelii Nuntiandi*, he states, "For the Church, evangelization means bringing the Good News into all the strata of humanity, and through its influence, transforming humanity from within and making it new."[14] Furthermore, the interior change is directed to convert "both the personal and collective consciences of people, the activities in which they engage, and the lives and concrete milieux which are theirs."[15] A key to teaching religious studies and cooperating in evangelization is recognizing what part of the evangelization process may be appropriate in the university religious studies classroom, and to what degree evangelization can be done in the classroom.

Instructive for the religious studies professor is Paul VI's contention that the goals of evangelization include "affecting and, as it were, upsetting through the power of the Gospel, [hu]mankind's criteria of judgment, determining values, points of interest, lines of thought, sources of inspiration, and models of life, which are in contrast to the Word of God and the plan of salvation."[16] Also instructive is his reminder that evangelization always takes "the person as one's starting point and always comes back to the relationships of people among themselves and with God."[17] Paul VI's vision meshes well with the Franciscan evangelical tradition, which stresses one-on-one relationships and maintaining a presence with others that helps draw them into deeper questions about faith. Paul VI's vision also recognizes a diversity of starting points for people, affirming the need to approach any evangelization with sensitivity.

Much like any university, educators in a Catholic, Franciscan, and liberal arts university encourage and welcome admission of students from all beliefs, and even those who are non-believers. Students are invited to be part of a community of learners in a liberal arts setting that, because of its Catholic identity, recognizes that religious studies courses are an integral part of the liberal arts curriculum, as well as one element in the development of well-rounded graduates. The demographic statistics at Viterbo University indicate that 40 percent of the students identify themselves as Roman Catholic believers, while 42 percent of the students identify themselves as Christian believers in a tradition other than Roman Catholic (primarily Lutheran, 23 percent). Of the other 18 percent, 11 percent indicate no religious affiliation and 7 percent indicate an affiliation with a non-Christian tradition. Furthermore, a large percentage of Viterbo students (45 percent) are first-generation college students.[18] One of the challenges of the first-generation college student is stretching his or her deeply held assumptions about life (including faith and religion). Perceived challenges to faith or religious upbringing can grow to a crisis when the student is unable to return home to parents who, having themselves been challenged in college, can help their child negotiate what is perceived as a challenge to his or her faith. Especially in religious studies classes, students frequently respond to new or challenging information as a denial of faith by the instructor. University religious studies courses do not reflect the kind of transmission of faith that the students have been used to in parish settings. The presumption by many students and parents is that the religious studies professors are acting in a way antithetical to the mission of the university and the well-being of the student.

Given what has been previously described, the role of the religious studies instructor in evangelization might be described as limited but important. It is limited because there is only so much one can do in one semester, three times a week for one hour. Furthermore, it is limited by the need to make sure that sufficient academic rigor is present in every course. The instructor's role is important because it potentially challenges students to ask deeper questions. Indeed, the very act of introducing academic rigor in the field of "religion" may be the catalyst that prompts students to ask deeper questions.

Pope Paul VI states that "The question of 'how to evangelize' is permanently relevant, because the methods of evangelizing vary according to the various circumstances of time, place, and culture, and because they thereby present a certain challenge to our capacity for discovery and adaptation."[19] The circumstances, the time, and the place that university instructors are given allow them to challenge the student believer to reach a deeper understanding of the Christian tradition to which he or she may have already made a commitment. The non-Christian believer, or the non-believer, is challenged to understand the basic beliefs of the predominant religious tradition of the United States, as well as the specific religious tradition which animates the university he or she attends. However, the instructor must still grapple with the best ways to deal with the diversity of student backgrounds present in the classroom.

Evangelization in the "Introduction to Theology" Course

Students at Viterbo University are required to pass two courses in religious studies. The first course, and a prerequisite for all others, is an "Introduction to Theology" course which fulfills a requirement of the core curriculum known as "Theological Inquiry." The second course can be chosen from any of the other various religious studies courses offered, and it fulfills a requirement of the core curriculum known as "Faith and Practice." Students are expected first to gain knowledge of basic concepts and vocabulary of the Christian tradition, far beyond that of parish religious education. Having done that, students are expected to be ready to converse in the theological concepts and vocabulary pertinent to other areas of religious studies.

If evangelization is to take place in the university setting, it is not solely the responsibility of the religious studies professor. Religious studies professors accept the challenge to educate students in the basic beliefs of the Christian tradition. Instructors also understand that students are all coming from different starting points, and, therefore even an introduction to basic beliefs will be sufficiently challenging for most if not all students.

The outcomes expected in the introductory course are as follows: (1) students gaining the ability to apply theological vocabulary through written and oral communication; (2) students analyzing how the practice of faith reflects the faith tradition's principles; (3) students demonstrating knowledge of various ethical and moral systems; and (4) students applying ethics and morals to contemporary life. The course is content-heavy, with a focus on understanding core Christian beliefs, their history, and vocabulary that helps support theological knowledge. Students are introduced to various ways core beliefs have been lived out throughout history, including discussion of periods in history where it might be suggested that the beliefs were not fully lived out. Further, students are introduced to points of divergence in Christian theology, giving time to both Protestant and Catholic understandings of various concepts such as sacraments, salvation, and grace.

The course is standardized so that all students leave the class with the same fundamental knowledge. All instructors use a common textbook, and assignments and tests have been standardized as well. One unique feature of the textbook is the inclusion of a homily in every chapter. Students are required to write papers that connect the homily with the theological content of the chapter. Believer or not, the student must engage the material in a way that indicates an ability to recognize when specific theological concepts are being utilized, and whether those concepts are being utilized correctly. For many believers, this may be the first time they have been required to understand a homily fully and relate it to a specific theological teaching. For some believers, the homily also provides a way to make the transition from the religious education program with which they were accustomed to the religious studies course they are now taking.

How does the introductory course evangelize? For believers, especially believers who may have an extensive parochial education, the course expands on and explains what they already know and challenges them to move beyond the heartfelt response to faith they may have developed to this point to a heartfelt response that includes a deeper understanding of their faith tradition. Believers are left to ponder how this new or expanded information helps them more fully develop their faith response, and what its impact may be for developing a more "adult" faith. Here, a nod to Paul Ricoeur's notion of "second naïveté" is appropriate. For the non-believer or other believer, the course offers exposure to the concepts and vocabulary of Christianity, perhaps for the first time, much like any other introductory course. These students are left to ponder why people in the Christian tradition believe what they believe and act the way they act, and consider what "integrity" means, given the relationship they see between belief and action. The hope, then, is that the non-believer or other believer is drawn to ask further questions about the Christian tradition. In this sense, evangelization takes place without intruding on any individual's starting point.

Evangelization in the setting described requires a focus on the basic components that make up Christian faith life, rather than enhancing the faith response, which is a key component of most parish religious education programs. Given the Catholic identity of the university even when there is a diverse population in the classroom, a thorough introduction to the Christian tradition that challenges the believer to learn more about the tradition to which he or she is faithful, while not imposing a "faith response" requirement on the non-believer, seems both appropriate for each student's education and respectful of their "starting point." Catechesis, in this setting, is an action that inevitably occurs. The Gospel is transmitted as the Christian community has received it, understands it, lives it, and communicates it, but the community's transmission must take into account the capacity for people to receive the Gospel.[20] How students receive the transmission of the Gospel depends on their openness to receiving it. The acceptance of the Gospel is an action that the religious studies professor cannot control.

Religious studies professors should also recognize that any evangelization that takes place on a university campus goes beyond what may happen in the classroom. Religious studies instructors can work in concert with other departments, such as campus ministry, without being expected to carry out the ministry of those departments. While campus ministry and a religious studies department may differ in their approach to evangelization, their varied methods are complementary and pieces of a larger whole that is evangelization in a university setting.

Franciscan Charism and Evangelization

Working at a Franciscan university, we at Viterbo take our cues about evangelization from the life and charism of Francis of Assisi. There is much to be said about Francis, but in the interest of time a brief summary should suffice to describe his approach to evangelization. There is a somewhat fabled story in our tradition about Francis and his brothers visiting a little village in the Umbrian valley. The friars spend the day praying with the villagers, caring for the lepers, and begging on behalf of the poor. On their journey home, a zealous young friar approaches Francis and asks, "This was a wonderful day, but when do we evangelize?" Francis replies, "We just did."

Francis understood that preaching the Gospel could take many different forms. His way of being in the world centered on following the example of Jesus Christ. Francis, so moved by the humility of God he recognized in the Incarnation, sought to follow in Christ's footsteps. Just as Christ had entered into relationships with the people around him, so too did the Saint.

Relationships became the focus of Francis's way of life and are at the core of the Franciscan way of life. Our Franciscan charism reminds us that how we are with people is more important than what we do. It is through our relationships that we, as did Francis, ultimately share the Gospel. There is a popular quote (often misused) incorrectly attributed to Francis, "Preach the Gospel, use words if necessary." This is not quite an accurate portrayal of Francis's charism, because it was not just in deed that he shared the Gospel. Francis liked to preach, but he was keenly aware that the preacher should not overshadow the content being preached. He reminded his followers that the Gospel must be allowed to shine and people must find its message through their own curiosity. For Francis evangelization was necessarily a fusion of both word and deed.

So what does this mean for our undergraduate classrooms? In light of the comments from our colleagues and drawing upon our Franciscan charism, we offer three concluding points. First, evangelization in the classroom is not about proselytizing, but about relationships—how we are with our students. The teaching and discussion of the Gospel (as well as other theological material) is a major component of our classrooms, but it is in our relationship with our students that the Gospel can truly come alive. Second, we must remember that our theological content does impact and challenge our students, and thus should be the focus. As theological students, we all have undoubtedly experienced conversion or revelatory moments in our studies. So too do our students. Theology by its very nature is instructive, challenging, and evangelical. It must be allowed to shine. Finally, our theology departments must work closely with our campus ministry offices, as together we can offer a holistic formative approach to our faith. We firmly believe that evangelization does not take place in isolation. It is the product of a multifaceted, integrated approach that utilizes both the classroom and campus ministry.

Notes

[1] Pope John Paul II, *Ex Corde Ecclesiae: On Catholic Universities*, 2.
[2] Ibid., 12.

[3]Ibid., 27.

[4]Theodore Martin Hesburgh, "The Challenge and Promise of a Catholic University," in Theodore Martin Hesburgh, *The Challenge and Promise of a Catholic University* (Notre Dame, IN: University of Notre Dame Press, 1994), 4.

[5]Catherine Mowry LaCugna, "Some Theological Reflections on *Ex Corde Ecclesiae*," in ibid., 120.

[6]"To Teach as Jesus Did," in *The Catechetical Documents: A Parish Resource* (Chicago, IL: Liturgy Training Publications, 1996).

[7]Ibid., 64.

[8]Ibid., 79.

[9]National Conference of Catholic Bishops, *Empowered by the Spirit: Campus Ministry Faces the Future: A Pastoral Letter on Campus Ministry, November 15, 1985* (Washington, DC: U.S. Catholic Conference, 1986), 21.

[10]Ibid.

[11]Ibid.

[12]Ibid., 2.

[13]Ibid., 14.

[14]Pope Paul VI, *Evangelii Nuntiandi* (Washington, DC: USCC, 1976), 18.

[15]Ibid.

[16]Ibid., 19.

[17]Ibid., 20.

[18]Statistics for this section are compiled by the Office of Assessment and Institutional Research at Viterbo University, La Crosse, WI. The statistics reflect undergraduate full-time and part-time students enrolled in the university in August, 2012.

[19]*Evangelii Nuntiandi*, 40.

[20]Congregation for the Clergy, *General Directory for Catechesis* (Washington, DC: USCCB, 2011). See especially paragraphs 1-33, which discuss the context of catechesis.

Challenges Theologians Face Teaching about Marriage and Family

Felicidad Oberholzer

Teaching sexuality, marriage, and family from a Catholic perspective is difficult to do in the culture in which we live.[1] Many of today's generation of Catholic college students, fifty years after Vatican II, have not been raised in a close-knit parish community imbued with traditional Church teachings and practices. Lacking experience and knowledge, and subject to much misinformation, these students tend to be readily critical or dismissive of what they think the Church teaches. Nevertheless, many will say they still believe in God, just not in any institutional religion.

The media has become the new catechist of our current generation, and it does a very effective job. The main messages are to seek pleasure, to identify yourself by what you own, to acquire as much as you can, to accept every person's opinion as equally valid, to deny there is an objective truth, and to regard sex as principally a pleasurable physical experience with a partner.

In this current state of affairs, how can one develop a course of study on the Church's teaching on sexuality, marriage, and family that has any hope of connecting with today's college students? How does one teach it in a way that reaches beyond their preconceived notions that the Church is stuck in the past and refuses to update her teachings? How does one help students realize the ways contemporary culture has shaped their beliefs, such that they uncritically accept a secular view of the world and are unaware that they do so?

After many years of taking on this challenge, I believe I have developed a basic strategy that has proved successful: create a dialogue between the students' contemporary Western culture and the counterculture of Catholic theology, using texts, guest speakers, and student activities. The students examine and begin to critique their contemporary culture's view of sexuality and family while comparing it to the countercultural perspectives drawn from the Catholic tradition. This task has to impact them personally if they are going to gain insight and internalize the good of the Church's teachings. While the strategy is simple in form, it has taken much effort to implement it effectively. What follows is an outline of select topics and activities of the course that illustrate my particular strategy. I do not include other regular content, such as sacraments, the vows of marriage, the wedding itself, finances, communication, consequences of divorce and procedure for applying for an annulment, fidelity, forgiveness, permanence, stages of marriages, raising children, dividing the tasks needed to sustain a home and family, or facing suffering and death.

One of the first challenges was choosing texts, and I have settled on three types. One is a standard college-level text written from a secular perspective on human sexuality and diversity in America.[2] The second is also a college-level text, a comprehensive and multidisciplinary anthology that includes contemporary perspectives on marriage and sexuality. Many of these are from a Catholic perspective.[3] The third is a reader I put together comprising key documents of the Church on marriage and family and select writings from theologians.

My class begins with an explanation that the course is not intended to convert them to the Catholic point of view, but that as a Catholic school we are educating our students about one of the largest and most influential religions in the world, with over 1.2 billion members, and its teaching about marriage and the family. They are free to have different views, and participate in discussions offering their own beliefs as a contrast.

We begin with basic theological foundations, starting with the biblical account of creation and the understanding that God, in a gratuitous act of love, created us as man and woman (sexual beings from the start) in God's image. To be in God's image is to share in the act of creation. First, we create human life and families. We create the structures of civilization, societies, cultures, language, science, the arts, agriculture, technology, a judicial system, and so on. Most of all, we create community through loving others, because being in God's image is to be in right relationship with others. Just as God is Trinity, a mystery of mutual love within God's self, so too are we, created in God's image, called to this same universal vocation, "to love" and "to be loved." Our sexuality reveals itself to be a core dimension of our experience of relating to others. We desire to move out from isolation to encounter the first step toward true love. Our vocation is love.

This topic introduces one of the biggest challenges—defining the meaning of the word "love." When the students define the word, the majority say it is a feeling of wanting to be with another person. Others equate it with having sex. We explore other uses of love, such as filial love, parental love, charitable love, and others. We discover that on a deeper level there is a common basis for all of these types of love. I propose Thomas Aquinas's definition of love as "to will the good for another," which can be applied to all these cases, and explore biblical references such as the one from the First Letter of John: "Dear friends, let us love one another for love comes from God. Everyone who loves has been born of God and knows God. Whoever does not love does not know God, because God is love" (1 Jn 4:7–8).

To the students, I propose two examples of acts of love that have little to do with feelings and everything to do with willing the good of another. We imagine a sleep-deprived mother with a newborn baby. The baby cries all the time and the mother can't seem to soothe her, even though she walks and rocks her. Is this mother feeling love toward her baby? No, she is feeling exhaustion, frustration, and stress. The only thing she wants to do is lie down and sleep. She wishes the baby would just be quiet. But does she love her? Yes, because in spite of feelings, she is caring for her. She wills the good of her child.

In the second example, we imagine a married couple of forty years, newly retired, and looking forward to exploring many things they had been waiting to see all their lives. The wife suddenly suffers a severe stroke, and in spite of medical care, will not recover her ability to walk or talk clearly, and cannot care for herself. Does her husband feel love when he has to change her diapers, spoon-feed her, bathe her, dress her, and care for her throughout the night? He probably feels anger over losing his companion. He mourns. Yet, is he loving her? Yes, he takes care of her tenderly and provides for all her needs living out his vow of lifelong fidelity.

The students know these situations are very real possibilities. Imagining themselves in these situations gives them deeper insight into the meaning of love. They gain a more discerning view of their culture's idea of love as a feeling. In particular, they begin to critique the projections that happen with romantic infatuation and the consequences of thinking this way about love. If love is proposed as a vocation, this seriously challenges their usual understanding of vocation dictated by their culture: to be successful, to make money, and to have what they want in life.

Our next step is to deal with sin. We begin in scripture with the story of the Fall in Genesis. The gift of free will enables us to love and reflect God's free act of love. Yet, it also allows for realizing desire for lesser goods. The tragic consequence of this choice in the Garden of Eden was a rupture in our relationship with God. The students tend to think of sin as individual transgressions against laws (lying, murder, stealing, etc.) and not as fundamental alienation from God. Consequently, so much other evil in the world (war, poverty, genocide, and discrimination) is not understood in terms of our inability to love. Unfortunately, looking at sin as transgression rather than alienation casts God in the role of judge (even executioner) and obscures the original truth that above all God is a loving creator and healer. Sin does not make God cease loving us because God always loves us. Rather, sin pulls the blinds down to experiencing and accepting God's love.

Christians believe that we are born into a world that makes it hard to love. This belief is what Christians mean by original sin where destructive or evil choices entangle people and prevent them from discovering truth, goodness, and love. Yet throughout the biblical account of salvation history, God assures his people that they are always loved and are offered not just forgiveness, but reconciliation and adoption in his incarnate Son Jesus, who came to teach us how to love, forgive, and serve one another in order to heal alienation. However, those who would have to give up their power and sinful ways rather than accept this love execute Jesus. The Christian believes that God always has the last word. Life prevails over death. Jesus is raised. Reconciliation is now realized in the risen Christ in his Church.

Having laid this theological foundation about love, I turn the class to the topic of sexuality. To live out a vocation of love is to live a life dedicated to serving God through loving others, being in relationship with our families, friends, neighbors, the poor and needy, and even our enemies. The key to living this vocation of love in marriage fully and well is through sexuality. Understandably, the students more or less equate sexuality with genital sex. But as the bishops from the United States have defined it, "Sexuality is a fundamental component of personality in and through which we, as male or female, experience our relatedness to self, others, the world and even God."[4] We relate to each other with our physicality, and even the incarnation of Jesus Christ, when God become fully human, "adds even greater dignity or divine approbation" to the incarnate goodness of our being embodied as sexual beings.[5] Thus, the mystery and meaning of being human—embodied, incarnate, and therefore sexual—is intimately bound up in the mystery and life of God as Creator, Redeemer, and Life-Giver. The bishops present human sexuality as a wonderful gift to be treasured, respected, and nurtured. Thus, they are able to speak positively about sex, a narrower reality that refers "either to the biological aspects of being male or female (i.e., a synonym for one's gender) or to the expressions of sexuality, which have physical, emotional, and spiritual dimensions, particularly genital actions resulting in sexual intercourse and/or orgasm."[6]

Students are often amazed that the Church speaks so positively and affirmatively about sexuality. They are surprised that our love toward anyone is expressed through our being either female or male, and that with the exception of marriage, none of these relationships have to do with genital sex, yet all deal with sexuality. It becomes clear that this is a counter-cultural point of view and warrants critique and comparison with the prevailing cultural view of sexuality. The key to doing this critique well is to have the students do the research and present their findings to each other. To this end, I have developed some exercises that have worked well, such as having the students look at the difference between sexuality and sex as the Church defines these terms and how they are portrayed by the culture through the media.

The students draw from cultural understandings drawn from music, TV, women's and men's magazines, video games, movies, pornography, sexting, and more. I ask them to write a short paper discussing the message their media choice gives about sexuality and then contrast it with what the Church believes. To facilitate the audio and visual aspects of their topics, they present their findings to their classmates. Here are a few examples from their presentations.

Much of the music the students encounter uses video as well as audio, so music videos were excellent examples of the power of this medium. One of the most disturbing was a song called "Tipdrill," containing the words:

> I said it must be ya ass cause it ain't ya face
> I need a tipdrill, I need a tipdrill . . .
> We throwin' money in the air like we don't
>   give a fuck
> Lookin for a tipdrill, I mean a tipdrill.[7]

A "tipdrill" (a tool with a twisted head but smooth body) is a woman whose body is deemed beautiful but her face ugly. The men featured in the song/video are enjoying their sex acts from behind so as not to see the woman's face. The money being thrown about is for purchasing these services. This was an extreme case, but so many more represent the same view of sex for physical pleasure and the power of money to purchase women for that pleasure. The eye-opener for many of the students was their realization that they were familiar with many of the songs but had never closely examined the lyrics or the view of sexuality they represented; this made them wonder how they may have been unconsciously influenced by them.

A presentation on video games featured a version of *Grand Theft Auto* where participants play at gaining points through criminal activity, including car theft and murder. In some versions of the game, one can play out having sex with a prostitute, but getting one's money back by killing her. Rape and killing score very high points. Again, viewing and reflecting on the underlying values of this entertainment in the context of our class was a real eye-opener for me and the students.

Attitudes about women's body image were revealed in a presentation on models, whose images are often not even true to life due to photo enhancement. Additional research on anorexia showed the devastating effect of the depiction of models on young girls. The use of sex to sell products was notable for its preponderance.

The students chose examples to use for the topic of the presentation. They began to see, as they discussed the presentations, how degrading many of the subjects chosen tended to be toward women by turning them simply into objects for arousing sexual pleasure. Through the presentations, it also became clear to my students how manipulative the media is in shaping our attitudes. They began to sense how much their identity was being determined by media's depiction of normal behavior. Regarding the formation of their sexual identity, something so fundamentally integral to their ability to relate to others, they were largely at the mercy of outside influences over which they had little control and no defense. An alternative view, as represented in the Church's tradition, became more promising to them. As one student commented, "It was astonishing to see and hear all of my classmates' presentations (as well as my own) about the different forms of sexual content in the media. I was not only baffled by all of the horrific information that was presented, but also at how ignorant I really was about it all and how unaware I was of how much it had influenced me."

As a response to the modern culture's view of sexuality, I have found it useful to explore the Church's teachings about the virtue of chastity. Most students are either not familiar with chastity or think it means not having sex or sexual feelings, so they are surprised to hear the Church's definition of chastity as a positive force for good and the essential virtue needed to live one's sexuality responsibly and appropriately, given each person's unique state in life. As the bishops in the United States have stated, chastity "truly consists in the long-term integration of one's thoughts, feelings and actions in a way that values, esteems and respects the dignity of oneself and others."[8] This means learning not just self-mastery with regard to lust and sexual actions, but also self-mastery in many other areas such as anger, greed, envy, pride, and the other capital sins. We must develop ourselves physically, emotionally, spiritually, and cognitively to become mature, virtuous persons capable of loving and receiving love. It is only in doing so that we learn to value our bodies, minds, souls, others, and all creation. This insight brings my students back to understanding that sexuality, which may end up being fully expressed in a vocation of marriage, religious life, or being single, is key to being fully human.

We discuss self-mastery in all areas of our lives and the need for God's grace to develop and live virtuously. The emphasis is not on what not to do, but on what one can learn to do. Through God's Spirit abiding, Christians believe grace abounds to help one live sexually whole and chaste lives, grace that is readily available in so many ways—in ourselves, our families, the Church, the Word of God, the sacraments, prayer, the lives and witness of Mary and the saints, and "in the recesses of each human heart, where prayer, conscience formation and discernment find holy ground."[9]

As the students work through other topics on marriage and family, there are other opportunities for contrasting ecclesial and secular views. Along with readings from their human sexuality textbook, I have a professor from another school lecture on anatomy, physiology, human sexual response, and contraceptives. As the students are on the whole very ignorant about how their bodies function, it is important for them to learn about how their reproductive systems work as well as the side effects of birth control. This lesson also serves as an introduction to Natural Family Planning. In the post-presentation discussion, the students realize that the presenting professor had assumed they were sexually active and that they often were casual about sex with others, and that they thought using a condom would protect them from all sexually transmitted infections and pregnancy. They also admitted surprise about the many side effects of most contraceptives—something downplayed in the text and even by their doctors.

We then read the sections from *Humanae Vitae* that include the four prophecies that Pope Paul VI made about contraceptives, and ask whether they thought any had come true:

1. Widespread use of contraception would lead to "marital infidelity and a general lowering of moral standards."[10]

2. A man who grew accustomed to the use of contraceptive practices might ultimately lose "respect for the woman, and no longer caring for her physical and psychological equilibrium, might come to consider her as an instrument of selfish enjoyment, and no longer as his respected and beloved companion."[11]

3. Widespread acceptance of contraception would place a

"dangerous weapon . . . in the hands of those public authorities who take no heed of moral exigencies."[12]

4. Contraception would lead men and women to think that they had limitless dominion over their own bodies and functions.[13]

They acknowledged that these prophecies sounded very familiar and that the so-called sexual revolution was not such a positive and freeing experience.

I also found that the testimony of Christian guest speakers, such as a gynecologist and a young woman who had an abortion, can connect positively with the students and is very effective for examining these questions critically.[14] In conjunction with these speakers, the class watches the *Nova* series episode *The Miracle of Life*, which shows the whole process of conception, gestation, and birth. They watch the wonder of human life developing through each stage and the miracle of the birth of a fully grown baby that had started with only two cells.

In the ensuing discussions, many reveal that they had never understood what was really involved in an abortion, even when they had had one, nor the development of the baby in the womb. They also contrasted the assumptions of a speaker from a state school with those of two women who were filled with faith. A number of these students told me later that they had not really examined why they were pro-choice and had changed their view.

My last speaker is a prominent professor of engineering from a prestigious university who speaks on Natural Family Planning. Hearing a thorough and coherent explanation of this much-maligned practice from a clearly intelligent scientist is very effective in getting the students to think about it seriously. His affirmation of the gift of fertility and the wonder of the human body makes clear the contrast between this positive method of family planning and the *prevent*-ative method of *contra*-ception. After this series of speakers, I have them list some advantages to not having premarital sex.[15]

The last exercise is one in which we examine consumerism and materialism. I have them examine various items such as clothes, purses, luggage, watches, engagement rings, and so on. They are to find one that is a reasonable price and one expensive. Pictures of both items are copied on one page and given out without the prices and brand names in a packet in which each has a number. I ask each student to fill in numbered blanks what they think each item costs. When the real prices are divulged, they realize they were unable to distinguish, for example, between a pair of jeans for $30 and a pair for $180, or a watch that cost $4.5 million compared to one that was $120. Again they realize how the attraction of social image, the media, and prestige influences their behavior.

In contrast to this popular message, we discuss readings from Church documents on consumerism and money, mainly from *Familiaris Consortio*:

> By taking up the human reality of the love between husband and wife in all its implications, the sacrament gives to Christian couples and parents a power and a commitment to live their vocation as lay people and therefore to "seek the kingdom of God by engaging in temporal affairs and by ordering them according to the plan of God." (*Lumen Gentium* 31)[16]

Such documents present marriage as a sacrament that is an enduring source of grace that guides and strengthens the couple to be good stewards of this world's goods and protects them from the forces of consumerism and materialism. Again, these readings are a welcome and empowering message for the students.[17]

Based on student evaluations and "What Have I Learned?" comments from the students, I am very confident about the effectiveness of my approach. They have been able to reevaluate their culture and realize how much they have been influenced by it. They have become more respectful of the teachings of the Church, understanding that they make sense and provide a way to lead a fulfilled life because of God's unconditional love.

Notes

[1]I would like to acknowledge the financial support from the Faculty Development Committee at Saint Mary's College of California, which enabled me to prepare and present this paper.

[2]William L. Yarber, Barbara J. Sayad, and Bryan Strong, *Human Sexuality: Diversity in Contemporary America* (New York: McGraw-Hill Higher Education, 2010).

[3]Kieran Scott and Michael Warren, *Perspectives on Marriage: A Reader* (New York: Oxford University Press, 1993).

[4]United States Catholic Conference of Bishops, *Human Sexuality: A Catholic Perspective for Education and Lifelong Learning* (Washington, DC: USCC, 1991), 8–9.

[5]Ibid., 10.

[6]Ibid., 9.

[7] Nelly, "Tip Drill Remix," on *Da Derrty Versions: The Reinvention*. New York: Universal Records, 2003.

[8]USCCB, *Human Sexuality*, 19.

[9]Ibid., 16-17.

[10]Paul VI, and United States Catholic Conference of Bishops, *On the Regulation of Birth: Humanae Vitae Encyclical Letter* (Washington, DC: USCC, 1997), sec. 17.

[11]Ibid.

[12]Ibid.

[13]Ibid.

[14]The obstetrician-gynecologist began her career as a doctor to help women. She had a life-changing experience when participating in an abortion procedure, which led to her conversion to Catholicism. Now in her successful private practice, she does not do abortions or give contraceptives. Instead, she teaches Natural Family Planning. The young woman who had an abortion tells the story of its serious long-term effect on her physical and psychological health and the healing that came when she finally, after the birth of her third child, went on a retreat with Rachel's Vineyard, a group that ministers to women who have had abortions. After this retreat, she was baptized and took all the sacraments, and was healed in her body as well as her soul.

[15]Some top ones were: (1) you can learn to know your partner and form a relationship together taking time to learn how to communicate, (2) no need to deceive your parents or others about what you are doing, (3) no worry about using birth control with all its dangers and side effects, (4) no danger of pregnancy or abortion, (5) no risk of having to raise a child as a single parent, (6) no risk of getting STIs that endanger future fertility or can be life-threatening, (7) time to form trust about fidelity, (8) no risk of guilt, anxiety, loss of self-respect, fear of commitment, or jealousy about previous relationships.

[16]John Paul II, *On the Family: Apostolic Exhortation Familiaris Consortio of His Holiness Pope John Paul II* (Washington, DC: USCC, 1982), sec. 47.

[17]For a final activity, I gave them a list of ten people (including Aung San Suu Kyi, Sonia Sotomayor, Sister Dorothy Stang, Elie Wiesel, Maximilian Kolbe, and Dorothy Day) and asked them to tell me why they are inspiring. Most of them could only identify two to three people at the most. Then I asked how many knew celebrities like Britney Spears or Kim Kardashian, and nearly everyone knew each person I named and all their personal info. They easily got the point.

PART III

IMPLICATIONS

The True Knowledge of Religion and of the Christian Doctrine

Robinson Crusoe as Catechist and Theologian

Curtis W. Freeman

The mere mention of the name "Robinson Crusoe" surely conjures up in the Catholic imagination troubling images of radical Protestantism: the lone individual, isolated from the church and its historic traditions, engaging in the dubious practice of private interpretation of the Bible. It also brings to mind an old story of another castaway who was rescued from a desert island. When after many years a ship finally reached him, he told the crew a story about surviving a terrible storm and being washed up on this island where he had lived all alone. "If you're all alone," one of the sailors asked, "what are these three buildings?" Gesturing to the first structure, he said, "That's my house." Pointing to a second, he said, "And that's my church." Then pointing toward a small hut off in the distance, he said, "And that one over there is the church I used to go to." The ship captain laughed and said, "You, sir, are surely a Baptist."

As Jesuit theologian Michael J. Taylor once argued, the Baptists have often championed this sort of individualism, for as he explained,

> The Baptist is a Christian not because he is a member of a Christian church but because he has accepted the absolute Lordship of Jesus Christ, whose life and redeeming message are unfolded for him in the Bible. If he has a norm for religious action, an authority to govern him, a creed

to teach him, it is the Bible, illumined by the light of the Spirit. The Baptist, armed with the Bible and guided by the Spirit, exercises supreme responsibility over his own soul before God and believes that no state, or religion, or group of ecclesiastics should dictate to him the religious principles that are to govern his life. He is a free soul under God and balks at anything or anyone that might compromise this freedom. Among Christians he stands out as the "rugged individualist," the "priest unto himself," the "Spiritual nonconformist."[1]

Some may wish to challenge this characterization. And though Daniel Defoe was not a Baptist, he was a Presbyterian dissenter in England after the Restoration of the monarchy who shared much in common with the Baptists. But as a Whig with deep anti-Catholic convictions that led him to participate in the Monmouth Rebellion aimed at the removal of the Jacobites and their perceived crypto-Catholic subversion of English Protestantism, his name still rightly arouses Catholic suspicions. Readers who were not worried before surely must now be confused by the suggestion of Robinson Crusoe as a catechist and theologian in search of what he called "the true knowledge of religion and of the Christian doctrine."[2] Nevertheless, it is a fitting text, not only because most Catholic readers are at least familiar with the story even if they know little about the history of Protestant theology, but because of what it has to say to Catholics about how dissenting Protestants understand and pass on the Christian faith. And in the interest of full disclosure, my attraction to the book began autobiographically.

The True Knowledge of Religion: Handing On the Faith

On December 25, 1912, when my grandfather was ten years old, his father gave him a copy of Daniel Defoe's novel *The Life and Adventures of Robinson Crusoe*. Years later, my mother passed on that same book to me. That my great-grandfather had given her father a copy of *Robinson Crusoe* as a Christmas present is not all that unusual.[3] It was precisely the sort of literature that young boys in turn-of-the-twentieth-century America were encouraged to read. And my great-grandfather was an avid reader and a collector of handsome editions of Dante, Shakespeare, Balzac, Poe, Tolstoy, Dickens, Darwin, Gibbon, and many more. It makes sense that he would want to introduce his son to the world of books. My first superficial encounter with Crusoe led me to believe that it was a kind of primer in the moral education for "manliness" that my parents sought to inculcate in me, but I suspect that something much more archetypal in the story was behind this Christmas gift.

As a young boy, my great-grandfather, O. M. Curtis, was deserted by his family in Ohio, where he was taken in and raised by strangers. He worked his way through pharmacy school in St. Louis and moved to the small north Texas town of Denton, where he married a young woman from a respectable family named Lizzie Smoot and opened a drugstore on the south side of the square. There his business flourished, and he became a prosperous and respectable citizen. He also joined the local Presbyterian church, which sent a signal that he could identify with pretty much everyone in the community, since Presbyterians were right in the middle of the social hierarchy, between Baptists and Methodists on one end and Episcopalians at the other. It is not surprising, then, that someone who had lifted himself up by his own bootstraps (so to speak) might identify with the story of a castaway merchant-adventurer as a kind of prose epic of economic self-sufficiency. And apparently it worked. My grandfather, Homer Smoot Curtis, eventually took over the family business, and he even became an Episcopalian as a sign of his upward mobility, confirming the old saying that Baptists become Methodists when they learn to read, Methodists become Presbyterians when they make money, and Presbyterians become Episcopalians when they inherit the family business.

The appeal of an economic reading was recognized by Karl Marx, who attacked *Robinson Crusoe* as a capitalist manifesto that simply underwrote the individualism of bourgeois society.[4] But whereas Marx portrayed Crusoe's religion as mere entertainment, Max Weber found in Crusoe an important symbol of the transformation from a religious to a worldly asceticism that embodied the spirit of Western capitalistic societies.[5] And yet, as Weber observed, inhabitants of the modern world who live into the economic existence of a secular vocation derived from an earlier Protestantism are entirely unable to understand or even imagine the religious inheritance that has been passed on to them in this vocation.[6] Indeed, the suggestion that the ideals undergirding contemporary social existence might be "puritanical" is repulsive to modern sensibilities, due in large measure to a caricature of Puritanism, which H. L. Mencken lampooned as the haunting fear that somewhere, somehow, someone may be happy.[7]

While it is true that *Robinson Crusoe* displays the germ of Protestant religion as it grew into an understanding of believers as having a secular vocation, it is also important to note that the inner and outer worlds of Defoe's fictional character are much closer to John Bunyan's *Grace Abounding to the Chief of Sinners*[8] than to Benjamin Franklin's *The Way of Wealth*.[9] Although there is undoubtedly truth to the economic reading, it seems more likely that my family's interest in Defoe's novel was about more than a story of self-sufficiency, for there is a deeper sense in which something of the Christian faith was handed on from my great-grandfather, to my grandfather, to my mother, and finally to me. And in this sense, as odd as it may seem, *Robinson Crusoe* functioned as a kind of catechetical instruction manual for handing on the faith. Following this insight, I want to explore what it might look like to read it as a catechetical and theological account of "the true knowledge of religion and of the Christian doctrine" for other castaways seeking to make a life in the modern world.

Such a reading recognizes that Crusoe stands as a transitional figure between the God-drenched world of English Puritanism and the lonely existence of modernity. For dissenters like Defoe, the "faith" that was passed on had its roots in something they called "the experience of grace." "True knowledge of religion" was experiential. But this "experience" was not a psychological permutation of human affection as described by William James,[10] nor an anthropological feeling of absolute dependence as suggested by Friedrich Schleiermacher.[11] Rather, it was a constellation of convictions and affections that bore the evidence of the presence and activity of God in the soul. Crucial to the experience of grace was a radical conversion, which entailed a process of self-examination as well as signs of regeneration. Consequently, the converted were often described as "experienced Christians," namely, those who could witness to their salvation by testifying to the work of grace in their lives. So Vavasor Powell, the Welsh dissenter and Baptist preacher, wrote in the preface to the immensely popular collection of conversion narratives entitled *Spirituall Experiences of Sundry Beleevers* that the "experience" of the forty-two Christians described in his book is "a Copy written by the Spirit of God upon the hearts of beleevers."[12]

Defoe begins Crusoe's conversion narrative in 1651, just two years before Powell's *Spirituall Experiences* was published. The story opens with an impatient young Robinson Crusoe longing for adventure, a desire which moved him to ask his father if he might go to sea. His father advised him that a calling in law was more fitting for a dissenter of life's middle station, warning that God would not bless him if he ventured off foolishly. Crusoe's father's advice was consistent with Puritan theologian William Perkins' argument in his *Treatise of the Vocations*, namely that "every particular calling must be practiced in and with the general calling of a Christian."[13] What this meant vocationally was that Christians were to show themselves to be Christians, not only in their congregation and in their conversation, but also in whatever worldly calling they might pursue. The hope of Crusoe's father, then, was not simply that his son might prosper as a lawyer, but that he might show himself to be a Christian in the practice of law.

At first Crusoe complied, but the lure of the high seas was too much. Against the advice of his father and the tears of his mother, Crusoe resolved to run away, and so with a friend he boarded a ship bound for London. When a storm nearly took both of their lives, his companion returned home. Crusoe briefly contemplated turning back as well, imagining that his own father like the father in Jesus' parable might also kill the fatted calf and celebrate his homecoming (Lk 15:23). Echoing his father's earlier admonition, the ship captain also issued a warning, urging him to take the storm as a sign that like Jonah, seafaring was not his calling. But even though the captain exhorted him that if he tempted Providence he would surely see the hand of Heaven against him, Crusoe followed the path of the Prodigal Son, determined to continue his rebellious journey, knowing full well it led to the far country. Then he added, reflecting on the nature of repentance:

> As to going Home, Shame opposed the best Motions that offered to my Thoughts; and it immediately occurr'd to me how I should be laughed at among the Neighbours, and should be asham'd to see, not my Father and Mother only, but even every Body else; from whence I have since often observed, how incongruous and irrational the common Temper of Mankind is, especially of Youth, to that Reason which ought to guide them in such cases, *viz.* that they are not asham'd to sin, and yet are asham'd to repent; not asham'd of the Action for which they ought justly to be esteemed Fools, but are asham'd of the returning, which only can make them be esteem'd wise Men.[14]

Crusoe recognized the irony of not being driven by shame of sinning, which he knew to be foolishness, but shame of returning, which he knew to be wisdom. Yet the thought of being humiliated by family and friends outweighed the reward of repentance. So he boarded a ship in London bound for Africa, in search of worldly fortune rather than pursuing an acceptable Christian calling in the law.

Following a successful voyage, Crusoe embraced his questionable calling as "a sailor and a merchant," though his prosperity was cut short when his friend and captain died unexpectedly. As he embarked on another journey, his ship was seized by pirates, and he was taken prisoner and brought with the crew to Morocco. After two years he broke free from his captors and was rescued by a Portuguese vessel which brought him safely to Brazil, where he established a prosperous plantation. But once again the call of the sea was too strong, and eight years to the day from when he left his father's home in England, Crusoe joined an expedition bound for Africa to bring back slaves for a group of Brazilian planters and merchants. The expedition soon went terribly wrong, as the ship was caught in a violent storm and foundered at sea. Robinson Crusoe alone among all the crew survived, as he was washed up on a deserted island where he remained for twenty-eight years.

AT LENGTH I SPIED A LITTLE COVE ON THE RIGHT SHORE OF THE CREEK

Crusoe soon began salvaging cargo from the wreckage of the ship, laboriously bringing it to shore, as in good Puritan fashion he let nothing go to waste that might be put to good use. Yet the more his plantation prospered, the more he sensed that he was running from his true calling. There in the far country he discovered something that had eluded him in his restless journey—freedom. This new liberty of soul came through an experience of grace one day in June of his first year on the island when he was seized by "a fit of ague." Afraid and alone, he began to pray: "Lord look upon me, Lord pity me, Lord have Mercy upon me."[15] His anguished prayers were followed by sleep, but his rest was interrupted by a terrible dream in which he saw a man descending from a black cloud filled with fire. The earth shook when this creature touched down, and as he approached Crusoe with a long spear, the ominous figure spoke with a most terrible voice: "Seeing all these Things have not brought thee to Repentance, now thou shalt die."[16] The notion that God speaks directly through dreams was a common feature of Puritan religion, as it is also of course a common feature of the Bible. For example, John Bunyan's conversion experience

likewise began with a vision, in which he saw a high sunlit mountain and himself shivering in the cold with a wall separating him
from the mountain and the sun's warmth.[17] And one need not look
further than any Puritan grave from the period to see how deeply
the angel of death permeated their imagination.

Crusoe awoke from his dream still sick with fever, yet the
memory of his disturbing vision lingered long after it passed.
Wondering why he was so afflicted, he took a Bible that he had
recovered from the ship. He opened it, and the first words that
caught his eyes were these: "Call on me in the Day of Trouble, and
I will deliver, and thou shalt glorify Me" (Ps 50:15).[18] He thought
to himself, "Can God deliver me from this Place?"[19] Days later,
after the fever had passed, he found himself still thinking about
God's promise of deliverance. It occurred to him that God had
delivered him, but he had not glorified God by being thankful
for his deliverance. So he knelt down and gave thanks to God for
his recovery from the sickness that brought him near death. He
resolved from that day forward to demonstrate his gratitude by
reading the Bible every day.

Over the course of his *lectio continua*, it struck him that all his searching had not brought him the one thing that would make him wise. Reading Acts 5:31, he came across these words, "He is exalted a Prince and a Saviour, to give Repentance, and to give Remission." Crusoe called out to the Lord, and again his prayer was answered. But whereas the first time he asked for deliverance from sickness, in his second request he construed his need for deliverance in a very different sense. For it now occurred to him that being a castaway from God was far worse than being a castaway from civilization. He cried out, "Jesus, thou Son of David, Jesus, thou exalted Prince and Saviour, give me Repentance!"[20] Yet his conversion was not so much an instantaneous event as it was a process. As John Newton later noted in his famous hymn, God's "Amazing Grace" first teaches the heart to fear (stage 1) before those fears can be relieved (stage 2) or finally celebrated in the hour of first belief (stage 3).[21] And so the Christian journey continues beyond conversion. For as James William McClendon observed, "If all is conversion . . . the Christian story ceases to be a story."[22]

Eleven years later, a third memorable event marked Crusoe's experience of grace. While walking on the beach one day about noon, he came upon a human footprint. For a moment he stood thunderstruck, as if he had seen a ghost. Sensing imminent danger, he retreated to his fortress. Terrified by thoughts of a cannibal invasion, or worse yet, of a satanic onslaught, he was unable to sleep. For months he was held captive to his fears. Then one morning, while lying in his bed, the familiar words of Scripture came into his thoughts: "Call on me in the Day of Trouble, and I will deliver, and thou shalt glorify Me."[23] Again he prayed for deliverance. Seeking a word, he picked up the Bible. It fell open to Psalm 27:14: "Wait on the Lord, and be of good Cheer, and he shall strengthen thy Heart; wait, I say, on the Lord."[24] A wave of inexpressible comfort washed over him, and he found himself able to trust in God's providential care.[25]

Some may nevertheless be suspicious that Crusoe's faith journey still smacks of the individualism that the Jesuit Michael Taylor lamented. Crusoe's father had in fact warned him that if he did not repent at home when he had leisure, he would be left alone with none to assist him.[26] Indeed, it might be argued that he did make his way alone and without assistance, and thus it might seem he encourages others to do the same. For unlike Bunyan's Christian, who always traveled with fellow pilgrims, Defoe's modern journey is a lonely one. Friends come and go, but most of the time Crusoe is alone. Yet such a reading fails to consider the striking way in which Defoe's fictional experiment was cast in the form of an autobiographical narrative that gave voice to other Christians journeying into the capitalist and individualist social world that was then emerging.[27] As such, the novel is an inherently social document set forth as a paradigm for other castaways in the modern world to discern the experience of grace.

"The Story is told," as Defoe states in the Preface, "to justify and honour the Wisdom of Providence," but noticeably absent is the quandary over the convert's status as elect or damned that so permeates earlier conversion narratives in the seventeenth century.[28] This is not to suggest that Crusoe's Christian journey is anxiety free, but it is a struggle arising from the *shame* induced by the knowledge that he deliberately and willfully disobeyed his father's advice, rather than a fear rooted in the certainty of his *guilt* because he is not one of God's elect. The autobiographical elements are surely a reflection of Defoe's own mental states as he made his spiritual and theological journey beyond Puritanism. But even though Defoe surely drew from his own experience in writing what he called an "allegoric history,"[29] the overall narrative structure enacts the biblical story, drawn from the parable of the Prodigal Son, the book of Job, and to some extent the book of Jonah. The result is a spiritual autobiography of "the true knowledge of religion" that remains relevant to all sorts and conditions of modern Christians, and not to sectarians alone.[30]

Yet this constructed identity still resonates with the experiential knowledge that was so appealing to Baptists and other evangelical Protestants who laid more stress on believing *in* God than on believing things *about* God. The contrast between *belief in* and *belief about* for Baptists and other evangelicals is roughly parallel to the *fides qua creditur* (the faith by which it is believed) and the *fides quae creditur* (the faith which is believed).[31] What was important for Defoe, and what still remains important for Baptists, is that the faith handed on be personal but not purely private. This emphasis on personal faith, however, should not be taken as a suggestion that doctrinal theology is unimportant. Indeed, *The Life and Adventures of Robinson Crusoe* was more than just a modern catechetical instrument. It was an attempt at a narrative theology for the coming faith amidst modernity, just as *The Pilgrim's Progress* was a kind of prose epic for an earlier era when modern individualism was first coming to the fore. Yet as it turned out, the theological vector of this emergent faith was more problematic than Defoe could have imagined.[32]

The Christian Doctrine: Teaching Theology

Twenty-four years of solitude for Crusoe were broken with the arrival of another human being, whom Crusoe rescued from being killed by neighboring islanders. He gave his companion the name "Friday" for the day of the week on which he arrived, and soon made it his business to teach his new understudy "every Thing, that was proper to make him useful, handy, and helpful."[33] Of first importance was language, including the grammar of the faith. Although he readily admitted that he was ill-equipped in the art of casuistry, Crusoe prayed that God would enable him to bring his student "to the true Knowledge of Religion, and of the Christian Doctrine, that he might know Christ Jesus, *to know whom is Life eternal.*"[34] Crusoe reluctantly took up the role of catechist by asking Friday a series of questions about basic doctrines and engaged him in reflecting on the bearing of each query for his own faith.

I . . . MADE IT MY BUSINESS TO TEACH HIM EVERYTHING

Crusoe's account of Christian doctrine has the familiar ring of Presbyterianism, yet he makes no appeal to the conventional language of the *Westminster Confession*, nor to its shorter or longer catechisms.[35] Instead, his catechetical instruction was based on a strict Biblicism without the aid of any creed or confession. Reflecting on his theological task, Crusoe appealed to the perspicuity of Scripture on matters which make one "wise unto salvation" because, he contends, the meaning is "so plainly laid down in the Word of God; so easy to be receiv'd and understood." He says that he learned this hermeneutical principle from his own experience, as he expresses, "the bare reading" of "the Scripture made me capable of understanding enough of my Duty, to carry me directly on to the great Work of sincere Repentance for my Sins, and laying hold of a Saviour for Life and Salvation."[36] But in this approach to Christian doctrine, Crusoe is far from alone. He is simply stating a widely shared belief among Protestants in the seventeenth century.

The Particular Baptists, for example, contended that the meaning of the Bible is sufficiently plain to be understood by anyone and everyone, affirming that "in this written Word God hath plainly revealed whatsoever he hath thought needful for us to know, beleeve and acknowledge, touching the Nature and Office of Christ, in whom all the promises are Yea and Amen."[37] Most dissenters held to this plain-sense understanding of Scripture, believing that "not only the learned, but the unlearned, in a due use of ordinary means, may attain to a sufficient understanding of them." Yet not everyone agreed that this clarity extended to the whole of the Scriptures. As the *Westminster Confession* attested, "all things in Scripture are *not alike plain* in themselves, *nor alike clear* unto all."[38] In contrast to Crusoe, who understood the Bible through and through as the plainly revealed Word of God, and thus accessible to anyone and everyone, other Christians held the Bible to be "both clear *and* obscure, not merely clear *or* obscure."[39] Reading for the knowledge of "the Christian doctrine" therefore required some hermeneutical assistance, as Scripture alone will not suffice, since creeds and confessions are necessary, they argued, to interpret it aright.

Crusoe's assertion that the "bare reading" of Scripture is sufficient for determining "the Christian doctrine," though set in the context of the mid-seventeenth century, actually reflects later events. During the time that Defoe was completing his novel, which was published in April of 1719, the dissenting ministers of London were embroiled in a bitter controversy. In February they assembled at Salters' Hall to debate the question of whether doctrinal orthodoxy with respect to the Trinity should be determined by *the Scriptures and* a confession of faith or whether *the Scriptures alone* were sufficient. Those who called for subscription to a confession in addition to the Bible became known as "subscribers." The other side, which insisted that "the Bible is the only perfect rule of faith," were called "nonsubscribers." When a vote was taken, the nonsubscribers won by a narrow majority of 57 to 53, leading one contemporary commentator to remark that "the Bible carried it by four."[40] But the issue was far from resolved, as the effects lingered for decades. Crusoe's reference to religious "Disputes, Wranglings, Strife and Contention" as "all perfectly useless" surely reflects the Salters' Hall controversy, and his affirmation of "The Word of God" as "the sure Guide to Heaven," clearly indicates that his sympathy was with the nonsubscribers.[41]

To his credit, Crusoe recognized that when it came to matters of Christian doctrine he had more sincerity than knowledge, and that in large measure he was actually instructing himself as much as his catechumen. When he reluctantly began laying a foundation of religious knowledge, he started by asking questions about God's creation and providential care, and from there moved on to the theme of Christ's redemptive work. On these subjects he found Friday remarkably receptive, but when their conversation turned to the Devil, Crusoe commented, "I found that it was not so easie to imprint right Notions in his Mind."[42] Friday wanted to know why, if God is all-powerful, he does not simply kill the Devil, or if he is all-merciful, why not just save everyone, including the Devil. Realizing they were headed down a path leading nowhere, Crusoe broke off the discussion. And he concluded his theological instruction with this observation, "I cannot see the least Use that the greatest Knowledge of the disputed Points in Religion, which have made such Confusions in the World, would have been to us if we could have obtained it."[43]

Disputed questions about the Devil, though placed on the lips of this aboriginal islander, undoubtedly represent the skeptical foolishness of the sort that dissenters like Defoe held in contempt.[44] As he contended in his *History of the Devil*, the reality of Satan is no excuse for shirking human responsibility, for

> Bad as he is, the Devil may be abus'd
> Be falsly charg'd, and causelesly accus'd,
> When Men, unwilling to be blam'd alone,
> Shift off these Crimes on Him which are their
>   Own.[45]

Nor could the questions of doubters guided by skeptics lead to any good end either, as the father in Defoe's *Family Instructor* explained to his children, saying, "And all the poor doubting Souls who are bewildered by Uncertainties, and bemused by the Learned

Perpelexities of these Men, must live, nay, which is worse, must die, in the same Uncertainty; not knowing *in whom they have believed*."[46] Indeed, Crusoe's theology reflects Defoe's aversion to speculative abstraction, as when he asked in his poem on the divinity of Christ, "How shall a Mortal Thought describe thy Being?" To which he answered that such conjecture is "Far above Nature's Reach, above her Sight."[47] Crusoe the catechist thus commended a theology of plain truths, similar to that described by the Catholic poet John Dryden, who observed that

> Faith is not built on disquisitions vain;
> The things we *must* believe, are *few*, and *plain*.[48]

Toward the end of his narrative, when he has been joined by two more inhabitants, Crusoe reflects on the place of religion in society. He observes that in his island kingdom were subjects of three religions: Protestant, Catholic, and Pagan. And yet unlike his homeland, in which there was an established church that only grudgingly tolerated dissenters, he notes, "I allow'd Liberty of Conscience throughout my Dominion."[49] Here the reader gets a glimpse of the practical value inherent in the politics of dissent. It echoes Defoe's earlier satirical tract, "The Shortest-Way with the Dissenters," in which he argued for the disestablishment of the Church of England by mockingly quoting high church calls to repeal the toleration of dissenters and "to root out this cursed race from the World."[50]

In many respects, *Robinson Crusoe* anticipated the emergence of modern religious freedom, which over time came to reverse the policies of state-sponsored persecution in favor of civil liberty. The experiential faith of Robinson Crusoe—a faith grounded more deeply in knowledge *of* God than in knowledge *about* God—would contribute to the common good of many who were not Defoe's fellow dissenters. The Whig party that Defoe earlier defended surely championed principles that came to be embodied in liberal democracy and in constitutional republicanism. Yet it was not an unmixed blessing. The Anglo-Puritan tradition, on which Defoe drew deeply, also handed on a long history of Rome-phobic attitudes, and the dirty secret of toleration was that it applied even less to Catholics than to dissenters.[51] Nevertheless, religious liberty, as Crusoe's short-lived island experiment suggests, was not merely a "loser's creed," but rather was put forth as a political good for all, as Roger Williams, John Locke, and Thomas Jefferson argued more forcefully.[52] And modernity received the complementary gift of religious pluralism at no extra charge. So despite the anti-Catholic sentiments of Defoe's novel, it was precisely this sort of vision of "true religion" that made it possible for Catholics, Protestants, Jews, and other people of faith to live together in a social space where *none* is established, and *all* are free.

Still, the close relationship between dissenting religion and republican politics did not come without a price. English Presbyterianism and other dissenters, chiefly the General Baptists, continued down the road laid out by revisions of "the Christian doctrine" that began at Salters' Hall, as the theology of non-subscription tended toward Socinianism and Unitarianism.[53] And as the theology of liberty became more deeply connected with Whig republicanism the old doctrinal orthodoxy faded as well.[54] These connections did not escape the perceptive notice of John Henry Newman, who saw in modern liberalism simply a revival of the ancient heresy of Arianism and its later iteration of Socinianism.[55] Yet for Crusoe, as for the father in Defoe's *Family Instructor*, the child of God must stand firm in faith and gaze not by foolish reason, seeking that which lies beyond the limits of human understanding:

> Believe and wonder, wonder and believe;
> Bring down our reasoning Follies to our Faith,
> To what we cannot comprehend, resign,
> And wait the glorious state where all our Eyes
> Illuminated from himself, shall see
> God as he is, and all be Gods like him.[56]

But perhaps the theology of Scripture evidence and plain truth was not to blame so much for what it said, as for what it left unsaid, making space for theological revisionism to redefine the nature of "the Christian doctrine."[57] This mixed legacy, however, does not diminish the fact that what Defoe produced in *Robinson Crusoe* was not simply the first modern novel, but a popular catechetical and theological account of "the true Knowledge of Religion, and of the Christian Doctrine." And as such, Crusoe anticipated the coming challenges that dissenting Protestants would face in handing on the faith and teaching theology. Yet as G. K. Chesterton once noted, the greatest part of the story may be Crusoe's simple inventory of things saved from the wreckage of his ship. It suggests that the future for Christians living in the wilderness of the modern world depends not on inventing the faith anew, but in retrieving the faith from the church and its ancient traditions.[58] And in doing so, perhaps Crusoe points a way for other castaways whose ecclesial ships have sunk as they seek to make a life on the desert island of modernity.

Notes

[1]Michael J. Taylor, *The Protestant Liturgical Renewal: A Catholic Viewpoint* (Westminster: Newman, 1963), 268.

[2]Defoe, *Robinson Crusoe*, ed. Michael Shinagel (New York: W. W. North & Company, 1994), 159. Subsequent references are to the Norton Critical Edition. I have taken Crusoe's line as the title of my paper.

[3]The illustrations included were taken from the edition of Defoe's novel that my grandfather received on Christmas in 1912, *The Life and Strange Surprising Adventures of Robinson Crusoe, of York, Mariner* (New York: R. H. Russell, 1900). The original sketches were done for this edition by Louis and Frederick Rhead, and are in the public domain.

[4]Karl Marx, *Capital*, trans. Samuel Moore and Edward Aveling, in Great Books of the Western World (Chicago: Encyclopaedia Britannica, 1952), 50: 33-35.

[5]Max Weber, *The Protestant Ethic and the Spirit of Capitalism*, trans. Talcott Parsons (New York: Charles Scribner's Sons, 1958), 176.

[6]Ibid., 155.

[7]H. L. Mencken, *A Mencken Chrestomathy* (New York: Knopf, 1949), 624. See also Mencken, "Puritanism as a Literary Force," in *A Book of Prefaces* (New York: Knopf, 1917), 197–283. That this stereotype still holds sway is illustrated in a recent political cartoon about the Republican struggle to coordinate a strategy for the Benghazi hearings in Washington. It pictured a Puritan in a crown hat with a burning torch and a Dominican friar with an instrument of torture tucked into his black robe. The friar is asking, "What?! *Witch Hunt?!* I thought today's theme was *Spanish Inquisition!*" *News and Observer*, May 11, 2013, 12A. When Puritans and Dominicans can be reduced to mere tropes for witch hunts and religious inquisitions, it is clear that Weber's point needs no justification.

[8]John Bunyan, *Grace Abounding to the Chief of Sinners*, ed. W. R. Owens (London: Penguin, 1984).

[9]Benjamin Franklin, *The Way of Wealth* (New York: Random House, 1930).

[10]William James, *Varieties of Religious Experience* (New York: Collins, 1960), 50.

[11]Friedrich Schleiermacher, *On Religion: Addresses in Response to Its Cultured Critics*, trans. Terrence N. Tice (Richmond: John Knox Press, 1969), 79.

[12]Vavasor Powel, *Spirituall Experiences, of Sundry Beleevers* (London: Robert Ibbitson, 1653). Powel does not use the term "copy" as a mere transcript of the original, but more in the sense of a specimen written by the Spirit of God, so that each specimen is evidence of the same author and each copy represents the same experience. *Oxford English Dictionary*, s.v. "copy," accessed May 28, 2013, http://www.oed.com.

[13]William Perkins, *A Treatise of the Vocations,* in *The Work of William Perkins*, ed. Ian Breward (Appleford, Abingdon: Sutton Courtenay, 1970), 456.

[14]Defoe, *Robinson Crusoe*, 13.

[15]Ibid., 64.

[16]Ibid., 65.

[17]Bunyan, *Grace Abounding*, § 53, 18. Bunyan states that his book *The Pilgrim's Progress* was delivered to him "under the similitude of a dream," to which the final line attests, "So I awoke, and behold it was a Dream," *The Pilgrim's Progress*, ed. N. H. Keeble (Oxford: Oxford University Press, 1984), 133.

[18]Defoe, *Robinson Crusoe*, 69. Defoe cites Psalms 50:15 in the footnote. Like Bunyan, Defoe's Scripture quotations are most often from the King James Version rather than the Geneva Bible. Valentine Cunningham, "Daniel Defoe," in *The Blackwell Companion to the Bible in English Literature*, ed. Rebecca Lemon, Emma Mason, Jonathan Roberts and Christopher Rowland (Malden, MA: Blackwell, 2009). Blackwell Reference Online. Accessed June 4, 2013. http://www.blackwellreference.com.

[19]Defoe, *Robinson Crusoe*, 69.

[20]Ibid., 71.

[21]"Amazing Grace," verse 2, in John Newton and William Cowper, *The Olney Hymns* (Bucks, UK: Arthur Gordon Hugh Osborn for the Cowper & Newton Museum, 1979; facsimile from the 1st ed. at Cowper & Newton Museum published in 1779). Although there was wide agreement among Puritans about the *ordo salutis,* which held that conversion was an arduous process preceded by preparatory stages, there was no consensus on the morphology of conversion; see Owens, Introduction to Bunyan, *Grace Abounding*, xxiii. For discussions of divergent morphological accounts, see Jerald C. Brauer, "Conversion: From Puritanism to Revivalism," *Journal of Religion* 58, no. 3 (1978): 233; Edmund S. Morgan, *Visible Saints* (New York: New York University Press, 1963), 90–91; Elizabeth Reis, "Seventeenth-Century Puritan Conversion Narratives," in *Religions of the United States in Practice*, vol. 1, ed. Colleen McDannell (Princeton, N.J.: Princeton University Press, 2001), 22–26; Patricia Caldwell, *The Puritan Conversion Narrative: The Beginnings of American Expression* (Cambridge, UK: Cambridge University Press, 1983).

[22]James Wm. McClendon Jr., *Doctrine: Systematic Theology, Volume II* (Waco, TX.: Baylor University Press, 2012), 141.

[23]Defoe, *Robinson Crusoe*, 114.

[24]Ibid., 114.

[25]It is no surprise, then, that the great nineteenth-century Baptist preacher Frank Boreham found the threefold deliverance of Crusoe to be paradigmatic of Christian experience. For Boreham concluded, "whosoever shall call on the Name of the Lord, the same shall be saved" (Romans 10:13). Frank W. Boreham, *A Handful of Stars* (New York: Abingdon, 1922), 32.

[26]Defoe, *Robinson Crusoe*, 6.

[27]So Charles Taylor argues more generally about Puritanism as a source of selfhood, in *Sources of the Self: The Making of Modern Identity* (Cambridge, MA: Harvard University Press, 1989), 184.

[28]John Stachniewski, *The Persecutory Imagination: English Puritanism and the Literature of Despair* (Oxford, UK: Clarendon, 1991), 7, 12, 40–42.

[29]Defoe, Preface to *The Farther Adventures of Robinson Crusoe* and Preface to *Serious Reflections During the Life and Surprising Adventures of Robinson Crusoe*, in *Robinson Crusoe*, Norton Critical Edition, 239-43.

[30]George Alexander Starr, *Defoe & Spiritual Autobiography* (Princeton, NJ: Princeton University Press, 1965), 3-50. Starr argued that although Baptists and Quakers contributed more to the production of spiritual autobiographies, unlike Defoe, "they gave rise not to fiction but to further Quaker and Baptist autobiographies" (*Defoe & Spiritual Autobiography*, x). While Starr is surely correct, as I have tried to point out, there is a striking resonance between Defoe's modern autobiography and the sectarian ones. On Bunyan's account of the spiritual autobiography, see Roger Sharrock, "Spiritual Autobiography in *The Pilgrim's Progress*," *Review of English Studies*, 24, no. 94 (1948): 102-20; and Owens, Introduction to Bunyan, *Grace Abounding*, xviii-xxiii.

[31]*Encyclopedia of Theology: The Concise Sacramentum Mundi*, Karl Rahner, ed. (New York: Seabury, 1975), s.v. "Faith," 500.

[32]I am using phrase "the coming faith" to denote the approach of theological liberalism, which I describe as "mainly about adjustment and accommodation to the modern world," in Gary Dorrien, *The Making of American Liberal Theology: Idealism, Realism, and Modernity, 1900-1950* (Louisville, KY: Westminster John Knox, 2003), 2:389.

[33]Defoe, *Robinson Crusoe*, 152.

[34]Ibid., 159.

[35]*The Westminster Confession of Faith* and *Westminster Catechism* (published in 1647), in *Creeds of the Churches*, ed. John H. Leith (New York: Anchor Books, 1963).

[36]Defoe, *Robinson Crusoe*, 160.

[37]First London Confession, VIII, Lumpkin, *Baptist Confessions of Faith*, 158.

[38]Westminster Confession, I.7, in John H. Leith, *Creeds of the Churches*, 3rd ed. (Louisville, KY: John Knox, 1982), 196.

[39]James Patrick Callahan, "*Claritas Scripturae*: The Role of Perspicuity in Protestant Hermeneutics," *Journal of the Evangelical Theological Society* 39, no. 3 (1996): 357. Emphasis added.

[40]Alexander Gordon, *Heads of English Unitarian History* (London: Philip Green, 1895), 33-34; Alexander Gordon, "The Story of Salters' Hall," in

Addresses Biographical and Historical (London: Lindsey Press, 1922); and John Shute Barrington, *An Account of the Late Proceedings of the Dissenting Ministers at Salters-Hall* (London: J. Roberts, 1719). Shute, later Viscount, Barrington was a Congregationalist and leader of the nonsubscribers.

[41]Defoe, *Robinson Crusoe*, 160.

[42]Ibid., 156.

[43]Ibid., 160.

[44]The father conversing with his children in the *Family Instructor* heaps scorn on "Deists and Hereticks" who question the plain and clear Scripture evidence for the deity of Christ. The father concludes that "we do not need these disputing Gentlemens determining of these Things so much as they imagine we do; let us search the Scripture, and seek the Guidance of the Spirit to interpret that Scripture, and to guide us to the knowledge of Christ, and he will guide us," Defoe, *New Family Instructor* (London: T. Warner, 1727), 351.

[45]Defoe, *The History of the Devil*, 2nd ed. (London: T. Warner, 1727), title page. Although Defoe himself accepted the reality of both "*God* and *the Devil*," because, as he argued, whoever "denies one, generally denies both," he nevertheless believed that Deists thought too little of the Devil while Milton thought too much of him, *The History of the Devil*, 22-23. Nevertheless Defoe never clearly explained his views on the nature and extent of evil personified.

[46]Defoe, *New Family Instructor*, 367.

[47]Defoe, "Trinity: Or, the Divinity of the Son," in the *New Family Instructor*, 369 and 384.

[48]John Dryden, *Religio Laici*, 431-32, in *The Poetical Works of John Dryden*, ed. George Gilfillan (New York: D. Appleton, 1857), 194.

[49]Defoe, *Robinson Crusoe*, 174.

[50]Defoe, *The Shortest-Way with the Dissenters: or Proposals for the Establishment of the Church* (London, 1702), 19.

[51]The "fears and jealousies" of Catholics are an indelible feature of English Protestantism, which fueled state-sponsored persecution of Catholics long after the so-called Act of Toleration in 1689 (John Coffey, *Persecution and Toleration in Protestant England 1558-1689* [Harlow: Longman, 2000], 90 and 134-60). The persistence of anti-Catholicism throughout the eighteenth and nineteenth centuries indicates that the shift from intolerance to tolerance was not linear; see Alexandra Walsham, *Charitable Hatred: Tolerance and Intolerance in England, 1500-1700* (Manchester: Manchester University Press, 2006), 300-22; and Scott Sowerby, *Making Toleration: The Repealers and the Glorious Revolution* (Cambridge: Harvard University Press, 2013), 79-96, 219-46, 259-63.

[52]Roger Williams, *The Bloudy Tenent of Persecution*, in *The Complete Writings of Roger Williams* (New York: Russell and Russell, 1963; reprinted, Paris, Arkansas: Baptist Standard Bearer, 2005), vol. 3; John Locke, *A Letter Concerning Toleration*, in *The Works of John Locke* (London: Rivington, 1824), 5:1-58; Thomas Jefferson, *A Bill for Establishing Religious Freedom*, published in 1777 but not approved by the Virginia legislature until 1786, in *The Papers of Thomas Jefferson* (Princeton: Princeton University Press, 1950), 2:545-47. A little noticed feature of Locke's *Letter Concerning Tolera-*

tion is that it equivocated on the question of religious freedom for Catholics. Locke's contemporary William Petty promoted "Liberty of Conscience as the inherent and Indealable Right of Mandkind," quoted in Sowerby, *Making Toleration*, 258.

[53]For a list of the publications by the subscribers and nonsubscribers at Salters' Hall see Hilarius de Synodis, *An Account of the Pamphlets Writ this Last Year each Side by the Dissenters* (London: James Knapton, 1720), 25-36. Among the Presbyterians there were 48 nonsubscribers and 30 subscribers at Salters' Hall. For a history of the theological devolution of Presbyterianism in England see C. G. Bolam, Jeremy Goring, H. L. Short, Roger Thomas, *The English Presbyterians* (London: Allen and Unwin, 1968), 151-74; and A. H. Drysdale, *History of the Presbyterians in England: Their Rise, Decline, and Revival* (London: Presbyterian Church of England, 1889), 489-515.

[54]Tim Harris, *Restoration: Charles II and His Kingdoms, 1660-1685* (London: Penguin, 2005), 300-09.

[55]Newman defines theological liberalism as a heresy because, he argues, "There is no existing authority on earth competent to interfere with the liberty of individuals in reasoning and judging for themselves," in John Henry Newman, *Apologia Pro Vita Sua*, ed. David J. DeLaura (New York: W. W. Norton, 1968), 223. See also Robert Pattison, *The Great Dissent: John Henry Newman and the Liberal Heresy* (New York: Oxford University Press, 1991), 100-4.

[56]Defoe, "Trinity: Or, the Divinity of the Son," in the *New Family Instructor*, 371. Defoe's free verse poem is read by the father as a conclusion to his long conversation with his daughter and son in which he leads them through Scripture teaching to affirm the full divinity and humanity of Christ.

[57]Matthew Kadane, "Anti-Trinitarianism and the Republican Tradition in Enlightenment Britain," *Republics of Letters* 2, no. 1 (2010): 38-54.

[58]G. K. Chesterton, *Orthodoxy: The Romance of Faith* (New York: Image Books, 1959), 64.

A Crisis in Catholic Identity

Lessons Learned from Catholic Relief Services

Christine Tucker

I would like to tell here a story about the transformation Catholic Relief Services (CRS) underwent as it faced a crisis in its identity, and to share the lessons that emerged. It is a journey filled with many challenges and convergences related to understanding Catholic faith and tradition, as well as to applying them to service on behalf of the poor and vulnerable overseas.

While the structure and mission of CRS and Catholic colleges and universities differ, we do share Catholic identity and values. Moreover, we also share the struggle to live them in a world that at times is easily disposed not to hear or appreciate them. In my judgment and from CRS's experience, these struggles are not tangential to carrying out our respective missions, but may be linked with our very survival. It is with this in mind that I share some key moments in CRS's journey in the hope that it may speak to the challenges facing faculty in Catholic higher educational institutions.

In its early years, CRS focused on providing relief—food, water, clothing, medicine, and solace—to refugees at the end of World War II. War Relief Services, as we were called at the time, worked through Catholic structures and religious congregations. When that mission ended, the U.S. bishops turned their attention to developing countries and the global concerns stemming from emergencies and poverty, renaming the organization Catholic Relief Services. As U.S. foreign policy began to focus on preventing the expansion of communism, CRS, by virtue of its American and Catholic identity, became a primary recipient of government funds. CRS became the largest supplier of surplus food for the purpose of feeding impoverished developing nations. Relief continued to be a major focus of operations, including in emergencies such as the crisis in Biafra and the Ethiopia famine. CRS also began to look at poverty reduction through development programs, primarily in agriculture and health.

The agency's approach to relief and development was fairly straightforward—give people some help to get them off the ground, and some skills so they can stay off. The first requires a transfer of resources—money, food, clothes, and such. The second requires a transfer of technical abilities. The shorthand would be the adage that that you give somebody a fish to eat so they are not hungry, and then you teach him or her how to fish so that person can continue to eat. Problem solved. Certainly that's what we thought at CRS for many years—that the alleviation of poverty was a technical problem that could be solved if we had enough resources.

Even as CRS did excellent work all over the world and helped large numbers of people lead healthier and more prosperous lives in the short term, some of us had nagging doubts about that equation. While working in South America watching CRS run large food programs that reached many people, I grew concerned as to whether the programs would have any real long-term sustainable impact once the resource transfers stopped. The American Dream, the idea that anyone could move out of poverty by pulling up his or her bootstraps, studying more, and working harder, just didn't exist for the poor. The political, economic, and social structures were such that the poor had no escape from the conditions they were born into. And the good produced by our development programs paled in comparison with these seemingly intractable conditions.

By 1991, communism was collapsing in other parts of the world, and with it, the Cold War paradigm that had driven so much foreign aid for the previous forty years. Yugoslavia was coming apart. Somalia began falling into chaos, as were many other African countries. Violence was erupting in virtually every region in the world. But the politics and social unrest that drove the violence were not seen to be addressed in our mission. Development work became difficult or impossible in some countries. All we could hope for in these circumstances were short-term responses while we waited for the political and social situation to stabilize.

During this period, many of our staff thought CRS was most successful when we were indistinguishable from our peers. Some went so far as to suggest that we take the word Catholic out of our name—to be identified as Catholic was seen as a liability, that we continually had to explain that we didn't serve just Catholics, that we didn't proselytize, that we didn't just hand out charity, but were a serious development agency.

It was at this point in 1993 that Ken Hackett became our new Executive Director. He faced a perfect storm. He had a mandate from our Board of Bishops to focus on our Catholic identity. Neither he nor we knew where that would lead. Staff morale was low. Our resources, which at the time were predominantly from the U.S. government, were in rapid decline. Without some dramatic change, we were a few years from going out of business.

Then the Rwanda genocide happened. The lives of 800,000 people were lost in just three months. Some of our staff and their family members perished. Others left the country—for good. Decades of "development work" were lost. Many felt a sense of hopelessness and despair. We wondered how we could not have seen the underlying tensions.

As all of these forces gathered, we knew that as an agency we needed a fundamental change if we were to be relevant to those we serve. We knew that the answer needed to be holistic. We started by looking at our field programming and strategic partnerships, fundraising strategies, and organizational management and culture, and some amazing, and surprising, history began to unfold.

We rediscovered our Catholic identity. We began to develop a renewed sense of who we were. In this process, we discovered Catholic social teaching.

Although we were familiar with emerging concepts in development theory such as "rights based programming," the concepts of human dignity, solidarity, subsidiarity, rights and responsibilities, and the common good found in Catholic social teaching were new to us not only as the Church's formal teaching but as principles that would be applicable to our work. Other concepts, such as the preferential option for the poor, had been part of our thinking but not in ways that provided new insights about what we needed to do. New windows for our outlook opened as we grappled with Catholic social teaching. We began to imagine what the world would look like if there were human dignity for all. Its principles gave us a whole new and exciting way of approaching what we did. Catholic social teaching was not just a set of theological or theoretical concepts, but became a very practical guide for what we believed in, what principles we espoused. It allowed us to rethink what we did.

Lesson #1: Both Catholic Identity and Church Teaching Matter

The discovery of Catholic social teaching didn't negate the positive professional characteristics of our agency, as many feared, but it did shape the questions we asked, the approaches we took and what we valued. As our thinking began to shift, we also discovered that we had been asking incomplete—and in some cases the wrong—questions about our relief and development work. We had been concerned about whether we would be more effective if we did, for example, more programs in one technical area and fewer in another. What we weren't asking about were the fundamental *relationships* within the societies where we worked. Whether there were structural problems related to class, ethnic, or political divisions built into these societies, leading to a lack of social cohesion. Whether these underlying tensions were keeping people in poverty. Whether these tensions were the root causes of the spreading violence.

This new perspective highlighted the threats facing not just local communities but entire countries and regions. We knew that even taking into account the different contexts and histories of each society, the violence and the intractable poverty we were seeing could not be attributed merely to the lack of relief and development. Thus, a continuation of an operational lens based on resource transfers and technical solutions alone would rarely, if ever, show long-term sustainable change. We realized that only by addressing the underlying tensions and the lack of social cohesion in areas where we worked would CRS be relevant into the twenty-first century.

We also saw that the Church worldwide was being called to play a significant role as defender of the rights of the poor; as a voice of the oppressed; as a witness to do good amidst corruption, torment, self-indulgent struggle, and exploitation; as a force for love where there is hatred; as a force for moderation where there is fanaticism. As an organization of the Church, we too were called to carry out our mission in new, more prophetic ways in society. Our identity as a Catholic organization gave us a moral imperative to address these challenges. It guided us to build a new plan with a foundation of moral courage, active peacebuilding, partnerships based on shared values, persevering reconciliation, and dynamic compassion for the poor and vulnerable.

The quest for a fuller sense of mission led us to make the promotion of justice, rooted in charity, our central organizing theme. This was to say that justice would be a new lens through which decisions would be informed and made. Justice was not another programming sector but something that needed to permeate and be incorporated within all CRS strategies, operations, and management.

Lesson #2: Start with Reflection and Make It Personal

As exciting as the new direction was, it was not sufficient to transform the agency. It reached only a small number of staff and was considered optional by many. Catholic social teaching and justice would only transform the agency if they touched everyone. This immediately raised several challenges.

The first was that there was no common understanding among the staff of Catholic social teaching and justice. Very few of the staff were familiar with the Church's social teaching, and many defined justice from a secular perspective, meaning to determine guilt or innocence, to seek retribution. Justice was not widely known to be about establishing relationships that would build peace and reconciliation, which are necessary to form the foundation for development. Even developing a common understanding faced multiple challenges. Sensitivities were high about our institutional motives for promoting Catholic teaching, because around the world our staff of more than four thousand reflected the communities in which they work. This meant that the majority was not Christian, and only a small minority was Catholic. Questions were raised whether these new directions were thinly veiled attempts to proselytize. For some, it was a sign that non-Catholics would soon be unwelcome.

Other challenges included the reality that a focus on justice was seen by many as threatening the roles that relief and development had played historically. To others, the implications were fraught with danger, ranging from concerns about the personal security of staff overseas, to a potential negative reaction from the existing CRS donor base, to a violation of individuals' personal ethical values. For others, concerns were raised that the shift would be done at the expense of professional standards and program quality—that the stronger the Catholic identity of CRS grew, the more our work would be perceived as "charity" rather than about serious development. In spite of the challenges, developing a common understanding was critical; unless leaders, staff, partners, donors, and other stakeholders were included in the new directions, there was a risk of derailing the entire process. Each of these fears needed to be identified, acknowledged, and addressed.

We started by providing foundational information about Catholic social teaching and justice that was accessible to everyone. To do this, we used terms such as "guiding principles," which focused on the values and principles inherent within Catholic social teaching without using language steeped in theological terms. After considering the meaning of the principles, staff discussed what these would look like in action and what difference the principles would make practically. After an introduction to justice, the staff was invited to tell their own stories about when they had seen injustice and to share their insights into how this should affect what we do.

Since these early reflections, CRS has continued to ensure that the staff understands the importance of our Catholic identity and its implications. We have continued to welcome all who wanted to work with us, including those who profess different religious and secular traditions. Yet our Catholic identity was, and remains, at the heart of our mission and operations.

Lesson #3: Justice Is Rooted in a Specific Context and Linked with Everyday Experience

The next step was to develop a tool that would help our staff to understand the context in which they lived through the perspective of relationships, and to build an operational framework for developing programs based on those relationships. While we would still support programs in sectors such as agriculture and health—and call on the expertise of our staff—one of the shifts required was that we support these programs by seeking to strengthen social cohesion and inclusion among all involved. It also meant a focus not solely on "rights," but on linking "rights and responsibilities" together in the local context. Some principles, such as subsidiarity and solidarity, took on new, critical meaning. We no longer limited our deliberations to whether we needed to feed someone a fish for today or teach him or her how to fish for tomorrow. The question was increasingly: "What about people who already know how to fish and have a fishing pole but don't have access to the river?"

Based on our understanding of our mission, the question that was most critical in guiding our decisions was previously, "What are the program options that make the most sense to solve relief and development problems?" The importance of our Catholic identity and the justice lens meant that we began to analyze issues from very different central questions:"What would justice look like in these circumstances? What are we called to do in order to create justice?" This distinct central guiding perspective led to new and exciting answers. For us, two big decisions emerged out of the contexts in which we were working. These related to HIV/AIDS and peacebuilding. Previously, from an exclusively relief and development perspective, we had decided to not engage with either of these issues. We didn't have the right technical expertise and it "wasn't our job." But once we looked at the context and the situation of the poor through the lens of justice, we felt we had to address them. They became "our job" because of our Catholic identity. If not us, who? If not now, when? Once this decision was made, we deliberately sought to get the expertise necessary to address them effectively.

Shifting again from relying solely on development theory and practices to a reliance on Catholic social teaching, we discovered the Church's teaching on integral human development (IHD). IHD promotes the good of every person and the whole person; combining economic, political, social, cultural, and spiritual dimensions. By incorporating both the concept and conceptual framework,

CRS was able to develop guidelines for program planning and evaluation. IHD gave us practical guidance for making sense out of a complicated world and for analyzing and explaining complex situations, and furnished a holistic checklist for guiding programming.[1] IHD enabled us to shift from approaching development within sectors (such as agriculture or health) as isolated technical problems to be solved independently of each other. Thus, while the approach required a marked conceptual shift, it was possible because it could be put into practice.

Approaching our work through IHD made several profound differences. One was to bring spiritual dimensions of individuals and communities into our framework as a positive asset.

Another profound difference was that our IHD framework incorporated peacebuilding into our programs.

For example, water programs are no longer developed merely from the perspective of supply and demand, without considering how they will contribute to greater social cohesion or to greater divisions within communities. Microfinance is no longer merely about generating savings, but about changing relationships within families and communities such that women are less vulnerable to domestic violence.

The change can also be illustrated by our work in emergency situations. While the creation of the justice lens grew out of an institutional crisis, the first major test came in 1998 at the time of another crisis—when Hurricane Mitch barreled into Central America with torrential rains and winds of 180 miles per hour. The storm killed more than ten thousand people and caused widespread devastation, particularly in Honduras. CRS's emergency response team kicked into high gear, saving lives and addressing the immediate needs of the people, and then helping with rebuilding. What was different this time was that we went through a deliberate process to ensure that the affected societies would not simply rebuild the poverty that existed before the hurricane, that the poor would be less vulnerable the next time disaster struck, that justice would be a cornerstone of our response.

The principle of right relationships took center stage as we worked for fundamental change in relationships that had the most impact on poor communities. Together with Church groups and local partners, we helped communities organize so they could work with local officials to advocate for their own needs. Domestically, CRS engaged the U.S. government to advocate for increased assistance to Central America, for debt forgiveness for countries most affected by Mitch, and for a temporary stop to the deportation back to Central America of people with expired—or no—visas. And we helped establish long-term relationships between dioceses in the U.S. and those in Central America, extending the role of the U.S. Catholic community from "donor" to "brother and sister."

There was an equally profound shift in our partnerships and relationships with U.S. Catholics, from being primarily about fundraising to serving them so that they could more fully live their faith in solidarity with the poor overseas. CRS sought to strengthen existing partnerships that would contribute to justice both overseas and in the U.S. CRS now reaches out broadly to serve Catholics so that solidarity with those in need can be integrated broadly into their lives, to pray, learn, act, advocate, and give. This has led to partnerships not only with dioceses and parishes but with many other Catholic institutions, including Catholic colleges and universities, movements, and religious orders.

Lesson #4: Allow the Spirit to Move

While the mission, values, and principles are shared across the agency, they are lived out in different ways depending on the individual, the physical location, and existing contexts. This means that the guiding question must be big enough to embrace all of them regardless of their differences. Catholic identity is not a box that can be checked off, or peripheral to mission. It is a continual process of reflection on how to live the Church's values, teaching, and tradition in a changing world. CRS has reshaped itself multiple times structurally and programmatically because of the world environment and the needs of those we serve. There was no long-term master plan which was determined at the outset. Nor could we, when setting our goals at the time, have possibly foreseen the path we would take over the next twenty years. To try to do so would have been a mistake even if it had been possible. Rather, progress was found through a continual series of short-term plans which allowed us to learn, plant new seeds, water others already planted, and see which bore fruit. It was the creation of a spirit of dynamic inquiry at the institutional level which allowed the spirit to enter and lead to each of the following steps.

Lesson #5: Called to Greater Boldness

CRS was created as the response to a call to greater boldness in addressing the suffering after World War II. Later, the call to boldness resulted in its presence in 100 countries around the world and contributions to the creation of Caritas Internationalis, a global confederation of 164 Catholic organizations. The adoption of a justice lens was a further response to a call for boldness in the face of violence and conflict. Faced with the profoundly secular society in which we live, we have learned that the challenge for our Catholic institutions when they seek vitality and relevance is not to blend more fully into that culture. Rather, it is to live Catholic identity and mission with greater boldness. It is "the courage to forge new paths in responding to the changing circumstances and conditions facing the Church."[2] Indeed, "In the two thousand years of Christianity, all the great movements in evangelization have been associated with forms arising from the radical nature of the Gospel."[3] A "business as usual" attitude can no longer be the norm.

In this rapidly changing world, we at CRS continue to struggle with how to alleviate poverty and promote integral human development as we look through the justice lens. We don't have technical solutions to alleviate poverty, although we do have technical expertise. We don't focus on resource transfers to alleviate poverty, although resources are needed and we, our partners, and those we serve all share our gifts and talents. What we do know is that the journey of love for one's neighbor through justice and charity is what the gospel demands of us.

The power that a reconsideration of our Catholic identity has brought to CRS can best be described in its impact on the hearts, minds, and lives of others. This is a story of people, brave, passionate, smart, inventive people, helping poor, desperate, vulnerable, sick, homeless, hungry men, women, and children, building and strengthening communities that foster charity, justice, and peace. It includes the stuff of epic novels. It is a story that is distinct from other faith-based organizations and international non-governmental organizations. If this story is neglected, no one will know. The loss would be less about the lack of details of the past as it would be about fewer opportunities to engage creatively with others in the future.

We are convinced that if any Catholic organization is to become the best version of itself it can be, including CRS, it needs the vibrancy of the larger Catholic community, its institutions and organizations that share each other's values and principles. The Catholic Church worldwide is being called to renew efforts to bring the love of God into the world concretely through service to the most poor, vulnerable, and marginalized. For the American Catholic Church, that call includes a challenge for more consistent witness to renew society and the world as a whole. As Catholic agencies and institutions, do we not believe that we have a role to play in furthering God's reign and transforming the world? If so, let us be bold together and seize the opportunities before us!

Notes

[1] Gaye Burpee, Geoff Heinrich and Rosanne Zemanek, *A User's Guide to Integral Human Development* (Baltimore: Catholic Relief Services, 2008), v.

[2] Synod of Bishops XIII Ordinary General Assembly, "The New Evangelization for the Transmission of the Christian Faith," *Lineamenta*, 2012, paragraph 5.

[3] Ibid., paragraph 8.

What We Have Loved, Others Will Love

Donna Orsuto

(Editors' note: The following essay was delivered by Donna Orsuto after she was honored with the 2013 Presidential Award from the College Theology Society on June 1, 2013.)

I have great respect for and appreciation of those who teach theology to undergraduates, and so to receive this 2013 Presidential Award is all the more meaningful. Thank you, Dr. Sandra Yocum, for this award, an honor I share with my colleagues in Rome.

For many years, my academic and administrative activities in Rome have been almost exclusively with graduate students: lay women and men at the Lay Centre and priests, seminarians, religious, and yes, some lay people at the Pontifical Gregorian University, where I teach. Recently, however, this work has expanded to include study abroad programs—for example, teaching a semester course for undergraduates from DePaul University and occasionally lecturing for various American colleges and universities with Rome programs. With my colleagues at the Lay Centre, I also organize international seminars for students, faculty, university presidents and administrators.

Instead of a formal scholarly paper, I was invited to share my vocational story in the context of the theme of the 2013 Conference: *Teaching Theology and Handing On the Faith: Challenges and Convergences*. My remarks are divided into three parts: first, a word about the "Roman" dimension of my vocation; second, the adventure of founding and building up the Lay Centre in Rome; and third, two pearls of wisdom I have learned in the last thirty-three years of academic and administrative activity in Rome.

The Roman Dimension of a Vocational Story

In 1979, with my newly minted BA in philosophy and religion from Wake Forest University, I made the decision to come to Rome for "one year" to volunteer at the ecumenical center "Foyer Unitas" and to study at the Pontifical Gregorian University. My decision was made largely because of the influence of three professors. Three Baptist professors (and ministers), Dr. Charles Talbert, Dr. Ralph Wood, and Dr. William Angell, each in his own way, enkindled within me a deeper appreciation of the Catholic intellectual tradition. Their encouragement, albeit indirect and perhaps even unintentional, helped me to rediscover my faith and to find my place again as a Roman Catholic at a time when I was seriously thinking about leaving the Church. These three professors, deeply rooted in their own expression of Christian discipleship as Baptists, were instrumental in helping me to discover that my vocation and mission, the particular way that God was calling me to live out my Christian discipleship, was as a Roman Catholic.

Dr. Charles Talbert stirred within me a profound love of the Bible and introduced me to the writings of many fine Catholic biblical scholars. This Baptist professor, who one day would become president of the Catholic Biblical Association, helped me to realize that the Word of God was just as central for Catholics as it was for other committed Christians. Dr. Ralph Wood introduced me to important Catholic literary figures, including Flannery O'Connor and Gerard Manley Hopkins, who continue to be companions on my journey to this day, and Dr. William Angell brought me and eleven other students to Rome and other European cities in January 1978 for a study abroad class on ecumenical theology. I was twenty years old at the time. It was in Rome, during the week of Prayer for Promoting Christian unity, while listening to Paul VI, that I experienced a deep longing to dedicate my life to work and prayer for Christian unity, something that has expanded over the years to encompass also a commitment to promote interreligious dialogue.

I shall be forever grateful to these professors and for their influence on me. They were great teachers, brilliant scholars, but above all men respectful of the distinctive personality of each student. This is an important dimension of university education. In the words of Blessed John Henry Newman,

> With influence there is life, without it there is none; if influence is deprived of its due position, it will not by those means be got rid of, it will only break out irregularly, dangerously. An academic system without the personal influence of teachers upon pupils, is an arctic winter; it will create an ice-bound, petrified, cast-iron University, and nothing else.[1]

These professors encouraged me to take a path less traveled, to embark on a Roman sojourn that turned out to be pivotal to my vocational journey. I am not the only person who has had such an experience. Two significant thinkers of the last century, Dietrich Bonhoeffer (1906-1945) and Thomas Merton (1915-1968), capture in writing the impact that Rome can have on a person. Just after his eighteenth birthday, Dietrich Bonhoeffer wrote to his twin sister, Sabine, "Just think, it is possible that next semester—I will be studying in Rome!! Of course, nothing is certain yet, but it would be absolutely the most fabulous thing that could happen to me. I can't even begin to imagine how great that would be!"[2] So in 1924, he came to the Eternal City, or to quote Eric Metaxas, Bonhoeffer "spun through Rome like a cyclone, absorbing as much of its culture as possible."[3] Rome became a classroom in which he could integrate all of his previous classical studies. Michelangelo's ceiling in the Sistine Chapel left a deep impression on him: "I was hardly able to move beyond Adam. There is an inexhaustible abundance of ideas in the picture. The figure of God reverberates with colossal power and tender love."[4] I should also note that in his diary, he registered a typical complaint about the Vatican Museums: "Terribly full. Only foreigners. Nonetheless the impression is indescribable."[5] A few weeks ago, nearly ninety years later, I was ploughing through the crowds at the Sistine Chapel with students from Cambridge Muslim College. These young Muslim students had the same reaction as Bonhoeffer. Rome is the "eternal" city after all.

And yet for Bonhoeffer, "The real significance of this trip . . . lay not in its culture-broadening aspect as a mini-grand tour or in its academic aspect as a semester abroad, but in its prompting his thoughts on the question that he would ask and answer for the rest of his life: *What is the Church?*"⁶ Somehow the experience of praying at St. Peter's and St. John Lateran helped this bright young Lutheran to grasp the universal notion of the Church. For him, Palm Sunday at St. Peter's was "the first day that something of the reality of Catholicism dawned on me, nothing romantic or the like, but rather that I am beginning, I believe, to understand the concept 'church.'" What struck him was "the universality of the church" which was "illustrated in a marvelously effective manner. White, black, yellow members of religious orders—everyone was in clerical robes united under the church. It truly seemed ideal."⁷ This experience of the Church in Rome at prayer was a "vivid illustration of the church's transcendence of race and national identity," and it had a deep effect on him.⁸

Thomas Merton, as a young and brash New Yorker, visited Rome in 1933, nine years after Bonhoeffer. In *The Seven Storey Mountain*, Merton wrote, "It was in Rome that my conception of Christ was formed. It was there that I first saw Him, Whom I now serve as my God and my King and who owns and rules my life."⁹ Merton's visit started with a rather harrowing experience with a Roman dentist who extracted an abscessed tooth. After surviving the Roman dental chair, he wandered through the ruins of Rome, but he eventually stumbled upon a "far different Rome."¹⁰ His visit to Sts. Cosmas and Damian, just across from the Roman forum, with its apse mosaic of Christ in judgement, confronted him as an "art full of spiritual vitality and earnestness and power."¹¹ On another occasion, he found himself kneeling in prayer, feeling embarrassed and self-conscious, but praying just the same, in the Dominican Church of Santa Sabina on the Aventine Hill. It was also in Rome, while visiting the Cistercian monastery of Tre Fontane, a site on the outskirts of Rome traditionally marking the place of St. Paul's martyrdom and where Cistercians first came in 1140, that the thought of becoming a Trappist monk passed through Merton's mind. Of course, it was only a youthful daydream at that point, and the fullness of that call would take many years to develop.¹²

The Roman experience marked Bonhoeffer and Merton for life. For Bonhoeffer, it was a liturgical anticipation of the unity of humanity, while for Merton it was the somewhat obscure stirring awareness of the Christ who calls. The accounts of Bonhoeffer and Merton resonate deeply within me, because I too discovered both Christ and the Church in a new and deeper way in Rome. I discovered that the Church consists not just of beautiful basilicas, but that we are the Church, bound together in a marvellous communion with Christ and one another, and that we are responsible for the Church's mission. This reality is artistically depicted in the mosaic of the vine and the branches in the basilica of San Clemente in Rome which rise from the life-giving waters of the cross to embrace the people of God: men, women, clerical, and lay. I also came to a deeper understanding of vocation. The call to follow Christ is neither simply the "wallpaper of our life" nor some sort of "background music." It is not just a career choice for a select few. No, vocation touches the core of who we are before God and for others. To quote John Henry Newman again,

> God has created me to do Him some definite service; He has committed some work to me which He has not committed to another. I have my mission—I never may know it in this life, but I shall be told it in the next. . . . I am a link in a chain, a bond of connection between persons. He has not created me for naught. I shall do good. I shall do His work.[13]

The Founding of the Lay Centre

My personal vocation has been intertwined with the founding of the Lay Centre at Foyer Unitas. My definite stay in Rome began in 1979 at the age of twenty-two, just after graduating from Wake Forest University, although the plan was to stay for "one year" to work at an ecumenical center called Foyer Unitas. Originally begun to welcome non-Catholic visitors during the 1950 Holy Year, Foyer Unitas underwent a major expansion in 1962 when the Ladies of Bethany, the Dutch religious order involved from its earliest days, relocated it to Piazza Navona. It was there that some of the official Protestant and Catholic observers and their families stayed during the Second Vatican Council. Significant gatherings of Council Fathers and theologians, including Karl Rahner, S.J., and Joseph Ratzinger, took place at Foyer Unitas during those exciting years of renewal. Some insights from these informal gatherings of

Council Fathers, theologians, auditors, and observers, often over a meal, may have even found their way into Council documents. After the Second Vatican Council, Foyer Unitas evolved into an ecumenical guest house, specializing in introducing non-Catholic visitors to Rome, and this is where I came first for the Wake Forest University study abroad program in 1978 and then eventually as a volunteer at Foyer Unitas in 1979.

The "one year" multiplied into many, and eventually in 1986, while working on my doctorate at the Gregorian University, the idea of the Lay Centre was born. The context is that the nuns had decided to close Foyer Unitas and move back to the Netherlands. At that point, Riekie Van Velzen, a Dutch friend and colleague, and I were inspired to build upon their ecumenical hospitality and start a "Lay Centre." I wish I could say that we had made a novena to the Holy Spirit and were praying piously in a Roman church when the idea came. Actually, we were in a bar. It was nine o'clock in the morning, a significant Holy Spirit hour, and we were only drinking cappuccino! A dream began to form: Why not set up a center for lay students who study at pontifical universities in Rome, a Lay Centre? The name "the Lay Centre at Foyer Unitas" captures the two dimensions of the initial inspiration. Yes, it was to be designed to foster the formation of lay students studying at pontifical universities, but in the spirit of Foyer Unitas. Foyer Unitas literally means a hearth of unity: and so "the Lay Centre at Foyer Unitas" was to become a place of welcome and warmth for lay students in the heart of Rome. Let me explain why this was such a strange idea at the time.

The pontifical universities were set up for training priests and seminarians. Rome is a somewhat clerical town, and this extends to the universities. In those days, the mid-1980s, there were just a handful of religious women studying in Rome and very few lay people. Progress had been made, though! For example, when Monika Hellwig was studying in Rome in the late 1950s, she wanted to do research at the Gregorian library. Please note: she did not want to get a degree from the university; she only wanted to do some research in our library. After numerous phone calls and conversations, she finally got permission to "use" the library. The fateful day arrived. She boldly crossed the threshold of the university, only to be escorted to a parlor where the books she wanted to consult would be delivered to her two at a time. She never actually set foot in the library, a space strictly reserved for male clerics and seminarians. I am proud to say that since 1999, the prefect of the Gregorian library has been a lay woman.

In 1986, nevertheless, the idea of a center for lay pontifical university students was still considered innovative. Even so, we forged ahead, above all because of the generous assistance of the Ladies of Bethany, who gave us nearly everything that they had, including chairs, beds, office furniture, and even a chalice gifted to them by Paul VI. On October 1, 1986, the doors of the Lay Centre opened. Over the years, it has doubled in size and expanded its activities. We have moved three times.[14] Students from every continent have made the Lay Centre their home in Rome: Catholic, Protestant, Orthodox, Anglican, Jewish, Muslim, and Buddhist.

What we are doing at the Lay Centre finds its inspiration in the renewal brought about by the Second Vatican Council. The empowering of the laity and the commitment to ecumenical and interreligious dialogue have their roots in Conciliar teaching. In its present location in one of the largest private gardens in the city center, the Lay Centre offers an oasis within the busy and noisy metropolis. The Lay Centre provides a unique niche in Rome not only by offering hospitality and a formation program, especially to lay women and men who study at the pontifical universities, but also by promoting a dialogue of life among people of diverse cultures and religions who choose to reside there during their academic sojourn in Rome. Hospitality and dialogue are also hallmarks for both the local and numerous international study programs that take place year-round at the Lay Centre.

Two Pearls of Wisdom

These many years in Rome at the Lay Centre have taught me many things, and by way of conclusion, I will share two pearls of wisdom I have garnered over the last thirty-three years in the "eternal city." First, some would say that Rome is eternal because it takes an eternity to get anything done. Others would say it is eternal because nothing ever changes. There is some truth in both statements. Sometimes too, in the Church, it seems that change takes not months or years, but decades and even centuries. Recently the new director of the Anglican Center in Rome, Archbishop David Moxon, at his installation on May 23, 2013, which incidentally took place at a Roman Catholic oratory, Caravita, recalled a proverb that really struck me: "If you want to go *fast,* go alone. If you want *to go far,* go together." He was referring specifically to the contemporary challenges facing ecumenical dialogue, but I believe its truth can be generalized. Church history teaches us that it pays off to have the patience to stick together, even though at times the personal cost can be quite high. This is a tough message, but I am convinced there is truth in it. Especially today, with the many internal divisions within the Roman Catholic Church, it is important to make a commitment to foster communion, the kind of communion which can only come from listening to one another and being attentive to the movements of the Spirit, even if we cannot move as quickly as we would hope.

The second point comes from St. Francis de Sales when he says, "Let us be what we are and be that well."[15] I would like to apply this saying to my own experience of dialogue. Over the years, I have had occasional opportunities to be involved in official Vatican interreligious dialogue (perhaps the most memorable was in Iran just a few days after 9/11), but more important than any official dialogue has been the daily dialogue of life that takes place at the Lay Centre, where I have built up deep and long-lasting friendships with people of other religious backgrounds. Sharing daily life, table fellowship and late night conversation, joys and sorrows, festivals, and routine activities like washing dishes or collecting food for the poor with other Christians as well as Jewish, Muslim, and Buddhist students week after week has taught me that the most important thing we can do to promote dialogue and understanding is, in the words of St. Francis de Sales, "Be what we are and be that well." Real dialogue disintegrates when we water down what we believe. And so, for example, I am quite free to express my belief in the real presence of Christ in the Eucharist to my Muslim and Jewish friends. I have always been struck by what Flannery O'Connor once said at a dinner party when Mary McCarthy commented that "When she was a child and received the Host, she thought of it as the Holy Ghost, He being the most 'portable' person of the Trinity; now she thought of it as a Symbol and implied that it was a pretty good one." Flannery O'Connor tells us that she responded in a shaky voice, "Well, if it's a symbol, to hell with it," but she later admitted, "That was all the defense I was capable of but I realize now that this is all I will ever be capable of saying about it, outside of a story, except that it is the center of existence for me; all the rest of life is expendable."[16] At the same time, it is equally important to allow others the freedom to live out their beliefs and, when appropriate, to support them by providing appropriate prayer spaces, respecting dietary needs, and celebrating festive meals with them on important religious holidays. Deep friendships abide when partners in dialogue are free to fully be and express who they are without compromise.

Conclusion

I began with the three Baptist professors who influenced me and helped me to discover my own vocation. I would like to finish with another incident from my days at Wake Forest University. I remember being at a reception and casually sharing with Dr. Betty Talbert my disillusionment with the Catholic Church. She wisely responded, "Ah, but there are many treasures in the Catholic Church." At that time, I sullenly asked myself, "What treasures? What is she talking about?" Looking back nearly forty years later, I can joyfully say that I have found these treasures and made them my own, and I hope that my life and yours is about handing on these treasures to the next generation. I end with a verse from William Wordsworth:
"What we have loved,
Others will love, and we will teach them how."[17]

Notes

[1]John Henry Newman, "Rise and Progress of Universities," in *Historical Sketches*, vol. 3 (London: Longmans, Green, & Co., 1888), 74.
[2]*The Young Bonhoeffer 1918-1927*, trans. and ed. by Paul Duane Matheny et al., vol. 9 of *Dietrich Bonhoeffer Works* (New York: Fortress, 2003), 78. See also Eric Metaxas, *Bonhoeffer: Pastor, Martyr, Prophet, Spy* (Nashville: Thomas Nelson, 2010), 47.
[3]Metaxas, *Bonhoeffer*, 50.
[4]*The Young Bonhoeffer 1918-1927*, 102. See also Metaxas, *Bonhoeffer*, 51.
[5]*The Young Bonhoeffer 1918-1927*, 89. See also Metaxas, *Bonhoeffer*, 50.
[6]Metaxas, 52.

[7]*The Young Bonhoeffer 1918-1927*, 88, See Metaxas, 53.

[8]*The Young Bonhoeffer 1918-1927*, 88, See Metaxas, 53.

[9]Thomas Merton, *The Seven Storey Mountain* (Boston: Houghton, Mifflin Harcourt, 1998), 120.

[10]Ibid., 119.

[11]Ibid.

[12]Ibid., 125.

[13]"Meditations on Christian Doctrine" (March 7, 1848) in *Meditations and Devotions of the Late John Henry Newman*, ed. Meriol Trevor (London: Burns and Oates, 1964).

[14]This is not quite accurate; you could perhaps say we have been in three locations: first Piazza Navona, then we moved to near St. John Lateran, and finally we are now in a beautiful monastery on the Caelian Hill perched above the Coliseum.

[15]*St. Francis de Sales and St. Jane de Chantal: Letters of Spiritual Direction*, ed. Wendy Wright and Joseph Power, trans. Peronne Marie Thibert (New York: Paulist Press, 1988), 111. In this letter, Francis writes to Mme. Marie Bourgeois Brûlart (June 10, 1605): "Let us be what we are and be that well, in order to bring honor to the Master Craftsman whose handiwork we are…. Let us be what God wants us to be, provided we are His, and let us not be what we would like to be contrary to His intention."

[16]*Letters of Flannery O'Connor: The Habit of Being*, ed. Sally Fitzgerald (New York: Farrar, Straus and Giroux, 1979), 125.

[17]William Wordsworth, *The Prelude*, ed. Jonathan Wordsworth (London: Penguin 1995), 2:446-47. See Michael J. Himes, "Communicating the Faith," in *Handing on the Faith. The Church's Mission and Challenge,* ed. Robert Imbelli (New York: Crossroad Publishing Company, 2006), 129.

Contributors

Andrew D. Black is a visiting assistant professor at Bucknell University, Lewisburg, PA. His research and teaching are in the areas of historical theology, American religious history, ecclesiology, ecumenism, and Jewish-Christian relations. His doctoral thesis at the University of Dayton, "A Vast Practical Embarrassment: John W. Nevin, the Mercersburg Theology, and the Church Question," received the 2013 Dissertation Award from the Center for Catholic and Evangelical Dialogue.

Mary-Paula Cancienne, R.S.M., is an assistant professor at Georgian Court University, NJ. She researches in the areas of theological environmental aesthetics, religion in a secular environment, and contemporary icons. She teaches undergraduate courses on the Christian tradition and theological ethics and graduate courses on ethics and pastoral counseling. She has published articles in the *Journal of the Mercy Association of Scripture and Theology* and for the Sisters of Mercy of the Institute of the Americas.

Christopher Collins, S.J., is an assistant professor at Saint Louis University. His research and courses are in the areas of systematic theology and spirituality. His publications include *The Word Made Love: The Dialogical Theology of Joseph Ratzinger/Benedict XVI* (Liturgical Press, 2013) and a forthcoming book from Ave Maria Press tentatively called *Three Moments: Ignatian Prayer of the Heart in Daily Life*. He has also published articles in *America, Review for Religious,* and *The New Jesuit Review*.

Emily Dykman is an assistant professor at Viterbo University, WI. Her research and courses are in the areas of lay leadership formation, missional theology, liturgy, sacraments, and pastoral ministry. Her publications include a collaborative textbook, *Christian Theology: Scripture, Tradition, and Practice*, and a prayer reflection in *Eucharistic Adoration: Reflections in the Franciscan Tradition*.

Curtis W. Freeman is Research Professor of Theology and Baptist Studies and director of the Baptist House of Studies at Duke University Divinity School. His publications include *Ties That Bind* (Smyth and Helwys), *Baptist Roots* (Judson Press), and *A Company of Women Preachers: Baptist Prophetesses in Seventeenth-Century England* (Baylor University Press). His current book project, entitled *Theology for Other Baptists: Catholicity, Confession, Community*, will be published in 2014 (Baylor University Press). He serves on the Baptist World Alliance Commission on Doctrine and Christian Unity and is the co-editor of *The American Baptist Quarterly*.

David Gentry-Akin is a professor of theology at Saint Mary's College of California, where he teaches primarily in the areas of scripture and fundamental theology. He also teaches in the college's Great Books Core Program and has led students in a pilgrimage to Rome each January for the past several years. He has published a variety of essays and book reviews. His most recent publication is "Fundamental Catholic Theology" in *Teaching the Tradition: Catholic Themes in the Academic Disciplines* (Oxford University Press, 2012), edited by John J. Piderit, S.J., and Melanie Morey.

Christopher Hadley, S.J., is a doctoral candidate in theology at Marquette University, Milwaukee. His dissertation will examine Hans Urs von Balthasar's use of distance as a category for Trinitarian theology. His other research interests include liturgical theology, Bernard Lonergan, and continental philosophy. He taught philosophy at Gonzaga University in Spokane, WA, as part of his Jesuit formation and has degrees in education, philosophy, and theology from Seattle University, Fordham, and Boston College.

Aurelie A. Hagstrom is an associate professor of theology and chair of the Department of Theology at Providence College, and obtained her S.T.D. at the Pontifical University of St. Thomas Aquinas [Angelicum], Rome. She teaches and publishes in the areas of ecclesiology, theology of the laity, and Mariology. Her work in ecclesiology focuses on the vocation, mission, and spirituality of the laity according to the Second Vatican Council. She is interested in how the laity are the church in the heart of the world and how they bring the world into the heart of the church. A recent publication is *The Emerging Laity: Vocation, Mission, and Spirituality* (Paulist Press, 2010).

Robert P. Imbelli, a priest of the Archdiocese of New York, studied in Rome during the years of the Second Vatican Council and was ordained there in 1965. He received his B.A. from Fordham University and his S.T.L. from the Gregorian University. After parish ministry in New York, he obtained his Ph.D. from Yale University. He has taught theology at the New York Archdiocesan Seminary and the Maryknoll School of Theology; and has been visiting lecturer at Princeton Theological Seminary and Fordham University. From 1986 to 1993, he was director of the Institute of Religious Education and Pastoral Ministry at Boston College, and he is currently associate professor of theology at Boston College. He is a member of the Steering Committee of Boston College's Church in the 21st Century Initiative. His articles and reviews have appeared in such journals as *Theological Studies*, *Pro Ecclesia*, *Worship*, *The Thomist*, *Communio*, *Commonweal*, and *America*. He is the editor of the Church in the 21st Century volume, *Handing On the Faith: The Church's Mission and Challenge* (Crossroad, 2006).

Anne-Marie Kirmse, O.P., is a member of the Sisters of Saint Dominic of Amityville, New York. She serves as the research associate in the Laurence J. McGinley Chair in Religion and Society at Fordham University, where she also teaches theology. She co-edited the book *The Legacy of Avery Cardinal Dulles, S.J.: His Words and His Witness* and is currently working on a biography of Dulles based on the twenty years she worked with him.

Michael Lopez-Kaley is an assistant professor of religious studies and philosophy at Viterbo University, WI. His research and teaching is in the area of systematic theology and theological ethics, specifically in Catholic social teaching and economic justice as well as marriage and family issues. His research is focused on the relationship between the scholarship of teaching and learning, especially in religious studies, and the virtue of solidarity in relation to economic justice.

Laura Nettles is a Franciscan Sister of Perpetual Adoration and an assistant professor at Viterbo University, WI. Her research and courses are in the areas of Franciscan theology, medieval Islamic philosophy, Christology, ecclesiology, and Catholic social teaching. She has published articles in the *Islamic Journal of Philosophy* and *Commercium*.

Felicidad Oberholzer is a professor of theology and religious studies at Saint Mary's College of California. She has also taught courses in other disciplines across all the schools in her college. She is a licensed clinical psychologist and a marriage, family, and child counselor in private practice and has done postgraduate work at the C. G. Jung Institute in San Francisco. Her research focuses on the intersection of theology and psychology.

Maureen H. O'Connell is associate professor of theology and chair of the Department of Religion at LaSalle University. She authored *Compassion: Loving Our Neighbor in an Age of Globalization* (Orbis, 2009) and *If These Walls Could Talk: Community Muralism and the Beauty of Justice* (Liturgical Press, 2012), which explores the arts as sources of ethical wisdom and catalysts for moral action. Her current research explores racial identity formation, racism, and racial justice on Catholic college campuses.

Donna Orsuto, originally from Ohio, is the co-founder and director of the Lay Centre at Foyer Unitas in Rome. She is also a professor at the Institute of Spirituality of the Pontifical Gregorian University. Her courses include History of Medieval spirituality, theology and spirituality of the laity, and friendship in the Christian Tradition. In addition to her book entitled *Holiness* (London: Continuum, 2006), she has written a number of scholarly articles in both English and Italian.

William L. Portier serves as the Mary Ann Spearin Chair of Catholic Theology in the Department of Religious Studies at the University of Dayton. He came to Dayton in 2003 after teaching for twenty-four years at Mount Saint Mary's University (Emmitsburg, MD), where he served as chair of the Theology Department (1989-98) and Henry J. Knott Professor of Theology (1997-2003). He is the author of *Isaac Hecker and the First Vatican Council* (1985) and *Tradition and Incarnation* (1994). His latest book is *Divided Friends: Portraits of the Roman Catholic Modernist Crisis in the United States* (2013).

Katherine G. Schmidt is a doctoral student in theology at the University of Dayton and a Lilly Graduate Fellow. Her research interests include American Catholicism and the intersection of theology and culture. She is currently writing about the theology of virtual space.

Matthew Lewis Sutton is an assistant professor at St. John's University, NY. His research and courses are in the areas of Trinitarian theology, Christology, Ecclesiology, and Mariology. His publications include a co-edited book, *On Suffering: An Inter-disciplinary Dialogue on Narrative and the Meaning of Suffering*, and a new book available now called *Heaven Opens: The Trinitarian Mysticism of Adrienne von Speyr*. He has also published articles in *New Blackfriars* and *International Journal of Systematic Theology*.

Christine Tucker is senior advisor at Catholic Relief Services. She has taught workshops on Catholic social teaching, Catholic mission and identity, and Catholic Relief Services' journey towards justice. Her publications include "Integration of Catholic Social Teaching at CRS" in the *Journal of Catholic Social Thought*.

Sandra Yocum is an associate professor in the Religious Studies Department at the University of Dayton and served as department chair from 2003 to 2012. Her publications include *American Catholic Traditions: Resources for Renewal*, co-edited with William Portier (The Annual Volume of the College Theology Society, 1996), *Joining the Revolution in Theology: The Col-*

lege Theology Society, 1954-2004, and *Clergy Sexual Abuse: Social Science Perspectives,* co-edited with Claire M. Renzetti, as well as journal articles and book chapters. She is president of the College Theology Society, 2012-2014.